Early Lexical Development

Early Lexical Development

Esther Dromi

School of Education
Tel Aviv University

SINGULAR PUBLISHING GROUP, INC.
SAN DIEGO · LONDON

Singular Publishing Group, Inc.
4284 41st Street
San Diego, California 92105-1197

19 Compton Terrace
London, N1 2UN, UK

© 1987 Cambridge University Press
© 1996 Singular Publishing Group, Inc.

Printed in the United States of America by McNaughton and Gunn

Library of Congress Cataloging-in-Publication Data Available

ISBN 1 56593-739-2

Contents

Tables

Figures

Foreword

In 1787, Dietrich Tiedemann, a German philosopher, published the first day-by-day record of a child's development – a diary study of observations of his own son. He concluded this landmark study with an eye to the future:

> This is as far as my observations go. Other business prevented me from their continuation. I greatly desire that others may make similar ones; it will then be possible to determine various things by comparison, and that important branch of psychology, too little exploited as yet, which studies the development of human facilities – the foundation of pedagogy – will make appreciable progress thereby. (Quoted in Bar-Adon and Leopold, 1971, p. 17)

Exactly two hundred years later, a developmental psycholinguist in an Israeli School of Education has given us a work that matches Tiedemann's desire. What we have here is a distillation of the similar studies that have been carried out through the intervening two centuries, topping them off with what is surely the most detailed study ever of the period between the emergence of first words and the appearance of first word combinations. This is the period which Tiedemann and his many successors have characterized in terms of limits in the child's abilities: "To combine several words in a sentence was still beyond his power" (1971, p. 15). Little Friedrich Tiedemann passed beyond this limit when he was 21 months old. When little Keren Dromi was 17 months old, her mother noted in her diary:

> Today it becomes evident to me that Keren does not face "programming-span" limitations or other constraints of production any longer. Most of her new expressions are two and multi-word utterances. It happened quite suddenly. (Chapter 7, p. 69)

The comparisons that Tiedemann hoped for, therefore, yield striking similarities: boy or girl, German or Israeli, eighteenth century or twentieth century – parents tend to agree that there is a period during which children apparently cannot say more than one word at a time, followed by a linguistic breakthrough. This we have known for a long time. What we have not been sure about, until the completion of Esther Dromi's work, is whether to characterize this period as a "stage" in development, and how precisely to characterize the child's successive attempts to find and create order in a one-word world. Having read Dromi's careful exposition and discussion of her remarkable data, we now know more than a dozen generations of careful parent-observers knew – at least with regard to one child's traversal through what was surely a developmental stage for *her*. And we know far more about the dynamics of "overextensions" and "underextensions" of word meanings – not to mention a new category of child language use, hitherto unnoticed: "systematic overextensions to only *one* irrelevant referent". And, perhaps more striking, we see how very frequently the child is simply "right on target" in the semantics and morphology of her word use.

I don't want to give away in advance the collection of important findings that emerge from this study. What we have here is the antidote to selective parental observation, and the proof that a naturalistic study can provide exquisite and reliable quantitative evidence for current theoretical issues in cognitive science. The Appendix presents the complete data on the course of development of a full lexicon of 337 words, recorded in 3,518 entries and registered with just the right level and amount of contextual information, over the 7 months and 12 days that marked the period in Keren's life that we can now, confidently, characterize as her "one-word stage". This data base – this *complete* lexicon – is insightfully used to evaluate the predictions of dominant current theories of the development of meaning in child language.

The evidence is in (though one will always, like Tiedemann, wish for data from more children and more languages). The arguments have been elegantly and carefully made. The reader is in for a good story, well told.

Dan I. Slobin
Department of Psychology
University of California, Berkeley

Reference

Tiedemann, D. *Über die Entwickelung der Seelenfähigkeiten bei Kindern. Hessische Beiträge zur Gelehrsamkeit und Kunst,* 1787. Reprinted, in part, in the English translation of Carl Murchison and Susanne K. Langer, in A. Bar-Adon and W. F. Leopold (eds.), *Child language: A book of readings.* Englewood Cliffs, N. J.: Prentice-Hall, Inc., 1971, pp. 13–17.

Acknowledgements

In the Fall of 1977, I started a Ph.D. program in Special Studies: Child Language. At that time I was a language clinician who, after having worked with language-impaired children, had come to perceive the normal development of language as miraculous. The present book reports on my scientific attempts to define and to study a set of specific research questions in order better to fathom this mystery. The book is based on my doctoral dissertation submitted to the University of Kansas, U.S.A., and my subsequent research on the early phases of verbal production which was conducted at Tel-Aviv University, Israel. The work was supported at various stages by the Bureau of Child Research at the University of Kansas, which supplied the recording equipment through Grant No. HD 00870 from NICHD and NIH Bio-med Grant 46985706, and by the School of Education at Tel-Aviv University, which awarded a research grant that supported research assistants and the English editorial work on the final version of the manuscript. The support of these institutions is gratefully acknowledged.

It was my good fortune to work in two highly stimulating intellectual environments over the ten years during which this project was conducted. I wish to express my deepest appreciation to all the people who guided me and provided invaluable assistance throughout those years. First and foremost, I thank my excellent professors and colleagues at the University of Kansas: Richard Schiefelbusch, John Wright, Frances and Floyd Horowitz, and Kenneth Ruder, who directed my studies and helped me discover how to conduct research in developmental psycholinguistics; Melissa Bowerman, the chairperson of my dissertation committee, strongly influenced my academic thinking. I am grateful for both her receptivity and her critical evaluation of my work during my graduate studies.

On my side of the Atlantic, I am indebted to my colleagues at Tel-Aviv University: Rina Shapira and Shimon Reshef, the previous Heads of the School of Education, who provided resources for the continuation of my research. Also to members of the Unit of Human Development and Education, who shared with me the joys and the sorrows of every step of this project. Special thanks to Ruth Berman, who opened the door for me to a new career, and with great interest and a supportive attitude followed my first steps in this field. I deeply acknowledge the help and encouragement of Sidney Strauss, the Head of our Unit, who, from the moment I first met him, spared no efforts in helping me establish an independent status as a researcher. I also thank Tamar Globerson, Rachel Karniol, Iris Levin, Dina Tirosh, Liliana Tolchinsky-Landsmann, and Tamar Zelniker for their critical comments and friendly support. My sense of accomplishment should be shared with Smadar Eilata and Michal Schleifer who helped in recording, transcribing, and analysing the data, as well as Dalia Ringwald and Michal Frid, who assisted in preparing the manuscript for publication. I particularly value the personal perspectives of Smadar and Dalia who were deeply involved in my research. I am grateful to Sara Kitai, my English Editor, for her meticulous reading of this manuscript, her invaluable comments on earlier drafts, and her highly professional attitude. Thanks are also extended to Michal Masiach who typed most of the chapters, and Susan Pinchas, who helped her.

During the past few years, I have had invaluable opportunities to discuss my work with my colleagues. I appreciate the input I received from: Eve and Herbert Clark, Peter and Jill deVilliers, Annette Karmiloff-Smith, Deborah Kemler-Nelson, Juan Pascual-Leone, Itzchak Schlesinger, Catherine Snow, and Jürgen Weissenborn. My greatest debt is to Dan Slobin, who expressed so much interest in my research, and who was the first to suggest that I publish it as a book.

I want to share the satisfaction of publishing a first book with my dear family who helped me to make this happen: my mother, Nira Ben-David-Mordel, and stepfather Jacob Mordel, my parents-in-law Rachel and Moshe Dromi, and my grandparents Sara and Benjamin Zaitzov. I also wish to mention my beloved father Joseph Ben-David, who did not live to read this book – a late fruit of the constant intellectual encouragement and the sound emotional background he had provided for me throughout my childhood. Words are insufficient to express my gratitude and appreciation to my husband Udi, for his co-operation and involvement in my professional plans in general, and in this project in particular. Finally, of course, I must thank my wonderful daughter, Keren, for being so loyal and patient and for indulging me while I observed her investigation of language.

E. D.

Notation

11(10)	Indicates age. Age is given in months and days; hence 11(10) is to be read as eleven months and ten days.
K	Keren
M	Mother
F or D	Father
(023)	Numbers in parentheses following word examples indicate the word number in the subject's cumulative lexicon (e.g., (023) means that this was the twenty-third word acquired by the subject).
Italicization	Hebrew words and sentences (in phonetic transcription) are italicized throughout, except in tables where they are underlined. Unless marked for penultimate, Hebrew words take final stress.
nor (sinor)	A Hebrew word enclosed in parentheses following another word indicates the adult equivalent for the child's approximation.
?	Utterance-initial or medial in Hebrew utterances, indicates a glottal stop.
'	Indicates English gloss. Parentheses are used in English glosses to indicate obligatory words in English that have no Hebrew counterparts, e.g. *bayit* '(a) house'.
/	Indicates end of a multi-word utterance.
/x/	Indicates exact repetition of a preceding utterance.
Pronouns	The shorter form 'he' refers to a generic child irrespective of his or her sex. The pronoun 'she' is used for anaphoric reference to K or to any other girl.
Styles of examples	Examples appear in two somewhat different formats. The discursive style represents an exact translation of entries in the handwritten record of the subject's speech; adult sentences are translated freely rather than literally. A more formal style, with both literal and free translation of adult sentences, is used for examples taken from transcriptions of audio-tapes.

To Udi and Keren

1   *Introduction*

It is widely accepted that an infant's entrance into human society begins with the start of language development, that is, when he first utters meaningful strings of sounds. Parents throughout the world eagerly await their children's first words, an event which occurs, according to most developmental charts, sometime during the second year of life. However, unlike the solid but naive body of knowledge concerning the relative importance of the inception of speech for the subsequent cognitive and social functioning of the child, the scientific body of knowledge of the periods that precede syntax is quite meager and the findings are still inconsistent. It is only during the last decade or so that intensive efforts have been devoted to the study of early speech and to pre-verbal communication.

The lengthy period of time throughout which children's production is limited to "one word at a time" (Bloom, 1973) has been the subject of a number of psycholinguistic investigations, most of them observational. Many of these modern studies were conducted by parent-investigators anecdotally describing specific aspects of the lexical growth of their own children. In other studies, groups of mothers were trained to record early speech, with researchers supplementing the mothers' diaries with periodic audio-recordings. Somewhat more systematic experimental studies of early speech production, as well as more scientifically controlled diary studies, have just recently begun to proliferate.

The present book focuses on research questions that are intrinsic to the scientific study of early lexical development. Various theoretical issues, along with the practical problems involved in studying the growing lexicons of children during the one-word stage, are raised and discussed here. The book examines the methodology of a disciplined case-study, as it reports on a case-study investigation of one child's entire lexicon of single words. This first chapter introduces the main topics, provides an overview of the empirical investigation, and offers an outline of the following chapters.

Identifying the issues

The term the *one-word stage* is commonly used to denote the period of time during which children extend their linguistic knowledge by adding new words to their growing productive lexicons. The first issue to be addressed in this book is the question of whether the mere emergence of new words can be seen in and of itself as proof that the one-word period is, in fact, a stage in language acquisition. Following a number of theorists (e.g., Flavell, 1971, 1982; Karmiloff-Smith, 1986; Wohlwill, 1973), I question the readiness of writers loosely to apply the term "stage" indiscriminately to any observable change in a child's behavior. Rather, I suggest that only those constructs within the linguistic system which show a certain degree of underlying uniformity and which have clearly identifiable boundaries can be considered real stages.

It is thus argued below that the mere emergence of comprehensible words is not by itself sufficient proof that a qualitative change in the underlying organization of the child's linguistic knowledge has occurred. Much stronger evidence than the identification of the overt addition of components is required before one can conclude that the one-word period is in fact a stage in language development. Such a conclusion should be based on findings indicating that during this period the child acquires a unique characteristic of the language previously missing from his linguistic system, and one that will be hierarchically integrated into this developing system in later stages.

The very utility of the psychological concept of stages (e.g., in Piaget's theory) to the specific domain studied here – language acquisition – is examined in this book, and quantitative details on the one-word period are presented. Thus, for example, questions such as exactly *when* children start to produce meaningful words; for *how long* they produce only one word at a time; *how many* lexical items children's lexicons contain prior to the first evidence of syntax; and *what* the rate of lexical acquisition during the one-word period is, are addressed below.

One of the main characteristics of the first words children produce is the fact that they are intimately connected with the non-linguistic context of their production. During the early months of speech, children utter words relatively rarely, most often when they interact with a familiar person in a familiar place (e.g., Greenfield and Smith, 1976; Rodgon, 1976). Therefore, it is extremely hard to interpret what a child says without being familiar with the context of the utterance. In other words, only if one integrates the spoken word with its non-linguistic context does it become possible to speak about the meaning of the word or its communicative function for the child.

The need for such an interpretative approach poses a difficult scientific problem. In discussing this issue, Brown (1973:152) questioned the very possibility of carrying out scientific studies of single-word corpora. As he sees it, the problem is not whether interpretation is legitimate or not, but rather how far we may be permitted to take it. Various authors have treated the issue of interpretation in different ways. In most cases, researchers have adopted existing theoretical models for classifying words, and by so doing have imposed limits on interpretation by establishing clear rules for the game.

This book will, therefore, examine the difficulties involved in classifying early words, reviewing and analysing previous attempts to classify single-word corpora according to parts-of-speech (e.g., Gentner, 1982; Nelson, 1973b), semantic relations (e.g., Greenfield and Smith, 1976; Rodgon, 1976), and various speech acts (e.g., Dore, 1974, 1975; McShane, 1980). Finally, I will offer my own model developed for the analysis of early words according to their reference to the real world (i.e., objects, events and relations).

The most logical eunderlying prerequisite for the generation of a productive lexicon is the learning of the conventional meaning of words. This process of meaning acquisition is dynamic, long-term and covert, and it involves complex interactions between two developing systems in the child: the cognitive and the linguistic. Over the last two decades, extensive theoretical and empirical efforts have been directed at the question of how young children acquire the semantics of natural languages. Despite the enormous amount of theoretical work in this area, very little is known about what determines the relative ease or difficulty of a word for a child, or how the meaning of each word develops and changes over time. As Carey (1982) has recently argued, the "state of the art" in the area of early semantics is still quite muddled, and does not lead to clear predictions.

In order to test competing models of meaning acquisition, the actual extension behaviors of words must be closely examined. The present book sets forth evidence regarding the development of word-meaning through the examination of the acquisition, extension and differentiation of one subject's complete lexicon of single words. Various theoretical models of word-meaning acquisition (Barrett, in press; Bowerman, 1978, 1980; Clark, 1973, 1983a; Nelson, 1974; Nelson and Lucariello, 1985; Schlesinger, 1982) are discussed, and their theoretical predictions are tested on the basis of a close observation of how the subject used each of her new and old words over time and in different contexts.

The study of individual children (or of a very small number of subjects) by means of natural non-intervening procedures is not a new practice in child-language research. Leopold's (1939) famous diary in which he documented the linguistic progress of Hildegard in English and in German is one example of a vivid portrait of a single child. Earlier diaries serving contemporary researchers for the purposes of secondary analyses are also available for students of child language (e.g., Clark, 1973; Ingram 1978). Harvard's famous longitudinal project (1960–70) of Adam, Eve, and Sara also sets the stage for the acceptance of a small number of subjects along with naturally obtained audio-recorded speech samples. The question of whether naturalistic studies are empirically solid, and whether their results can be tested for generality, is of major scientific importance. Therefore, both the principles and the practical concerns of the application of case-study methodology are discussed in this book.

Case-study methodology is described and contrasted with other methods of naturalistic research. It will be shown that a disciplined and well-planned case-study does meet the requirements of both external and internal validity, and inter-judge reliability. Several suggestions for testing the reliability and the generality of case-study findings are offered in the text by means of a number of examples taken from the case-study analysis of the early lexical development of one child – the subject of the present investigation.

Description of the data

The main body of data that is considered in this book comes from my own daughter Keren, who was the subject of my disciplined case-study investigation of early lexical development. Throughout the entire one-word period of production, I recorded the linguistic development of my first-born child – a native Hebrew speaker – utilizing a pre-planned set of rules for data collection and data organization. The child's verbal productions were collected with almost no sampling for a period of 32 weeks between the ages of 10(12) and 17(23). I concentrated primarily on recording the appearance of new words and the repeated uses of the same words in different linguistic and non-linguistic contexts, and I could therefore pinpoint the emergence of each new word and study how it was used by the child over time.

Three independent means were employed for collecting natural speech:

(a)   a continuous handwritten diary which included extensive descriptions of the phonological forms together with the linguistic and non-linguistic contexts of production. This record contained detailed information about new words and repeated uses of old words;

(b)   nine audio recordings ranging in length from 55 to 180 minutes recorded no more than three weeks apart. These samples provided a representative picture of Keren's ordinary speech at specific points in time; and

(c)   four 30-minute video-taped play sessions of the subject interacting with one of her parents.

The combination of data-collection procedures was adopted to compensate for the drawbacks inherent in each individual procedure. It also provided the means for conducting five different measures of reliability and validity on the data.

In the course of data analysis, each of the subject's productive words was scored on a weekly basis on three independent dimensions: (a) morpho-phonemic changes in the form of the word; (b) the development of the word's reference; and (c) the development of the word's extension. The analysis of word reference was carried out in order to determine whether a given word was an object word, an action word, a modifier, a social word or an indeterminant word which named both action and object, or modifier and object. The analysis of a word's extension was aimed at comparing the range of application of a word to its conventional meaning in adult Hebrew. Four categories were employed: underextension, overextension, regular extension and unclassified.

By repeatedly scoring each word it was possible to measure the developmental processes over time. Since every change in the child's lexical development was identified in real time, the processes observed could be evaluated from two complementary perspectives:

(a)   by examining all the behaviors recorded during any given week, it was possible to evaluate developments across the entire lexicon;

(b)   by considering one word across time, it was possible to evaluate the developmental history of a given word with reference to the time that had passed since it first appeared in the child's speech (i.e., the "age" of the word).

Outline of Chapters 2 through 12

Chapters 2 through 6 acquaint the reader with the main theoretical issues that are studied in this book. Studies directly relevant to the questions raised in the preceding sections are reviewed.

Chapter 2 focuses on the question of whether the one-word period is indeed a stage in language development. It explores the essential set of underlying conditions needed to determine whether a given slice in a sequence of behaviors constitutes a developmental stage. Following the general discussion, more specific claims as to the status of the one-word period in relation to the preceding (i.e., pre-verbal) and subsequent (i.e., combinatorial) phases of production are considered. The chapter concludes with a summary of quantitative measures for the one-word period derived from various published materials. Despite the methodological drawback of collating findings from diverse studies, some very general linguistic characteristics of the stage do emerge from available information on a variety of subjects.

Chapter 3 deals with the difficulties that are involved in classifying single-word utterances. During the last few years several attempts to classify single-word utterances by applying different taxonomies have been reported. Despite the various attempts to classify early words according to parts-of-speech, semantic relations, or pragmatic functions, very little discussion of the theoretical or practical complexities inherent in this procedure appears in the literature. For example, little attention has been paid to the distinction between taxonomies that are used as a data-reduction tool as opposed to taxonomies that employ categories which supposedly have "psychological reality" for the child. Little information has been provided as to the type of evidence needed to determine the class membership of words.

Issues such as the difficulty (or ease) of the process of assigning words to a class, or the consistency and functionality of superimposed categories as tools for studying early lexical development, have been virtually neglected (Bowerman, 1976). Chapter 3 discusses the means that can be used to determine the reference of words to real-world objects, actions, and the relationships among them. It also critically reviews a number of classification systems that have been proposed for categorizing single-word expressions (e.g., Bloom, 1973; Nelson, 1973b; McShane, 1980).

Chapters 4 and 5 are devoted to the study of word-meaning acquisition. Chapter 4 orients the reader to the main considerations that must be taken into account when studying early meanings. The distinction between intension and extension (Anglin, 1977) is explained in Chapter 4, and some practical suggestions are offered as to how the extension of a new word can be determined. The chapter concludes with a summary of the evidence on the extensional properties of early words, in particular the tendency of young children to overextend the meaning of words to various referents which lie outside the adult category for the same word.

Chapter 5 does not provide a comprehensive review of the theoretical literature available on the subject of word-meaning acquisition, but is rather designed to acquaint the reader with the most central theoretical models of the acquisition of meaning, as well as to direct attention to the issues that are most closely related to the present investigation. Besides critically reviewing each model of meaning, the chapter presents specific predictions that each model makes on the course of extension of early words.

Chapter 6 concludes the theoretical introduction of the book. It considers philosophical and practical issues involved in conducting a naturalistic investigation of early speech. Since naturalistic studies are quite common in child language, but are rarely accepted outside developmental psycholinguistics, it seems advisable to explore their necessity and advantages as well as disadvantages. The basic assumptions of qualitative research and the main principles of data collection, data organization, and data analysis are discussed. Moreover, a special attempt is made to contrast the disciplined case-study methodology with other types of naturalistic studies. The chapter addresses the following specific questions: (a) why and when a case-study approach should be considered by child-language researchers; (b) the ingredients of a full-scale case-study of early speech; (c) the methods of measuring the scientific truth of a disciplined case-study; and (d) the limitations of case-study research.

Chapters 7 and 8 describe my own case-study investigation of the early lexical development of one subject. Chapter 7 reports in detail the methods of data collection and presents the system by which the comprehensive quantity of data was prepared for later analysis. Five different measures of reliability and validity created to test the truth value of the data are described, and their numerical results given.

A comprehensive set of operationalized rules was developed to classify words according to their reference to real-world contents and to their scope of extension. The five categories of reference and four mutually exclusive categories of extension are defined in Chapter 8. A number of examples from Keren's data are cited to illustrate the specific rules and the criteria for their application. The chapter concludes with a short description of the coding procedure and the computer analysis that was conducted for the present research.

Chapters 9 through 11 report the principal findings in regard to Keren's early lexical development. Quantitative results are reported in Chapter 9. The curve of the child's lexical growth throughout the period of investigation is presented, showing that new words entered her lexicon very slowly in the initial phase with a sudden increase in the acquisition of new words about two months prior to the emergence of word combinations. A considerable slowdown in learning words was noted towards the end of the stage.

In Chapter 10, the findings in regard to the development of reference are presented. The distribution of the child's words in the five different categories of reference is given for every month of study. The correspondence between the child's reference and adult classification by parts-of-speech was tested and it was found that a surprisingly high correspondence is exhibited between the two.

The findings on the distribution of the different classes of extension are presented in Chapter 11. The present analysis shows that some words were used by the child initially in very restrictive settings only (underextended), while others were applied too broadly from the outset (overextended). A surprisingly large number of words (45 per cent of all words analysed) could not be assigned to any specific category. Some of these unclassified words were empty words to which constant meaning could not be attached (e.g., *avoda* 'work'), while others were idiosyncratic. A number of unclassified words were undifferentiated words that were used as cover terms for whole situations, or "scenes". They were thus concurrently extended to objects and actions, as well as to relations among them.

Chapter 11 addresses such questions as: Does the child apply the same basic rules for learning the meanings of words throughout the one-word period? Does the child alter her strategies at a specific point in time? If, in fact, the child changes her way of treating the relationship between a word and its meaning, when does this change occur?

The final chapter of the book (Chapter 12) tests the generality of the case-study findings, integrates them and presents their theoretical and practical implications. Here, the major findings are summarized and compared with other evidence on children's early lexicons. It will be shown that the principal findings as to the size of single-word vocabulary, the rate of lexical growth, and the basic patterns of meaning acquisition were not idiosyncratic to the subject of the present case-study research. Published reports, as well as additional diaries of Hebrew-speaking children, reveal overwhelming similarities in the processes for learning new words, and in matching conventional meanings to them. Thus, Keren's data seem representative at least of middle-class infants reared in Western cultures.

Chapter 12 offers concluding remarks as to the status of the one-word period, its fundamental structure, and its function in establishing the connection between words and their underlying conventional meanings. It will be shown that there is a great difference between the beginning and the end of the one-word period. Whereas at the beginning each word is learned slowly and as a special case, at the end of the period most words are learned quickly and are immediately attached to their correct conventional meaning. I shall argue that the one-word period is indeed a stage in acquiring language since it meets the strict criteria set by psychologists for determining stages in development. During the one-word stage, which extends over eight to twelve months, children learn how symbolic meanings are conveyed by words, and which principles to follow in order to apply words in the right contexts to convey conventional meanings.

It will be claimed that only some words are initially learned by the child as undifferentiated cover terms for whole situations. Such words are used as verbal labels for a set of different elements and relationships that belong to the same scheme. Unclassified words are usually acquired early and are applied to various objects, actions, and relationships for a lengthy period of time, sometimes even beyond the limits of the one-word stage. Most of these words are frequently heard by the child in repeated everyday contexts which do not facilitate referential differentiation. Many situational words are never modeled to the child in contexts which reinforce a clear word-referent pairing.

The considerably large number of words which are regularly extended by the child from their outset indicates that strong ties exist between non-linguistic categorization abilities and early lexical development. The present study shows that children concurrently apply various strategies for mapping words onto their underlying meanings. It is argued here that the generally accepted categorical model, in which concepts are described in terms of underlying features, cannot account for all of a child's early meanings. I propose that categorical models of meaning must be supplemented by an alternative representational model that invokes the notion of schemes (Mandler, 1979, 1983), or holistic processing (Kemler-Nelson, 1984).

My findings indicate that the vast majority of the early words that are learned by the child are extended to subsets of referents in the corresponding adult category or to an overlapping set of referents. Only a few words are extended to referents that do not belong to the basic adult category for the same word. Overextension, then, is not as common a phenomenon as some theorists have predicted. Overextensions are recorded late in the developmental history of each word, and are usually applied to outside referents on the basis of similarity of components. The evidence from the present case-study investigation indicates that a child's ability to perform componential analysis of referents is not an early development.

The book concludes with a discussion of the relative significance of the syntactic structure of parental input, and the transparency of the contexts of acquiring new words to the establishment of word reference. It is proposed that more detailed analyses of the linguistic and non-linguistic contexts in which words are learned should be carried out in order to verify the theoretical claims that are derived from the present case-study investigation.

The one-word period and stages in language development[1]

When my daughter Keren was age 24(14), and well into the phase of producing well-formed Hebrew sentences, she spent an afternoon visiting with her grandmother. During that visit, Keren was introduced to a little girl, Sharon, who was about her age and whom she had not met before. The two girls played together. After returning home I recorded the following conversation between my daughter and myself:

M: *kereni,*   *sixakt*   *im šaron?/*

      kereni   play   with Sharon

$$\left[\begin{array}{l}\text{past, 2nd person,}\\\text{feminine, singular}\end{array}\right]$$

'Kereni, did you play with Sharon?'

K: *at*   *yodaat,*   *sharon*   *tinoket/*

      you   know   Sharon   baby

$$\left[\begin{array}{l}\text{present,}\\\text{feminine, singular}\end{array}\right]$$

'(Do) you know, Sharon (is a) baby'

hi   *lo*   *medaberet/*

she   no   talk

$$\left[\begin{array}{l}\text{present,}\\\text{feminine, singular}\end{array}\right]$$

'She (does) not speak'

hi   *omeret*   *rak*   *milim/*

she   say   only   words

$$\left[\begin{array}{l}\text{present,}\\\text{feminine, singular}\end{array}\right]$$

'She says only words'

Keren's naive hypothesis that talking in single words does not really mean "true" speaking is of relevance to the main issues of this chapter, which will examine the questions of whether the occurrence of the first meaningful

[1] An earlier version of this chapter was presented at the 1983 Tel-Aviv University Annual Workshop on Human Development. I would like to acknowledge the invaluable discussions of this presentation by L. Tolchinsky-Landsmann and I. M. Schlesinger. Special gratitude is extended to I. Levin and S. Strauss for their careful comments on earlier drafts of this chapter. Thanks are also extended to R. Berman, E. Clark, and to A. Karmiloff-Smith who encouraged me to reconsider some of my earlier claims.

words is a juncture in development that reflects a significant shift in the child's modes of representing or processing language, and whether single-word productions differ qualitatively from either pre-verbal or multi-word constructions. The chapter consists of four sections. The first section discusses the utility of the cognitive concept of stages to the specific domain of language development. The second and third sections review existing claims as to the status of the one-word period in relation to the previous pre-verbal phase, and the subsequent multi-word phase of production. The concluding section summarizes quantitative details of the one-word period.

Stages in language development

The utilization of the concept of stages raises an immediate association with the Piagetian structure-based model of cognitive development. Piaget suggests stages as a heuristic for seeking links across widely differing domains of human functioning: spatial, social, physical, linguistic, conceptual, etc. The model describes development as a fixed series of overarching stages, characterized by different modes of representation, from perceptual to formal, that are common to all areas of knowledge. For Piaget, the passage from one stage to the next is explained by the achievement of new cognitive structures. The construction of these new structures is the result of an interactive process between pre-existing structures and various aspects of the child's environment (1926, 1950).

Piaget's central claim of horizontal structure or "structure of the whole" has been questioned at different argumentative levels on both theoretical and empirical grounds. Some writers are sceptical of the claim that as development proceeds, qualitative shifts can be noted synchronically across the board in different tasks of unrelated contents (e.g., Brainerd, 1976, 1978; Levin and Simons, 1986). Others have asked whether the qualitative shifts that do emerge in development in the different domains of human functioning are all of the same nature. Thus, there are writers who claim that since the developmental literature is replete with evidence of asynchrony, inconsistency and heterogeneity across tasks, stage-related structures cannot characterize an individual's mental processes in a global fashion, but must only qualify specific knowledge or intra-domain achievements (e.g., Turiel and Davidson, 1986).

The most radical opposition to the classic structuralist model of development utterly rejects the notion of cognitive stages. Non-stage psychologists (e.g., Fodor, 1975) would argue that the same representational or computational systems characterize cognition at all ages, and that the varying performance profiles of subjects at different ages do not result from qualitative shifts in underlying structures, processes, or representations, but are linked rather to an increasing access to the same structure by the adoption of new strategies of information processing (see Keil, 1986, for an analysis of the differences in the approaches of stage vs. non-stage theorists). In light of (a) the diversity of opinions concerning the intrinsic value, underlying meaning, and usefulness of the concept of stages to the general cognitive developmental theory (Flavell, 1971, 1982; Flavell and Wohlwill, 1969; Wohlwill, 1973), and (b) the complexities noted in the application of a stage-model to a specific domain, there seems to be a genuine need for a clear statement of what the term "stage" in language development actually means.

The first question to be raised in this regard is whether the notion of stages is at all functional for the study of language acquisition. Secondly, researchers must consider the issue of what might serve as a set of identifying (essential) criteria for determining whether a given period in language acquisition does, in fact, constitute a developmental stage. A survey of the contemporary psycholinguistic literature reveals that the term "stage" appears quite deliberately in almost every text that describes how children learn to talk. Illuminating examples might be McNeill's oft-cited cognate, the "holophrastic stage", or Brown's well-known figures of stages I through V as defined in terms of children's MLU scores (1973: 56). A relatively newer term, "the pre-linguistic stage", has also been coined recently and is frequently referred to in work describing how infants convey communicative intentions prior to the emergence of conventional words (e.g., Bates, Camaioni and Volterra, 1979; Bates, Bretherton, Shore and McNew, 1983; Carter, 1978a and b, 1979). The readiness of writers to apply the term "stage" indiscriminately to any observable change in a child's overt behavior has been criticized by Wohlwill (1973), Flavell (1971), and Karmiloff-Smith (1984, 1986a, b). These researchers argue that the term must be reserved only for those changes in human functioning which are caused by a genuine qualitative shift, or for the construction of new representational systems in an individual's knowledge system (see also Mounoud, 1982, 1986).

I have argued elsewhere (Dromi, 1986) that, in principle, a stage-model is very useful for describing language development. My main justification for this position is rooted in the fact that language is by nature a highly complex system which is hierarchically organized. In such a system, it is sometimes possible to detect intra-domain developments that reflect underlying structural reorganizations. Several conditions, however, must be specified before the status of "stage" may be conferred upon a given slice of language development.

The first step in identifying a stage in language development requires the definition of its starting and ending points. This, however, is not sufficient in and of itself. It is, further, obligatory to state explicitly which qualitative features differentiate this period from preceding and subsequent periods in the sequence of language stages. A stage must usually span a recognizable length of time (see Karmiloff-Smith, 1979, 1986 for the distinction between micro- and macro-stages in development), and emergent behaviors during a given stage should constitute a novelty. Some underlying uniformity must be identified in a number of events that may initially appear heterogeneous before one can conclude that these behaviors evolve from the same underlying structure or process and hence belong to the same stage. The transition between stages must be overtly marked in the pattern of the behavioral growth of the phenomenon studied.

According to Fischer (1980), Fischer and Canfield (1986), and Globerson (1986), behavioral spurts play a central role in determining structural changes. If a child's performance is measured at optimal levels and at short intervals on a continuous scale, a spurt in his behavior will inevitably be identified at some point during measurement. This spurt usually indicates the transition from one stage to the next (Fischer and Corrigan, 1981). Finally, the utilization of stages for developments within a specific domain implies that precursor behaviors must constitute necessary but not sufficient conditions for the attainment of subsequent developments (see also Sugarman, 1983b).

The following section will consider the most prominent claims cited in child-language literature with reference to the issues raised here. It will be seen that the only theoretical issue that has been discussed is that of continuity or discontinuity between the pre-verbal and verbal stages, or between the one-word stage and the combinatorial two-word stage that follows it. In other words, it is the issue of transitions that so far has exclusively occupied the researchers' attention.

Continuity or discontinuity: the transition from pre-linguistic communication to the one-word period

A survey of contemporary studies of the early phases of verbal production reveals that very little attention has been paid to the question of whether the one-word period is a developmental construct that meets certain psychological criteria necessary for it to be considered a stage in language development. In what ways do single words differ from vocalizations of the late sensorimotor period? How can we explain the transition from one level of production to the next? These are questions that have been touched upon and that are relevant to the issue of stages. Convincing evidence that single words are in no way similar to the previously used forms of communication is needed to substantiate the claim that the emergence of the first meaningful words is a developmental novelty. Only if the difference between producing single words and vocalizing different speech sounds is not simply a matter of degree is it legitimate to assume that a marked change in the underlying representation of the linguistic knowledge is achieved at the beginning of the one-word stage.

It is generally accepted today that infants are involved in effective communication with their primary caretakers much before they begin to talk. Early evidence has been recorded of intentional communication towards the latter half of the first year of life, usually two to three months before the emergence of recognizable speech (Bates, 1979; Bruner, Roy and Ratner, 1982; Carter, 1978a; Sugarman, 1978, 1983a). During the last months of the pre-linguistic period, infants utilize both gesture and speech sounds to gain adults' attention and/or to carry out basic pragmatic acts such as imperatives, declaratives and volitions (Bates, 1979; Dore, 1974, 1978). Since functionally based pre-linguistic vocalizations are the antecedent behaviors of true words, the relationship between these vocalizations and real words must be examined. Two theoretical questions have been raised as to this relationship: Is there a continuity or discontinuity between the two periods? Is pre-verbal communication a prerequisite for the acquisition of conventional speech?

Sugarman (1983b) argues that both continuity and discontinuity must be assumed between pre-verbal and verbal communication. In her opinion, *intentional signaling* must be clearly tied to later linguistic achievements. However, it is extremely unlikely that communicative developments (i.e., the co-ordination of person and object schemes) can ever account for the details of the linguistic system itself. While Sugarman describes the relationship between the pre-verbal and verbal periods in a two-way model, other researchers have opted either for continuity or discontinuity in their discussions of the transition into meaningful speech.

In a detailed paper that discusses the transition from babbling to first referential words, Dore, Franklin, Miller and Ramer (1976) argue that between these two modes of production children utter phonetic forms that, although they have no identifiable referential meaning, are produced regularly by the child for a specific pragmatic function. Dore and his colleagues postulate that these phonetic consistent forms (PCFs) are not real words since they have no reference. They argue that the children who utter PCFs have not yet reached the representational level that is needed for learning meaningful words. According to Dore *et al.*, children arrive at the level of word production suddenly, by an instantaneous insight into the function of words, that is, the naming of objects. A very similar explanation is offered by McShane (1980), and Lock (1980), who also believe that the transition from no words to words is abrupt and can be explained by a mechanism of insight.

At odds with the "naming insight" explanation are Carter's (1978a, b, 1979), Bates's (1979), Gillis and DeSchutter's (1984), and Barrett's (1986) accounts of how children develop referential meaning. These authors argue that reference develops gradually by the repeated use of the same words in different contexts. The two key terms used by this second group of researchers to explain the transition into speech are "symbolization" and "decontextualization".

> There was no single moment when the performative structures could be said to "sprout" propositions. Instead, words as symbolic vehicles with

corresponding referents emerged gradually out of the action schemes of sensorimotor communication. (Bates, Camaioni and Volterra, 1979:125)

Gillis and DeSchutter (1984), who carefully followed the linguistic development of one child during the transition from pre-verbal communication to early speech, judge the transition to be long and gradual. Their Dutch-acquiring subject extended the transitional period for a number of months during which he acquired no new words but rather used a small number of old words in different repeated contexts. Gillis and DeSchutter hypothesize that, during the plateau stage which precedes considerable vocabulary growth, the child develops conceptual skills that constitute necessary conditions for the use of words referentially.

An additional point which must be considered when discussing the child's transition into true speech is that of the difficulties in determining which sounds in the growing linguistic system of the young child are real words. At the outset of speech production a child's words may be highly idiosyncratic. At this phase it is often difficult to differentiate between an actual word and the countless sounds which are produced by the infant in the course of a day (Braunwald, 1978). Without a clear definition of what a meaningful word is, it is extremely difficult to address the question of when the single-word period begins. As Dore *et al.* (1976) report, the two most frequently used criteria in the literature for identifying early words are:

(a)   the approximation of the child's forms to adult words, and
(b)   the consistent use of sounds in relation to objects and/or situations

Veneziano (1981) has added a third criterion for identifying meaningful words in children's early speech. She argues that during the early phases of production both the properties of the sound itself and the properties *ascribed to it by a familiar conversational partner* constitute important and indissociable factors in isolating true words. Therefore, in order to identify early words, an interactional value should be attributed to each sound, and the question of whether sequences of sounds are comprehended by an adult listener should be considered.

The arguments cited above clearly demonstrate that there are still contradictory views as to the relationship between early vocalization and first words. Some researchers argue for continuity in the transition into language while others hold for a sudden insight which instantaneously changes the child's understanding of what language can do. Clearly, there is a need for a workable definition of a meaningful word, since early words very often do not resemble adult words either in form or in content. Without such a definition and a very close ongoing observation of the growing linguistic system of the child, it would be very hard to get a clear picture of how children enter the one-word stage. The definition of a meaningful utterance that was employed in the present investigation is given below in Chapter 6, along with a description of a reliability measure that was conducted to insure that this definition could serve independent judges in identifying meaningful words in the ongoing vocalization of the subject. The discussions in Chapters 8 and 12 touch on the question of whether the one-word stage begins at a specific point in time, or whether children enter it gradually.

The relationship between single- and multi-word expressions

Exactly when the one-word period ends and children move up to the next level of multi-word utterances is an empirical question that has hardly been examined. Various claims regarding hypothesized underlying relations between one-word productions and early word combinations have, however, been made. Such claims are relevant to the discussion of whether or not the one-word period constitutes a linguistic stage and are therefore summarized below.

McNeill (1970), a proponent of the extreme nativist view, applies the term "holophrastic stage" to the early period of production during which children use single-word utterances. The term "holophrase" refers to single-word utterances which correspond to complete adult sentences (Ingram, 1971; Rodgon, 1976). According to McNeill (1970) (and other nativists, e.g., Fodor, 1975, 1980), children are endowed from birth with the underlying representations of the universal grammatical rules of language. Therefore, the underlying representations of fully grammatical sentences are present in the child's mind even when, in fact, he is producing only single-word utterances. The limitations hypothesized by McNeill to account for the phenomenon of holophrastic speech are reduced short-term memory, low attention span, and severe programming deficiencies. Such constraints are gradually removed through maturational processes, and this is reflected in the child's growing ability to construct longer utterances and finally grammatical sentences. McNeill makes a strong claim for only quantitative differences between holophrastic speech and later speech, since he considers it impossible for the child to develop a knowledge of syntax on the basis of previous experience with single words. Since McNeill argues that no qualitative differences exist in the child's underlying characterization of his linguistic knowledge during the different phases of production (the one-word period, the period of early syntax, and the period of late syntax), it would seem that he does not attribute to "holophrastic speech" the status of a developmental "stage".

Bloom (1973) was the first to dispute McNeill's arguments. She claimed that the reason one-word-stage children do not produce sentences is that they do not know the syntactic rules of their language. According to Bloom, single-word utterances are not "holophrases"; rather, they are simple linguistic entities that the child produces while focusing on single aspects of situations. During the early phases of the one-word period, children are unable to deal with more than one aspect of a situation at a time, and they therefore produce single words *one at a time*. Towards the end of the one-word period, children start to differentiate between different aspects of the same situation, and also refer to them verbally. However, they still have no knowledge of syntax, and as a consequence they now utter sequences of single words. Bloom argues that there is in fact a qualitative difference between the one-word stage and later stages of linguistic development. In her opinion, the difference lies in the underlying knowledge of syntactic rules which is present only when the child produces multi-word utterances.

These two contradictory views as to the relationship between the one-word period and the early period of word combining has generated a controversy among researchers as to whether *discontinuity* or *continuity* exists between the one-word period and subsequent periods in language acquisition. Bloom's (1973) proposal that there is discontinuity between the two has not gained wide support and has been rejected by both Greenfield and Smith (1976) and Scollon (1976) on different grounds.

Greenfield and Smith's investigation of the different ways children use the same single-word utterances throughout the one-word period led them to the conclusion that although this period seems to be static in syntactic form, it is remarkably dynamic in terms of growth in semantic content. They do not assume that the concept of a sentence is present in the mind of children who produce only one-word utterances. Rather, they suggest that in the course of the one-word period, children develop their ability to convey complex messages by means of combining words with non-linguistic elements. Finding that the semantic relations expressed by single words (e.g., agent, action, location, possession, etc.) are also conveyed by later speech, they argue that: "Between early language and matured language ... the basic organization may be the same" (1976:223).

Scollon (1976, 1979) highlights still other aspects of continuity between the one-word period and the early phases of multi-word speech. In the speech of his subject he identified *vertical constructions*, and he argues that these sequences of utterances are constructed in a topic/comment organization that conveys a single complex message. Since such constructions were present in speech samples recorded during both the one-word period *and* the multi-word period, Scollon concludes that in terms of their discourse structure, the single-word stage and the multi-word stage are basically the same. According to Scollon, during the prolonged single-word period, the child practices the main prerequisites for syntax which are then directly transferred to multi-word structures.

The arguments cited above indicate that there is no one predominant view as to the status of the single-word period in the sequence of linguistic growth. Most researchers, although on differing grounds, argue for continuity and a gradual transition into the more advanced level of speech. Bloom, however, vigorously objects to this view. One goal of the present investigation is to provide additional data relevant to this very interesting question of whether the one-word period is indeed a distinct stage in linguistic development, manifesting unique characteristics with respect not only to subsequent stages but also to preceding ones.

Quantitative measures of the one-word period

Most charts describing the milestones of early development suggest that between the ages of one and two years an infant typically learns from 30 to 300 new words (Nelson, 1973b). This gross estimate is far too general and does not allow for predictions in regard to the age at which children can be expected to produce their first meaningful words, the regular size of single-word vocabularies, and the rate at which children can be expected to acquire new words throughout the one-word period.

Contemporary psycholinguistic studies of the beginning of speech provide only general estimates of the quantitative characteristics of early vocabularies. These estimates are either derived from anecdotal and more qualitative analyses of underlying processes involved in learning to talk, or are based on calculations of the number of new words produced by subjects in a given recorded session, a method which provides only partial evidence since it is based on a comparison between types and tokens in two successive recordings.

From a methodological point of view, it does not seem desirable to collapse the findings of diverse studies in order to arrive at an overall picture of the quantitative characteristics of the one-word period. Data deriving from a variety of investigations are not comparable since researchers employ varying definitions of what constitutes a meaningful word and adopt different sampling procedures, methods of recording data and techniques of data analysis. Despite these reservations, some very general outlines do emerge from existing studies. These outlines are presented below and will be used later (see Chapters 8 and 11) to test the generality of the results of the more continuous and exact measures obtained in the present research.

When do children first start to utter meaningful words? Nelson (1973b), who studied the early lexical development of 18 English-speaking children, reports that her subjects reached the level of ten different words at a mean age of 15 months (the exact ages ranged from 13 to 19 months). Similar results were obtained by McCune-Nicolich who recorded ten different words during a 30-minute audio-recorded session for two of her subjects at the ages of 14 and 15 months, respectively (Anisfeld, 1984:80). Gillis and DeSchutter (1984), who very carefully studied the development of the lexicon of one Dutch-acquiring subject (by video-taping the child twice a week for over one hour at each session), found that the first word was acquired around the subject's first birthday, and that he reached the level of eight different words when he was 19 months old.

Somewhat younger ages for the emergence of first words have been suggested by other investigators. Bloom (1973) reports that Allison's record of single words began when she was nine months old. Braunwald (1978) identified the first meaningful word in Laura's speech when she was 9(8). Greenfield and Smith's subjects were 8(19) and 7(22) when their first words were recorded. Among researchers who studied their own children, Bowerman (1978) is the only one who reports that her daughters' first object names were learned when the children were just over one year old. Eva and Christy were 13 and 14 months, respectively.

For how long do children produce only "one word at a time"? The scientific information about this question is quite limited. Braunwald (1978) reports that at 20 months Laura's linguistic development conformed to Brown's (1973) description of Stage I (i.e., the early period of word combination). Bloom's (1973) study was concluded when Allison was 22 months of age. Although Bloom (1973:110) states that at that time Allison spoke in sentences, she does not specify the grammatical constructions or frequency of these utterances. Greenfield and Smith (1976) are the only researchers who provide an exact cut-off criterion for the one-word stage:

> The data reported in this volume end at a point where single word utterances were in the minority for the first time. (1976:31)

Nicky was 21(8) and Matthew 22(0) when their speech samples fulfilled this criterion. With this information in hand, it is reasonable to conclude that children start to utter meaningful words around their first birthday and continue to produce single-word utterances for a period that ranges between eight and twelve months.

How many items does a child's complete lexicon of single words contain? Nelson (1973b) used an arbitrary cut-off point of 50 words for the lexicons she examined. She argues that the slower learners had vocabularies of about 50 words at the age of two years. Moreover, most children in her sample started to combine words into phrases at that age level. Other information that is relevant to the question of vocabulary size comes from Braunwald (1978). Although Braunwald was not directly interested in this question, she reports that by the age of 15(12) Laura had acquired her first 50 words, and that by the age of 20(0) she produced 391 different words. Even though Laura was a Stage I speaker at the second count, it seems evident that she acquired far more than 50 single words before starting to construct phrases.

Support for Braunwald's figure for a single lexicon comes from a study which was conducted in 1926 and is summarized by McCarthy (1954) and reported in Anisfeld (1984:79). This study found that during the first half of the second year of life, infants learn between three and 22 new words; between the ages of 18 and 20 months they increase their vocabularies by 96 additional words; and from the age of 21 to 24 months they acquire another 154 words. On the basis of the limited evidence cited above, I estimate that single-word lexicons contain over 250 words. I hypothesize that the discrepancy between Nelson and other researchers can be explained in part in methodological terms. This discrepancy, however, clearly points to the need for a more systematic examination of children's early vocabularies.

The question of how many different words children's lexicons contain prior to the first evidence of syntactic ability is only one quantitative issue. A different and yet related problem is the rate at which new words are learned throughout the one-word stage. Does the learning curve of single words display specific characteristics? Nelson offers the following description of the rate of growth of the first 50-word lexicons of 18 subjects:

> The usual course of acquisition was a slowly accelerating pace with a strong positive increase at the end of the period when the maximum rate was achieved. The maximum rate, however, varied for individual children from 10 to 66 words per month. (1973b:36)

While the trend described by Nelson was typical of the majority of children she observed, it was not true for all of them. Similarly, Braunwald (1978) presents a monthly-rate calculation of Laura's lexical growth between the ages of 9(8) and 16(0) (1978:505 Table 4). She found that during the early phases of the study her daughter added words at a slow rate in contrast to the few months that followed the acquisition of the first 52 words. Between 17 and 18 months of age a dramatic increase in the rate of acquiring new words was noted by the investigator:

> During this interval, Laura added 80 new words to her cumulative lexicon. For whatever developmental reasons, she was suddenly able to increase rapidly the number of words in her vocabulary. (1978:505)

Braunwald was not the first researcher to report on a sudden spurt in lexical development. Other researchers also described a sudden increase in children's vocabularies at different times during the one-word stage. Bloom (1973) identified two distinct phases in this prolonged period on the basis of differences in lexical behavior. During the second phase, which in Allison's case lasted about four months (between the ages of 17 and 21 months), the following lexical characteristics were noted:

(a)   the subject's vocabulary became more stable with a noticeable decrease in the mortality rate of new words;

(b)   the frequency of use of existing words increased significantly; and

(c)   many new words, especially words for objects, were added to the child's lexicon.

Bloom (1973) attributes these characteristics to the child's cognitive achievement of the concept of "object permanence". She argues that before children fully recognize that objects continue to exist even when they are out of sight, the concepts to which object words are attached are not stable enough to support consistent usage.

The hypothesis that a causal relationship exists between the attainment of object permanence and the growth of lexicon was tested by Corrigan (1976, 1978, 1979), who reports that following the attainment of the 6th rank of object permanence in Uzgiris and Hunt's (1975) scale, a spurt in lexical growth is noted. Similar findings have been observed for longitudinal and cross-sectional subjects at about the age of 18 months.

In a number of recent studies of early speech (Benedict, 1979; Halliday, 1975; Gillis and DeSchutter, 1984; McCune-Nicolich, 1981; and McShane, 1980), researchers refer to this spurt in vocabulary development, finding that it is observed during the second half of the one-word period and soon before word combinations emerge. Halliday (1975:41) reports that between the ages of 16(15) and 18(0), 50 to 100 new meanings evolved in Nigel's language system. These were expressed by means of conventional words, whereas earlier meanings had been expressed in very idiosyncratic ways. McShane (1980) observed a sudden increase in the size of vocabularies of six children. He argues that this spurt is a direct reflection of the main achievement of the one-word stage, namely, insight into the naming function of words (see also p. 14 above). According to McShane, after experiencing this insight, children learn many more words and also begin to construct sentences.

McCune-Nicolich (1981) similarly reports a sudden rapid change for the rate of lexical acquisition in all of her five subjects. She claims that the lexical spurt is recorded between 19 and 20 months of age, immediately after an initial lexicon of 30–50 words is established. In Gillis and DeSchutter's 1984 opinion, the rapid rate at which new words are learned following on an extended plateau can be seen to indicate that the build-up of a productive lexicon is a gradual and continuous process. Gillis and DeSchutter's subject, who initially learned new words very slowly, showed a distinct change in the rate of acquisition of new words at the age of 19 months. At that point he learned 92 different words in the short period of two months.

How long children continue to learn new words at this increased pace is another question to be considered. It is mainly the left side of the acquisition curve that has been investigated thus far. Only one study tested the relationship between the rate of lexical growth and the transition to syntax. Anisfeld (1984:107) reports that in McCune-Nicolich's five English-speaking subjects, as MLU value exceeded 1:0, a clear slowdown in the learning rate of new words was noted. This finding may indicate that the one-word stage is coming to an end, and therefore more evidence in regard to this issue would be of major value. I would suspect that the fact that researchers other than McCune-Nicolich have failed to document the slowdown in lexical growth stems primarily from methodological considerations (see Fischer and Corrigan, 1981). Once a child's lexicon exceeds 50 or 100 words, it is extremely difficult to study it closely (Nelson, 1973b). Only in a study involving systematic daily recordings can one obtain the amount of information needed to develop a precise and complete picture of the shape of the acquisition curve of new words.

Summary

Some general outlines of the quantitative features of the one-word stage have been given above. It seems that children start to utter their first meaningful words around their first birthday. They then continue to produce only single words for a considerable number of months, possibly eight to twelve. Initially, new words enter the child's lexicon slowly, but at some point the rate of acquiring new words changes radically. When exactly the spurt in lexical growth is noted does not appear to be precisely documented. Investigators also differ in their views as to the relationship between this spurt and the attainment of specific cognitive or social skills. The exact shape of the acquisition curve throughout the one-word period has yet to be examined. There is some evidence indicating that towards the end of the period the acquisition rate slows down.

In light of the meager and still inconclusive data, one goal of the study reported below (Chapters 6 through 10) was to examine directly the quantitative aspects of the one-word period in one child. As I shall demonstrate, an attempt was made to determine whether clear boundaries of the period can be identified. Other aspects that were examined include the rate of lexical growth during this period and the total number of words that are learned by the child before she moves into the stage of uttering two- and multi-word constructions.

3   Classification systems of single-word utterances

Words, the building blocks of human language, refer to a variety of real-world entities, among them objects, actions, and relationships (Anglin, 1977). In adult language, words carry lexical meanings and are used to construct grammatical sentences. Yet how can we determine the reference of children's first words? This is a complex question which is directly relevant to the present work. When children utter single words "one at a time" it is not always easy to decide whether a given word refers to an object, an action, or a certain relationship. Consider the following example discussed in Bowerman (1976). Whereas Bowerman's own daughter used the English verb *close* for closing doors and pushing chairs up to tables, another child produced the English noun *door* in exactly the same contexts. Was *door* an action word in the speech of the second child or *close* an object word in the speech of the first? How are we to deal with linguistic and contextual information that supports contradictory assumptions?

Although a number of investigators have distinguished between words for objects, words for action, and words for attributes, processes, and states, the grounds for determining the category membership of early words have not always been explicitly defined. Some investigators have classified early words purely on the basis of phonological resemblance to adult forms, superimposing categorization systems developed to analyse more matured speech onto single-word corpora. The present chapter introduces various taxonomies which have been proposed for the analysis of single-word speech. Space is devoted to a discussion of the critical distinction that exists between systems that are used to determine psychologically real categories and those which are applied as methodological means for data reduction. The chapter emphasizes the need for a close examination of repeated contexts in which the same word is uttered over time. It is argued that early words may change their reference from one recording to the next and that, although they may at times resemble adult forms, they are apt to convey very different meanings. Since lexical acquisition is a highly dynamic process, it is recommended that the evaluation of the class membership of words involve an ongoing process that measures changes in repeated contexts.

Why categorize early words?

Although many investigators have made attempts to classify early words (e.g., Gentner, 1978, 1982; Nelson, 1973b), very little discussion appears in the literature as to why this procedure was performed. The grounds for determining the category membership of words are also very rarely defined explicitly and in most instances no clear-cut rules for assigning words to specific classes are given.

On the more interesting theoretical level, classification systems may reveal the existence of psychologically real categories that are functional in the child's linguistic system. On the practical level, however, classification systems can serve as instruments for summarizing and organizing data and discerning regularities. In his survey of taxonomies of early semantic relations of Stage I speech, Brown (1973) argues that a set of semantic relations (e.g., agent and action, object and location, possessor and possessed) may represent real categories, i.e., categories that are functional in the comprehension and production of sentences by children. The identification of psychologically real categories in the speech of young children bears directly on the study of semantic development. Therefore, when researchers talk about different classes of words they must be explicit as to whether the classes are considered to be real for the child or were merely generated to simplify the analysis.

Assume, for example, that it can be proved that the lexicons of young children consist of only two types of words: open class words and closed class words – functors (e.g., Bloom, 1973; Braine, 1963). If the two classes show different developmental routes (e.g., closed words entering the child's lexicon either earlier or later than open words), the hypothesis that two types of words do exist might be accepted. Bloom's (1973) attempt to identify two periods in the prolonged stage of one-word speech was based on her distinction between substantive and functional words. Bloom argues that functional words, which express relations among different objects (and are based on similar experiences the child has had with a variety of different objects), are the dominant class of words used by the child during the early phases of production. Only after achieving the concept of object permanence is the child able to represent conceptually the objects to which substantive words make reference, and therefore the child learns many more substantive words during the second half of the one-word stage.

Bloom is not the only researcher to base her theoretical explanations on findings suggesting that there are distinct, psychologically real categories in the child's speech. Another attempt of a similar kind is Gentner's (1975, 1978, 1982) explanation of why the acquisition of verbs lags behind that of nouns. Gentner argues that there are clear differences between the underlying representations of nouns as opposed to verbs. Nouns typically – especially in child speech – encode object concepts composed of concrete, tangible, and highly imaginable category members. In contrast, verbs, or "relational terms" in Gentner's terminology, encode concepts that consist of perceptually less constrained elements with a variety of different potential conflational patterns (i.e., ways in which semantic elements are combined). This difference explains why nouns are acquired earlier than verbs, and also why nouns outnumber verbs in the early lexicons of children.

In an experimental study, Huttenlocher, Smiley and Charney (1983) tested the hypothesis that different subclasses of action words can be identified in the speech of two- to three-year-old children. Huttenlocher and Charney examined how children use verbs to encode both their own actions and the actions they observe. They found that children describe their own actions earlier than actions that are performed by others, and that they verbally encode movement patterns (e.g., run, jump) well before they talk about goal-directed actions (e.g., get, put). These findings clearly indicate that it is possible to show that psychologically real subclasses of words do exist in the child's lexicon.

On a more practical level, researchers have often used pre-planned taxonomies as a research tool for reducing and organizing data. In previous studies of the one-word stage, single-word utterances have been classified according to: (a) adult parts-of-speech (e.g., Goldin-Meadow, Seligman and Gelman, 1976); (b) grammatical categories that correspond to parts-of-speech (e.g., Benedict, 1979; Gentner, 1982; Nelson, 1973b); (c) semantic relations (e.g., Greenfield and Smith, 1976; Rodgon, 1976); and (d) pragmatic categories (e.g., Dore, 1973, 1974; Halliday, 1975; McShane, 1980). In studies such as these, a taxonomy is usually selected as an instrument for research in order to facilitate the answering of certain theoretical questions. The most common queries have involved identifying similarities and differences between child and adult linguistic systems; determining the relative proportions of words in different classes in the child's speech; and determining the order of emergence of the different categories as a function of the relative linguistic complexity of the classes in question.

Greenfield and Smith's (1976) study is a good example of the use of a taxonomy that was originally developed for the description of adult speech. These authors used Fillmore's (1968) case-grammar model to analyse single-word expressions. They found that during the one-word period, children learn to use the same word to express a variety of semantic relations. This constitutes the main evidence for their claim that there is continuity between early language and mature speech (see also Chapter 2 above).

Nelson's (1973b) argument that the high proportion of nominals in the speech of her subjects reflected a fundamental distinction between referential and expressive communicators is another example of the application of a taxonomy as a means of formulating a theoretical argument. The procedure of calculating the relative proportions of different types of words has been used by other researchers for similar purposes. Gentner (1982) performed such an analysis on early speech samples of children acquiring four different languages. Her goal was to test her hypothesis that conceptual rather than linguistic factors account for the early emergence and high frequency of nouns relative to verbs in the lexicons of young children.

Several investigators have classified words in such a way as to enable them to test the order of emergence of specific linguistic forms or functions. Greenfield and Smith (1976), Halliday (1975), and McShane (1980) present findings on the order of acquisition and the development of different semantic case relations and various pragmatic intentions. These authors sought to explain their findings by testing the relative complexities of the categories they had devised and imposed on the data. They predicted that the more complex a category, the later it would emerge in children's speech.

Since there may be a number of motivations for categorizing early words, and as some obvious anticipated difficulties in the actual classifying procedure still exist, it would seem that when selecting a set of categories to facilitate the scientific study of early speech, these categories must be clearly defined and explicitly motivated. If a categorization system is constructed on the basis of an *a priori* assumption that its classes are functional constituents in the child's linguistic system, such an assumption should be overtly marked. By the same token, when categories are borrowed from adult speech and superimposed on child samples, such a procedure should be reported and justified. The type of evidence required to assign a given word to a specific class should also be clearly stated. When researchers anticipate difficulties in the actual application of their categorization code, these should be identified and optional solutions suggested. The following section is a critical review of taxonomies which have been used by various researchers to classify single-word utterances. It is organized in historical perspective, and points to some of the weaknesses in existing systems.

Content-based categorization systems of single words

The first two classification systems proposed for the analysis of children's single-word lexicons were those of Bloom (1973) and Nelson (1973b). Although they differ from each other in their internal structure and in the criteria used for determining the category membership of a given word, both are based on the assumption that child categories are semantic in nature. Since part-of-speech analysis is a strictly formal tool based on the combinatorial possibilities or "privileges of occurrence" of words, this instrument is completely irrelevant when pre-syntactic speech is being analysed (Brown, 1957). Bloom, Nelson, and other child-language researchers, recognizing the consequences of applying part-of-speech analyses, have therefore proposed semantic or content-based categories to avoid this obvious incompatibility.

Bloom (1973:68–70) distinguishes between two classes of words: substantive words that refer to classes of objects or events, and function words that encode relationships among objects and events. Words are allocated to one class or the other according to the phonological resemblance found between child and adult forms. Thus, using the form of the word as her main guide for classification, Bloom suggests words such as *chair* and *cookie* as typical examples of substantive forms, and *up*, *away*, and *more* as examples of function forms. She holds that during the first few months of single-word production, function words dominate the child's lexicon and are used repeatedly in various contexts, whereas during the same period substantive forms are learned infrequently, are uttered inconsistently, and show a high mortality rate (i.e., they often drop out of use). The relative rate of acquisition for substantive words, Bloom argues, changes considerably towards the last months of the single-word period when these words constitute the major class of actively used words and are recorded frequently and consistently.

As reported earlier, child forms have largely been categorized according to their phonological resemblance to adult model words. Bloom (1973) may also have used behavioral clues to determine the category membership of words, but she does not specify any explicit set of rules she may have followed, and completely neglects the issue of possible mismatches of meaning between child forms and adult model words. Similarly, she does not directly address the question of whether the two classes she identified were psychologically real for the subject. Since the evidence is not clear that the two classes are indeed different, it seems that the distinction may have been superimposed onto the child's system rather than actually reflecting functional differences in it.

Nelson's categorization system is much more elaborate than Bloom's. It consists of five classes of words that originate from grammatical distinctions, but are defined and illustrated in terms of a child's differentiation of real-world entities. Thus, "nominals" in Nelson's system refer to the objects or things in the world, and "action words" are those that describe demand or accompany actions.

In Nelson's study, words were classified on the basis of mother's descriptions of the contexts in which they first occurred. This fact has been criticized in the literature (e.g., Bowerman, 1978). McShane (1980), for example, criticizes Nelson for confusing pragmatic and semantic considerations in the course of analysis. McShane argues that the assignment of the word *door* to the category of action words merely because it was first recorded when the child expressed her wish to go outside is a clear violation of semantic rules. (The example of *door* is the only one cited by Nelson to illustrate her coding system.)

In sum, Nelson's system, although original, suffers from the lack of comprehensive discussion of rules and examples. Moreover, Nelson fails to discuss the difficulties she faced in classifying her words according to the system of analysis in question. Another weakness of the system is the fact that words are classified on the basis of a single-context description. This is a very serious problem in view of the common observation that early words are not very stable in terms of the contexts of their initial applications.

Despite the weaknesses of Nelson's system, it should be noted that this first attempt to describe emerging grammatical knowledge in semantic terms was followed by other studies which either replicated or mildly modified Nelson's original system. Benedict (1979) adopted the system and examined the first 50-word lexicons of eight children, considering comprehension as well as production. Braunwald (1978) replicated Nelson's analysis of the first 52 actively used words of her subject Laura. In a more recent study, Gentner (1982) used a modified version of Nelson's classification system to analyse speech samples of one English-speaking subject and of six subjects acquiring languages other than English.

Gentner's classification system consisted of four main categories: (a) nominal terms, (b) predicate terms, (c) expressive terms, and (d) indeterminant terms. Gentner collapsed the two categories of action words and modifiers into one which she called "predicate terms". In addition, she generated a category for words she could not classify. This new addition is of great importance, since, as will be argued below, some words in the early lexicons of children are used ambiguously or in multiple ways. Gentner performed this analysis in order to discover whether the pattern observed for English-speaking children – nominals emerging earlier than predicate terms – is a universal of language development. She hypothesized that such a universal, if confirmed, would support her claim that conceptual rather than linguistic factors account for the relatively later acquisition of verbs than nouns.

Two pitfalls are apparent in Gentner's study. First, she is not explicit enough about the data-reduction procedures she followed. Her analysis was conducted on data collected for various purposes by other researchers and is not described in any detail. She neglects the issue of how the data were prepared for secondary analysis, and specifies neither whether she followed a strict rule in determining the placement of a word in the child's cumulative lexicon, nor whether words were classified on the basis of their first occurrence or repeated uses.

The second problem in Gentner's (1982) work is even more serious. Although her study was directly related to the correspondence between adult parts-of-speech and child categories of meaning, she ignores the possibility of mismatches between the two. Gentner asks why *nouns* are learned before *verbs*, and provides an answer based on the relative proportions of *nominals* and *predicate terms* in the speech of children, but she did not test the degree of correspondence between the child categories and adult parts-of-speech. Braunwald's (1978) and Griffiths and Atkinson's (1978) finding that some words in the child's initial lexicon show complete mismatch with adult meanings explains why a measure of correspondence between the categories of the child and those of the adult must precede any conclusion as to the relative distribution of specific classes of words in the child's early lexicon.

Semantic relations and single-word corpora

The most detailed attempt to describe the "structure" of single-word utterances by the application of a categorization system was that of Greenfield and Smith (1976). These authors documented the linguistic development of two English-speaking children throughout the one-word stage, superimposing the case-grammar model of analysis, as proposed by Fillmore (1968) and Chafe (1970), onto the speech samples they collected. Greenfield and Smith's classification system consists of twelve classes of words. Each class is defined according to the semantic relation expressed by the utterance. Since semantic relations must be determined by the combinatorial properties of at least two words, a single-word expression is analysed by integrating it with its non-linguistic context. Thus, in the proposed system, a distinction is made between the referential use of a word (e.g., *daddy* for the entity DADDY), and the relational use of the same word (e.g., daddy to indicate possession relationship between DADDY and some other entity, or for indicating DADDY's semantic role as an agent or the patient of an action).

The order of emergence of the twelve different classes in the speech of the two subjects was found to be substantially the same. This finding supported the authors' theoretical claim that during the one-word period children learn to express new combinatorial meanings in already known words. The ongoing developmental process of learning how to use words to convey new semantic functions (i.e., case relations) is held by Greenfield and Smith to be the most significant achievement of the one-word period.

The most critical question concerning Greenfield and Smith's (1976) study is whether superimposing case-grammar analysis onto the limited and unripe linguistic system of the child is justified. Several examples cited by the authors to illustrate their system raise serious doubts as to the psychological reality of the classes for the child. Consider, for example, the two following classifications: the word *bow-wow*, said when hearing a dog barking outside, was assigned to the category of "indicative object", while a person's name, said under very similar circumstances when the child heard a sound made by this person, was assigned to the category of "agent". A similar example is the classification of the word *fan*, produced when the child expected a fan to be turned on, to the category of "object". Here the classification as "object" reflects the assumption that the child attributed inanimate properties to the fan and that he knew that a person was going to turn the fan on. These examples and several others indicate that Greenfield and Smith's analysis was not carried out independently of adult knowledge of the grammatical categories of words. It would seem, therefore, that in many instances the classification of an utterance was motivated by adult linguistic intuition rather than by non-linguistic cues provided by the child or the context.

The direct inclusion of the non-linguistic context in the representation of the meaning of an utterance is also problematic in Greenfield and Smith's methodology. Such a methodological procedure requires much stronger justification than is presented by the authors, as well as reliability measures to demonstrate that the contextual distinctions that were made could be detected by other observers.

Finally, Greenfield and Smith seem to have confused pragmatics and semantics. At least two of the categories they applied are pragmatic rather than semantic. The category "performative" was defined as "utterances that occur as part of a child's actions" (1976:50) and "volition", the basic function of which is "to obtain some desired response from the person addressed" (1976:51), was defined as a particular kind of "performative". It is not very clear why the authors considered the communicative functions of utterances in classifying them according to what they characterize as *semantic* meanings. Should vocalizations that occur in one context (e.g., embedded in action schemes) be analysed as semantically different from the same vocalizations in other contexts? Perhaps some of the confusion is created by the authors' use of terms in other than their usual meanings. The term "performative", for example, was borrowed from Austin's taxonomy of different types of verbs. It is unclear how words that were classified by Greenfield and Smith as "performatives" are related to Austin's original definition, if at all. Should the words *hi* or *bye bye*, said by the child while waving, be seen as precursors or prerequisites of performative verbs to be learned later?

To summarize, Greenfield and Smith's attempt to investigate the development of meaning during the one-word period is both ambitious and comprehensive; yet the very richness of the interpretation procedures they applied has given rise to a number of weaknesses. It seems to me that in analysing single-word expressions it is very often extremely difficult to decide whether the child is overextending the meaning of an existing word to an irrelevant referent, or is referring to some semantic relation that he or she is able to notice. Consider, for example, the case of a one year old pointing to a new briefcase and saying *daddy*. Is the child calling the briefcase by the "wrong" name or is he saying *daddy* to indicate his appreciation of the relationship of *possession* between daddy and briefcases? I suspect that the adoption of any single interpretation of such an example is highly biased (Schlesinger, 1982, and Personal Communication, October 10, 1983), and it is thus inadvisable.

Pragmatic-based classification systems

The mid-seventies witnessed a substantial increase in the number of studies which focused on the question of how young speakers convey various communicative intents. Pioneering attempts to describe one-word expressions in a pragmatic theoretical framework were made by Dore (1974, 1975), Halliday (1975), and McShane (1980). Dore and McShane defined a set of speech acts (Austin, 1962; Searle, 1969) operationally, and supplied evidence on the relative frequency of their use by children. Halliday (1975) used his own classification system, defined in terms of pragmatic constituents, to describe the emergence of pragmatic functions in the speech of his son, Nigel.

The orientation of these three pragmatic studies is in sharp contrast to the more structurally based studies of Bloom (1973), Nelson (1973b), and Greenfield and Smith (1976), which investigated the development of grammatical devices to convey meaning. The later studies concentrated on describing the different communicative intentions and ignored any issues related to the linguistic devices used to express these intentions.

McShane's classification system is a representative example of this tendency to disregard structure while emphasizing the role of communication. It is highly elaborate and encompasses three distinct levels of analysis (see McShane, 1980:71–9). On the basis of his findings (and similarly to Dore, 1974, and Halliday, 1975), McShane argues that the pragmatic functions of language emerge prior to the acquisition of the conventional means for expressing them verbally. According to McShane, pragmatic functions that are more interactive in nature, such as directing, attending, giving, and protesting, emerge before the pragmatic function of naming. The use of words to name objects is a late-emerging phenomenon that is achieved only toward the end of the one-word period, and it constitutes the crown of early language development. According to McShane, shortly after realizing that words stand for objects, children understand that they also refer to actions, attributes, and other aspects of their environment. This recognition (which he explains as an insight into the function of language) makes the child capable of producing word combinations, and helps him verbally to encode experiences that are removed from the here and now (see also Chapter 2 above).

The main difficulty with the pragmatic descriptions of early speech is that they sidestep the problem of classifying words according to their meanings. McShane (1980) uses Nelson's example of *door* (which she classifies as an action word) to illustrate his point that the pragmatic function of a word (i.e., a request to go outside, in Nelson's example) should be treated separately from its grammatical description. He argues that the utterance *door* in the context of opening a door in order to go outside "is just a request", and therefore should be classified as such with no reference to its meaning or content. I cannot agree with McShane. I find this proposal to be weak, since it completely ignores semantics. Was it mere chance that the child produced the word *door* as a request to go outside? Why did he pick this form (rather than any other) verbally to encode an experience in which doors play such a prominent role? I propose that the development of pragmatics must be considered together with the development of meaning (i.e., reference). I cannot see how it might be possible to study the use of words in different contexts without closely examining the development of their reference.

Identifying the reference of early words

The previous sections have outlined the evident limitations of classifying single-word corpora according to systems based solely on phonological, semantic, or pragmatic considerations. We have seen that resemblance of form does not necessarily indicate similarity of reference, and that context description does not always reveal the reference of a child's new word. It is obvious that the identification of an early word's reference is not an easy empirical task. One way of attacking this problem is by conducting analyses of repeated uses of the same word in different contexts and over time. This solution was originally proposed by Braunwald (1978), who conducted a diary study of the early development of lexical meaning, providing several examples illustrating how the development of the meaning of a single word can be traced over time. She shows that in the early phases of lexical acquisition many words do not share meanings with similar adult forms. The word *ba*, for example, was initially used by Laura (Braunwald's subject) both as a label for round objects and as a request word for more milk. Braunwald hypothesizes that the English noun *ball* was the model word for Laura's *ba*. The word *bow-wow* was initially used for any noise audible in the house and coming from the outside, as well as for the sight of dogs and cars.

Early undifferentiated and ambiguous uses of new words were also noted by Valsiner and Lasn (n.d.), who investigated the development of the meaning of a number of Estonian expressions. These authors found that during the early phases of production some words changed their reference. The words "thank you", "food", and "out to the yard" were initially used by all the subjects in anomalous contexts. For example, the word *aitah*, "thank you", was uttered by the subjects when asking for objects, while playing with objects when no transfer was observed, and while giving objects to other recipients, and also as an acknowledgement immediately after receiving objects. The children gradually stopped uttering the word in certain contexts (usually the non-relevant ones), and preserved it in the context of receiving, which is the more common context in adult speech. On the basis of their finding, the investigators argue that initially children may not use words referentially, but rather as a functional means of communication. At this point the meanings of early words are essentially fuzzy. Valsiner and Lasn (n.d.) argue that since word-meaning acquisition is a lengthy process of context differentiation, the measure of changes in contexts of use must be the ultimate goal when trying to trace the early development of reference.

A third attempt to explore the reference of words by looking at different contexts of occurrence is that of Griffiths and Atkinson (1978). These researchers argue that there is a notable gap in our understanding of how words for actions (i.e., verbs in adult grammar) are learned by the child compared to what is known about children's acquisition of terms denoting concrete reference (i.e., nouns in adult speech). Moreover, as Bowerman (1976) warned, they found that what are nouns in adult speech are not always used as object words by the child. By carefully examining the contexts in which four subjects produced the word *door*, Griffiths and Atkinson discovered that this word was initially used by the subjects as a "doing word". These authors therefore claim that a close examination of repeated contexts for uttering the same word is obligatory in identifying the reference of early-acquired terms.

In line with these studies, the investigation reported below (Chapters 6 through 10) proposes a classification system developed for the categorization of single-word expressions based on their repeated occurrences in different contexts. It categorizes words on the basis of their reference to real-world contents. The system consists of a set of five mutually exclusive classes (i.e., Object Words, Action Words, Modifiers, Social Words, and Indeterminant), which were selected on the basis of the *a priori* plausibility that they may be psychologically real for the child. Each category is explicitly defined and illustrated by examples taken from Keren's data (see Chapter 7). In the context of the present research, the identification of five different classes of reference facilitated comparisons with other investigations of the single-word period and were also used to test the correspondence between adult parts-of-speech and child reference for the same words.

4   *The meanings of early words*

Learning the conventional meanings of words is a dynamic, long-term, and covert process that involves complex interactions between two systems developing in the child: the cognitive and the linguistic. Over the last two decades, extensive theoretical and empirical efforts have been directed at the question of how young children acquire the lexical semantics of natural languages. Despite the enormous amount of discussion on the subject, a number of crucial questions still remain open, awaiting scientific investigation. Very little is known about what determines the relative ease or difficulty of a new word for the child. It is not at all clear how initial meanings of words are to be characterized. No suggestions are available as to the best way to represent changes over time in the meaning of the same word. The type of relationships that exist between the growing conceptual abilities of the child and the processes that underlie early lexical acquisition are also not fully understood. Is the course of meaning acquisition dependent on the age of the child, on his cognitive–symbolic abilities and the different linguistic experiences he absorbs with time? Most researchers assume that children extract information about the conventional meaning of a word from hearing the word used repeatedly in various non-linguistic contexts. It is believed that through repeated experiences with a new linguistic construct, children generate hypotheses about the underlying meaning of that construct and how it should be used. Yet how do initial meanings evolve out of early experiences with words? What is the role of the linguistic input to the child and how do linguistic inputs interact with the non-linguistic contexts to generate mental representations of word-meaning?

The present chapter introduces the basic principles which researchers need to consider when they study the evolution of early meanings. It reviews available data as a necessary background for the presentation of competing theoretical models of word-meaning acquisition in the following chapter.

The distinction between the extension and the intension of words

There are serious philosophical, theoretical, and methodological problems in the study of *word-meaning*. The problems lie beyond the scope of child-language research and hence will not be directly discussed here. Philosophers and semanticists have proposed several alternative ways for dealing with the most intriguing question of how to characterize the meaning of a word (summaries of the different models are given in Kempson, 1977; Lyons, 1977, vol. I). In this section I choose to concentrate on one model for representing the meanings of words, a model which clearly distinguishes between two levels of lexical meaning – that of extension and that of intension. As argued below, this distinction is primarily relevant to the analysis of the meaning of first words, when the initial application of new words and the growing lexicons of young children during the second year of life are tested.

Anglin (1977) has provided an explicit explanation of how the meanings of words can be represented at two distinct levels. For Anglin, each word is a term of reference which functions as a speech unit that is associated with meaning. The meaning of a term of reference consists of both a set of referents and a set of properties that the individual believes to be true for these referents. Anglin's (1977) definitions of the terms "extension" and "intension" clearly illustrate the differences between the two levels of analysis:

> *Extension*: The extension of a term of reference includes all the objects which an individual is willing to denote with that term of reference.
>
> *Intension*: The intension of a term of reference is the set of properties which an individual believes to be true of the instances of the category denoted by that term. (1977:27)

In a model that distinguishes between extension and intension, the meaning of a word such as *animal* can be characterized as follows: *extension*: cow, horse, cat, dog, elephant, etc.; and *intension*: animate, eats grass or meat, does not speak, has four legs and a tail, etc.

It is extremely difficult, perhaps even impossible, to examine scientifically how the intension of an early word emerges and develops over time. Controlled experiments, such as the ones described in Anglin (1977) for older children, in which children are asked to define words and to state properties of classes of particular instances, cannot be conducted with one-year-old subjects (see Barrett (1986), and Gelman and Markman (1986, in press), on experimental studies of comprehension and category formation with very young subjects). It is, however, possible to test the initial extension of first words and how the extension of these words changes over time. In fact, most researchers who have studied the early development of word-meaning, either in production or in comprehension, have based their arguments on examples of the different uses of words by the child (e.g., Barrett, 1986; Bowerman, 1978, 1980; Clark, 1973, 1975; Reich, 1976). That is to say, most discussions of the development of meaning are based on reports of the referential use of words or their extensional behaviors.

It would seem to me that researchers of early lexical development should deal with the theoretical and methodological difficulties they face in trying to reveal the covert processes that underlie early semantics. Before we can apply the model proposed by Anglin (1977), two questions must be considered. On the philosophical level, we must determine whether we can acknowledge the distinction between intension and extension, and whether we are ready to accept data on extension as sufficient evidence for making inferences about intensional meanings (see Merriman (in press), who attempts to do so). On the more practical level, it is necessary to test whether it is at all possible to identify the extensions of words by examining descriptions of how these words are used by the child. The following sections address these two questions.

Difficulties in determining the extension of an early word

In Chapter 3 above, the difficulties involved in identifying the category membership of early words were discussed. It was indicated that nouns in adult speech are not always used by the child to refer to object referents. Some preliminary evidence was presented to show that there is sometimes a complete mismatch between the child's and the adult's meaning for the same word. Most discussions on the meanings of early words are based on anecdotal descriptions of the contexts in which children utter them. Very little attention, however, has been paid to the question of whether the uses of words directly reflect their meaning or extension. During the early phases of production, and in particular throughout the one-word stage, children often produce a word when its referent in terms of adult language is absent from the immediate context. Apparently children sometimes produce words in connection with an entity that is somehow associated with the referent of the word. Greenfield and Smith (1976) have argued that in such cases the child is trying verbally to encode a semantic relation such as possession, location, dative, etc. that exists between the immediate referent and the absent one. When a child points to her doll's crib and says *doll/doll/*, how is one to know whether the word *doll* is extended to the referent CRIB or whether the child is indicating that this crib is her doll's? Most researchers have completely neglected the issue of how one identifies and eliminates association from the description of a word's extension, and vice versa (e.g., Greenfield and Smith, 1976; McShane, 1980; Rescorla, 1980).

In his pragmatic classification of early one-word utterances, McShane (1980) distinguishes between three subtypes of statements. One type is *association.* McShane offers the following definition of the associative use of a word:

> Association: names uttered in the absence of the referent but in the presence of some object, person, location, etc. associated with the referent . . . Cases of apparent overextensions of a referent are not regarded as instances of Association. (1980:74)

Note that McShane is aware that some misuses of words may reflect "apparent overextension" behavior, but he fails to provide criteria for determining when a word is extended to a new referent rather than used to indicate association.

Rescorla (1980), faced with the same problem of determining whether a word is the name of the immediate stimulus or not, regards associations as a subclass of overextension. She distinguishes between analogical, categorical, and predicative overextensions and claims that a predicative overextension is a statement about the relationships between an immediate referent and an absent person, object, property, or state. Rescorla, however, fails to provide explicit instructions as to how to make the distinction between the qualitatively different classes of overextension that she identifies (for further criticism of Rescorla's system, see Merriman, in press).

Braunwald's (1978) thorough discussion of the distinction between a cognitive mismatch and a semantic extension illustrates how careful the researcher must be in studying the earliest words learned by the child. According to Braunwald (1978), the child's early words become meaningful through repeated successful communicative interactions with the parents, during which adjustments are made by both the parents and the child. Braunwald argues that the match between a word and its referent can be viewed from two different perspectives, that of the adult and that of the child. From both points of view, the matching task involves inferring the meanings of words from the possibilities or alternatives within the situational context in which they are uttered. The problem of semantic match, Braunwald suggests, is related to the clarity and consistency with which the adult models the word to the child, as well as to the salience of the referent in the child's early environmental experiences.

Braunwald describes the evolution of the meanings of two early words in the lexicon of her daughter, Laura, in order to illustrate the distinction between a semantic mismatch and an overextension. In the two examples, the significant role of the adult who models the word to the child is highlighted. The word *bow-wow* was used by the child as a multi-purpose word referring to the sound and sight of dogs, cars and other engines. Braunwald states that:

> Superficially, *bow-wow* is an inexplicable semantic extension based on sound and/or movement. However, when the etiology and evolution of *bow-wow* are considered, Laura's global reference is neither a semantic extension

based on a critical feature of dogs nor an example of the early overinclusions cited by Bloom (1973) as instances of chained concepts (Vygotsky, 1962). Rather, it is symptomatic of the problem of match which Laura must solve. (1978:520)

Braunwald argues that the word *bow-wow* was modeled to the child in opaque and inconsistent situations, and therefore she failed to identify its referents and produce it referentially.

The development of the word *tree*, which also showed unconventional uses, differs from *bow-wow* in that it provides a clear case of semantic overextension. The child started to use the word for a large tree in the front yard. Not surprisingly, the tree which was readily perceived by the child was consistently labeled by Laura's babysitter as a *tree* in a routine of pointing to it. After making an initial correct match between the word *tree* and a referent, Laura started to use the word for the referent 'shoe' (her own orthopedic shoes had a thick, barklike sole). Here, Braunwald claims, Laura extended the word in order to expand the range of situations about which she could talk. Braunwald (1978) argues that: "*tree* became in effect a homonym in which situational context and behavioral cues clearly disambiguated the reference" (1978:524).

The above discussion clearly indicates that the extensional properties of early words cannot be identified by looking at a single instance of a misuse. Only a close observation of how the child repeatedly uses the same word in various situational contexts may reveal its referent in each case, or the scope of its extension at a given point in time. Researchers must, however, be very careful not to consider all occurrences of a word as equivalent to each other. It is important to evaluate the history of a word and how consistently it is used by the child over time. In chapter 8 below, I propose a set of critical rules for the analysis of the extensional behaviors of early words. These rules were generated after serious consideration of the problems that have been discussed in this section.

Quantitative information about extensional behaviors of early words

The relationship between the child's and the adult's extension of a specific word may in principle take one of the following five logical forms: identity, partial overlap, mismatch, underextension, or overextension (Anglin, 1977: Clark, 1983a; Reich, 1976). In the available literature on the acquisition of word-meaning, the most commonly described and discussed extensional behavior is overextension. This preoccupation with the phenomenon of overextension and concomitant neglect of underextension (Anglin, 1977) is interesting. To the best of my knowledge, very little is known about extensional behaviors other than overextension and underextension. No reports have been published on the prevalence of regular extended words (i.e., words that never show either overextension or underextension in production), or words that show irregular patterns of extension (i.e., semantic mismatches as termed by Braunwald (1978), or illustrated by Barrett (1986) for the word *chuf-chuf* in his own son's lexicon). The paucity of empirical investigations of the early uses of words as compared to the abundant theoretical discussion of models of word-meaning acquisition (see Chapter 5) may explain in part the lack of quantitative data on the relative distribution of extension types in the initial lexicon of the child.

The major diary studies reviewed by Clark (1973) reveal that the phenomenon of overextension has been recorded in the speech of children between the ages of 1(1) and 2(6). Clark argues that this phenomenon is universal, and that it is characteristic of many words that are acquired by the child. Although Clark does not explicitly discuss how frequently overextensions occur, her preoccupation with this phenomenon gives the impression that overextension is almost intrinsic to the process of learning the meanings of new words. Clark's emphasis on overextension has recently been criticized on two grounds. First, Anglin (1977) and Reich (1976) argue that diary studies (Clark's primary source of evidence) tend by their very nature to suggest that the direction of development is from the general to the specific, because the data collected are biased towards overextension: when the child uses a word inappropriately it is noted down, but when the child does *not* utter a word in the presence of an "appropriate" referent, no record is made.

The second claim against Clark concerns the finding that no specific stage in the period of lexical acquisition is characterized by overextension (Nelson, Rescorla, Gruendel and Benedict, 1978; Rescorla, 1980). Rescorla (1980), who sampled the speech of six children at the one-word stage, found that only 33 per cent of her corpus of 445 different words were overextended one or more times. An even lower proportion of overextended words, between seven and 20 per cent, was reported by Barrett (1978, 1986), Gruendel (1977), and Nelson (1982). Researchers skeptical about the frequency of overextensions have also suggested that it may not be a uniform phenomenon, but that there may be different types of overextensions (e.g., Bowerman, 1978; Rescorla, 1980), and that it may be a late rather than an early phenomenon in the developmental path of the extension of new words (Barrett, 1986; Bowerman, 1978, 1980).

The phenomenon of underextension has received far less attention than that of overextension. Some researchers, however, have provided anecdotal examples of very restricted early uses of words (Barrett, 1986; Bloom, 1973; Bloom and Lahey, 1978). Lewis (1959) notes that his son initially applied the word *fafa* (flower) only to pictures of flowers and not to real flowers (cf. Bloom and Lahey, 1978:120). Similarly, Bloom (1973) observed that her daughter restricted the word *car* to cars moving on the street which were seen from her living room window. Reich (1976) describes in detail the development of the meaning of *shoe* for his son between eight and sixteen months, and also concludes that initially the meaning of the word was very narrow.

From the limited amount of evidence on the phenomenon of early underextension, one can make the following generalizations: (a) underextension occurs during the early phases of lexical development, and only methodological failures in identifying it have created the impression that meaning develops from the general to the specific; (b) underextension occurs both in comprehension and in production; and (c) there are several kinds of underextensions: underextension to a specific subset of objects, to specific agents, or to specific situations (see Chapter 8 for operative definitions of the subtypes of underextension). Two controlled experimental studies that were conducted with relatively older children provide considerable support for the above claims. Anglin's (1977) ambitious attempt to explore the range of word extension indicates that both overextensions and underextensions exist in the speech of pre-school children in comprehension and production alike. Anglin's set of systematic experiments showed that children exhibit individual differences in the extent to which their words manifest overextension and underextension behaviors. Differences were also found for the various concepts tested. In addition, the nature of the stimuli presented contributed to the relative frequency of extension types. For his youngest group (ages 2(6)–4(0)), the number of underextensions was greater than the number of overextensions. The frequency of both types of extension decreased with age. A later study by Kay and Anglin (1982) offers further support for the hypothesis that overextension and underextension alike occur both in comprehension and in production. This study also found that underextension occurred more frequently in production than in comprehension. Taken together, then, the experimental results show that, with enough methodological sophistication, one can achieve a better description of how the extension behaviors of first words are to be characterized. The question of whether various types of extension can be identified through a comprehensive longitudinal observation of the repeated uses of each word in different contexts over time remains open. This question will be addressed below in Chapters 11 and 12.

Why do children overextend words?

Proposed explanations of why children overextend words shed light on the more general question of whether early uses of words actually reflect their meanings. Let us consider three opposing views on the subject.

Clark's (1973, 1975) suggestion that words are overextended because the child as yet has only partial meanings for them is representative of the view that overextensions are straightforward guides to word-meaning.

Other researchers who have hypothesized that early uses of words reflect their meanings are Barrett (1986), Bowerman (1978, 1980), and Schlesinger (1982). Bowerman developed her argument about the underlying prototype structure of the child's categories (for some words) on the basis of data on early uses of words. It is clear that Bowerman, who provides descriptions of repeated uses of the same word, believes that the misuses of words are not accidental. Schlesinger's (1982) claim that overextensions are simply examples of a word paired with a "non-standard" referent is in accord with Bowerman's and Clark's views that early uses of words do indeed reflect their meanings. In Schlesinger's model, an overextension is regarded as a manifestation of word generalization. The child may generalize words to either "correct" or "incorrect" referents, from the standpoint of the meaning of the word in adult speech. Since Schlesinger argues that underlying concepts develop concurrently with the words rather than before them, he can explain overextension and regular extension as reflections of the same process of generalization.

In a recent work in which Barrett presents his model of meaning acquisition, he argues for parallelism between the comprehension and the production of early words. He maintains that the underlying representation of each word's meaning explains how the child uses it both in production and in comprehension, and that therefore early uses do reflect underlying meanings. The semantic representation of each word changes with time and becomes progressively more differentiated as the linguistic experience of the child grows. Barrett (1986) claims that early undifferentiated uses of words indicate that the semantic representation of a word consists of holistic event-bound representations; later associative overextensions imply an underlying representation of a prototypical exemplar and an ability to identify principal features that characterize this exemplar. The rescission of overextension, according to Barrett, clearly indicates that the child is able to abstract contrastive features and to assign words to semantic fields.

Not all the investigators who have conducted research on the acquisition of word-meaning take overextensions as straightforward reflections of meaning. Bloom (1973), Clark (1983a), Huttenlocher (1974), Nelson, Rescorla, Gruendel and Benedict (1978), and Nelson and Lucariello (1985) provide different answers to the question of why children overextend words. Bloom (1973) and Clark (1983a) argue that children overextend words in order to improve communication. In situations in which the child is in need of a word that has not yet been acquired, he substitutes for it an existing word in his vocabulary. According to Bloom, then, children apply a word inappropriately even if they know that the word is not the most desirable one. They do so in order to satisfy their listeners and keep the interaction flowing.

Huttenlocher (1974), Thomson and Chapman (1977), and Fremgen and Fay (1980) also argue that overextensions are merely the result of the child's strategy in getting along with a limited vocabulary. These researchers report that children who overextend words in spontaneous productions tend not to do so in comprehension. Thomson and Chapman (1977) and Fremgen and

Fay (1980)[1] carried out individualized comprehension tests with young subjects in order to test Huttenlocher's (1974) claim that overextensions are not observed in comprehension. In these individualized tests, each child was tested on the comprehension of words he had overextended in production. The researchers presented each child with several set of pictures and asked him to show the "correct" picture for each tested word. The results of the two experiments confirmed Huttenlocher's (1974) anecdotal observation that children do not overextend words in comprehension, even if they do so in production. These researchers therefore conclude that the overextension of a word in production does not necessarily indicate that the overextended referent is included in the underlying concept attached to the word.

What does cause overextensions, then? Thomson and Chapman (1977) and Fremgen and Fay (1980) concur with Huttenlocher's (1974) original claim that overextensions are due to production deficiencies in the child. More specifically, Huttenlocher hypothesized that children initially face problems in the retrieval of words. She argues that: "It is easier to retrieve object information on the basis of a word than it is to retrieve word information on the basis of an encounter with an object" (1974:366). The difficulties in production are usually observed, according to Huttenlocher, when the child has several similar object or action schemes linked with different words. Huttenlocher assumes that in such cases the words are stored in close proximity to each other, so that one is sometimes incorrectly selected when another is needed. Huttenlocher's procedural explanation of overextensions in production coincides with Rice's (1980) detailed analysis of why discrepancies may be identified between children's responses to experimental comprehension and production tasks.

I cannot accept Thomson and Chapman's (1977) and Fremgen and Fay's (1980) conclusion that overextensions are the direct reflection of production deficiencies alone. I believe that the type of evidence which can be produced by experimental procedures such as the ones they designed cannot support such a definite conclusion. Even if children do tend to pick an appropriate picture in a forced-choice experimental paradigm, we cannot exclude the possibility that the underlying concept attached to the test word has other referents in addition to the most prototypical one, including some that may be irrelevant in terms of adult language.

As Schlesinger (1982) argues, a procedure that could prove the hypothesis of only a production deficiency would be one that showed that children refused to choose a picture when asked to do so if no picture of a correct referent was included in the array presented to them. Such an experimental procedure cannot be attempted with children as young as those tested by Thomson and Chapman or Fremgen and Fay. Another experimental task,

---

[1] Fremgen and Fay's (1980) methodology was slightly different from that of Thomson and Chapman (1977). These differences, however, are not relevant to the present arguments, and therefore are not discussed.

however, could be designed to allow subjects to choose more than one picture for a test item. If, in fact, in second choices children did pick less conventional referents as possible candidates for inclusion in the set of objects associated with a word, then it would be legitimate to conclude that the claim made by Thomson and Chapman, and Fremgen and Fay was erroneous. This was done by Kuczaj (1982), who draws attention to the methodological problem noted above. Kuczaj confronted children aged 1(9)–2(4) with a forced-choice task in which they were allowed to make sequential choices of "correct" referents. His findings clearly indicate that children indeed tend to choose the most prototypical referent first, and then also go on to choose less prototypical referents when given the opportunity to do so.

A third attempt to explain the phenomenon of overextension is that of Nelson, Rescorla, Gruendel and Benedict (1978). These researchers believe that words are linked to already existing concepts that do not undergo change. The overextension of a word, according to this model, reflects the active attempts of the child to identify the boundaries of the concept. When the child overextends a word, he indicates that he perceives some sort of similarity between the "extended" referent and certain referents in categories of his own devising. Thus, when the child points to a half grapefruit and says *moon*, he is trying to convey his conviction that *the grapefruit is like a moon*.

Nelson *et al.*'s (1978) interpretation of overextensions as analogies is open to criticism. It is not at all clear that all overextended words are based on the perception of analogies. Rescorla herself (1980) has identified other types of overextensions (e.g., categorical and predicative). Moreover, I question whether Nelson *et al.* had enough evidence to conclude that children overextend words in order to comment on similarities between referents. Do children overextend words only when describing objects and making statements about them? The proposal does not provide an explanation for overextensions of action words or for overextensions across classes of referents (e.g., overextensions of *gi* ('giddi-up') to both riding actions and to objects on top of which the child can sit (Bowerman, 1978)).

In sum, there is no agreement among theorists on the question of whether extensions of words (and especially overextensions) reflect the meaning that the word has for the child. Further, naturally produced data as well as experimental evidence on comprehension and production are needed in order to test opposing arguments. It is important to differentiate between fortuitous misuses of words and consistent ones. It must be discovered whether overextended words are always recorded as statements (as Nelson *et al.*'s "analogy" interpretation would seem to predict), or whether they are sometimes uttered in other speech acts as well (e.g., as requests). The distribution of different overextension types must be explored, as well as the extent to which the predictions made by each proposal are supported. An attempt should also be made to find out whether the child's age and linguistic experience have any effect on the type of extensions and the frequency in which each is observed in production and/or comprehension under various conditions. It is hoped that the study reported below, in which an attempt was made to follow these suggestions, will shed further light on the issue.

5   Competing theoretical models of word-meaning

In the previous chapter we examined some of the principal phenomena and major difficulties that are associated with the empirical study of the meaning of early words. The present chapter reviews the main theoretical models that have been proposed in the last twelve years (1973–85) in an attempt to explain these phenomena. These models were all constructed to explain the puzzling question of how very young children construct meanings for their first words. The competing models are presented in the historical order of their publication. Clark's and Nelson's pioneering work in this area serves as our starting point, since their models laid the ground work for most later theories. As some of the authors have since revised, extended, or even abandoned their original ideas, I will consider the major claims as initially presented and then cite the chief criticisms that led to more recent developments. The following review is designed to illuminate the main hypotheses, point to principal weaknesses, highlight differences among models, and, most especially, to examine the predictions that evolve from each model. Special reference is made below to those predictions that can (and will) be tested by actually observing how young children start to use the first words they acquire.

The Semantic Feature Hypothesis – E. V. Clark

Clark's (1973, 1975, 1977) Semantic Feature Hypothesis (SFH) was constructed within the framework of the more general componential semantic models of Postal (1966) and Bierwisch (1970), who described meanings of words as composed of a set of universal primitives that are likely to be derived from human percepts. The universal primitives are clustered according to somewhat language-specific combinatorial rules, and they constitute the underlying representation of words' intensions. In her early writings, Clark argued that during the initial phases of production, children use words for which they do not yet know the full adult meanings. The initial representation of the meaning of a new word is assumed to be incomplete, including only a subset of the semantic components that are associated with the same word in adult language. The complete meaning of a word is acquired gradually by the addition of meaning components to the underlying semantic definition of the word. Clark hypothesized that upon hearing a new word, the child observes one or two of the most salient features of the object or the event to which the word is applied, and infers that these are the only semantic features that are associated with the meaning of that word.

Since initially the definition of a new word is incomplete, the child makes many referential errors in using it. Thus, it is commonly recorded that children initially produce the word *doggi* for all [+ four-legged] animals regardless of the fact that the underlying semantic meaning of "dog" in adult language includes other features as well (e.g., [+ furry], [+ small], [+ is barking]). Through repeated experiences with a new word, the child realizes that his or her use of the word does not correspond with the way it is used by adults. Thus, the child further differentiates the conditions for its use, adding new features. This differentiation gradually brings the child's semantic representation of the word closer and closer to that of the adult. In other words, the list of criterial features or components in the child's definition of a word grows until the acquisition of its conventional meaning is complete and the word's extension is as narrow as it is in adult language.

Clark developed and supported her model on the basis of both a secondary analysis of old diary studies that contained descriptions of the early uses of new words, and experimental data she collected on the acquisition of words in specific semantic domains (e.g., spatial adjectives, time expressions, deictic verbs). Clark argued that the following major predictions of her theory were supported by empirical findings:

(a)   many overextensions are observed in the early speech of young children. Most overextensions in Clark's samples were based on identifiable perceptual similarities among the several referents to which the same word was applied. The most commonly observed similarities were attributes of objects such as shape, movement, sound, size, texture, and taste;

(b)   within the same semantic domain, terms varying in number of cumulative criterial features are acquired in order, from the simpler to the more complex. That is, progress within the same semantic field is from the general term (which includes fewer and broader features) to the more specific one (which includes more, and more precise, features);

(c)   in acquiring antonym pairs or semantically contrastive terms, the positive term (e.g., *more, tall*) is learned earlier than the negative term (e.g., *less, short*). Clark invoked the theory of linguistic marking (Greenberg, 1966; Richards, 1979) in order to explain this finding. She argued that marking contributes to greater semantic complexity, and therefore negative terms, which are linguistically marked, are learned late.

The Semantic Feature Hypothesis has elicited an immense amount of debate and further research. Nelson (1974) was the first to voice strong criticism of Clark. She argued that Clark's model does not deal with the most important level of cognitive organization, namely, the conceptual level. According to Nelson, the conceptual level operates between the percepts of the child and the words he or she acquires, and it is therefore erroneous to translate lexical meanings directly to perceptions. She held that objects are perceived by the child as unanalysed wholes, and that they are categorized by principles of function rather than by principles of form.

Bowerman (1978), who recorded in detail the early lexical development of her two daughters, found only partial support for Clark's claim that overextended words are applied to sets of referents on the basis of shared criterial attribute(s) (or semantic features). Bowerman questioned the generality of Clark's model because it could not be invoked to explain "complexive" overextensions, which were present in the lexicons of her two subjects (1978, 1980). Bowerman's claim that the SFH is not comprehensive enough to account for all the data available was later supported by other investigators as well. Some researchers argued that Clark disregarded evidence on phenomena other than overextension primarily because she dealt with diary data and very selective examples (Anglin, 1977; Barrett, 1978). Richards (1979) and Carey (1982) questioned the generality of the model in light of contrary experimental evidence that they cited from researchers other than Clark. They showed that Clark's prediction that general terms are acquired before more specific ones within the same semantic field did not always hold (see also Merriman, in press), and that Clark's treatment of English antonyms suffered from experimental biases.

Carey (1982:366–8) claimed that Clark's model "has not borne the test of time" simply because componential analysis of word-meaning does not work even for semantic domains that have yielded convincing componential analyses (spatial adjectives, polar terms, etc.). Carey's opinion that semantic models of early speech cannot be componential is motivated by new models of natural concepts that put forth the claim that natural categories are not organized around sets of necessary and jointly sufficient bipolar features (see also Labov and Labov, 1978; Rosch, 1977; Merriman in press; and the following discussion on pp. 51–3, 56).

Schlesinger (1982) also questioned the claim that a simple abstraction of universal perceptual attributes determines the range of the applicability of a word. Schlesinger argued that a set of binary properties, such as Clark invokes, is too rigid and therefore not appropriate for capturing the psychological processes that are involved in the acquisition of word-meaning. He emphasized that when children learn the names of objects, they have to appreciate complex configurations of attributes that are often culture-related and language-specific, and to differentiate between them. Therefore, Schlesinger maintained, the assumption of a set of supposedly universal binary features cannot explain how the child learns the names of objects, since it is plainly too simplistic.

In her 1983a article on early meaning, Clark herself summarizes the main criticisms that have been voiced in child-language literature against the SFH. Clark acknowledges that her theory suffers from four major problems:

(a)   the vague criteria for identifying potential candidates that may serve as possible semantic primitives in the child's linguistic system;

(b)   the focusing of the theory on the process of the addition of semantic features, which explains only how meanings become narrower and not how they are broadened and become more generalized;

(c)   the clearly mistaken assumption that features are always learned from the general to the specific, since they are organized in a top-down fashion; and

(d)   the finding that overextensions are much rarer in comprehension than in production and that therefore this phenomenon may not be the result of an incomplete underlying semantic representation, but may reflect, rather, a communicative strategy for stretching existing vocabulary.

Although Clark believes that the SFH makes fairly good predictions about the relative order of acquisition of related meanings (1983a: 819), she agrees that the model should be replaced by a much more general model of meaning that makes stronger and more powerful predictions. Her new proposal, termed the Lexical Contrast Theory (LCT), appears below.

The Functional Core Hypothesis – K. Nelson

In 1974 Nelson published her criticism of the Semantic Feature Hypothesis and presented an alternative model of word-meaning acquisition. Nelson questioned the ability of young children to carry out detailed feature analyses of the referents they encounter. She claimed that objects are initially perceived by the child as functional wholes, and therefore are assigned to a specific category on the basis of function (i.e., what they can do and what one can do with them). Only after the child has had the opportunity to explore the functional relationships in which the object can participate is he able to treat it as a member of a known category. Once a functional core concept is formed, the child assigns a label to it. In the functional core, objects are organized hierarchically. One object is located at the top of the hierarchy, and it forms the functional core of that category. Nelson argued (1973a, b, 1974, 1978) that functional information about objects dominates perceptual, contextual, and affective information about them. That is, functional information defines a category, whereas perceptual information helps only in identifying objects as possible candidates for that category.

Nelson's main body of evidence derived from the content analysis she performed on the 18 fifty-word lexicons of English-speaking children (1973a, see also Chapter 3 above) and a series of experimental studies that were designed to test her hypothesis that functional characteristics are of primary significance for infants in grouping objects together. Nelson (1974) maintained that the very first words that children use are names of highly functional objects (i.e., objects that move or that can be physically manipulated by the young child). This observation suggests that the first terms of reference are linked to already existing concepts that have a functional core. Only after abstracting the defining functions of objects (e.g., that balls can be thrown, rolled, and bounced), do children abstract formal characteristics which serve the secondary role of identifying other candidates for that category. Nelson's (1973b) experiment exemplifies this point, as well as illustrating her research program. In this study, 15–20-month-old subjects were presented with nine ball-like objects varying, in terms of their resemblance to a real ball, in either form, function, or both. The subjects were asked to show a ball before and after playing with the objects. The results indicated that while earlier choices were random, later ones that followed a ten-minute session of play with the objects were based mainly on functional similarity. The researcher concluded that once subjects have the opportunity to explore the functional properties of an object they may even change their minds as to its category membership. Therefore, it is clear that functional properties always override static perceptual characteristics in the making of such decisions (see a review of other experiments in Nelson, 1978).

Nelson's theory has been challenged by other researchers. Bowerman (1978), for example, criticized it for only providing an explanation as to how object words are learned. A theory of the acquisition of word-meaning, according to Bowerman, must account for a variety of phenomena within a common theoretical framework. A further problem with Nelson's model is that data collected by several investigators (e.g., Barrett, 1978; Bowerman, 1978) have shown that at least some early words are not learned in action contexts. Moreover, Bowerman (1978) describes several instances in which her daughters overextended words on the clear basis of shared perceptual attribute(s), rather than any similarity of function. She cites examples of Eva's different uses of the word 'moon' that clearly indicate that the child disregarded known differences in the functional properties of the various referents.

Schlesinger (1982) has taken issue with Nelson's basic assumption that when children start to use new words, they have already attained non-linguistic concepts to which these words are attached. Schlesinger points out that no independent evidence is available to show that non-linguistic concepts are established prior to the learning of words. An alternative proposal presented by Schlesinger is that words and concepts develop concurrently, with words in most cases delimiting the scope of a given concept by defining its borders (Schlesinger, 1977, 1982).

Along similar lines, Merriman (in press) notes the neglect of the linguistic input dimension in Nelson's model. Merriman maintains that many early words are onomatopoeic or are the result of clear attempts to reproduce adult-model sound patterns, so that it is ill-advised to rule out entirely the possibility of an abstruction process based on a match between regularities of sound patterns and real-world experiences.

Merriman (in press) discusses a number of other basic shortcomings in Nelson's theory. The hypothesis that function overrides form is problematic because without abstructing formal properties there is a danger that a category will never be delimited. How, for example, does the FCH explain the necessary distinction between a concept that is based on the identification of the many functions of one object (i.e., ball = [+ rolls], [+ is bounced], [+ is thrown]) and a concept which is based on a common function of different objects (i.e., round=balls, circles, hats etc.)? It seems quite clear that the only way an infant can recognize that the same object is engaged in different functions is by abstracting static features that recur and are constant across the various contexts of repeated actions.

Nelson's proposal that functions must be more salient than formal features is counter-intuitive since, as Gentner (1978, 1982) argues, formal features are much more differentiated, constant and distinguishable from background than are actions. Furthermore, in real-world experiences, form and function are strongly tied to each other. The fact that children alter judgments on the basis of functional experience does not rule out the possibility that they also consider perceptual information when making judgments. Justifiably, Merriman (in press) claims that the results Nelson obtained in support of her hypothesis derived from an experimental design which was incomplete because she never tested whether children alter judgments after gaining additional knowledge about static characteristics of stimuli that are difficult to define. Proof that children tend to alter judgments after gaining functional information through active engagement with different objects cannot be sufficient reason to reject an alternative hypothesis that the relative importance of perceptual cues for categorization is as great as, or perhaps even greater than, that of functional cues.

> It may be that the chief difference between formal and functional features does not involve their necessity or diagnosticity, but the manner in which they are verified. Formal information is usually immediately apparent in the perception of an object, but reception of functional information may require extended viewing or manipulation. (Merriman, in press: 15)

The final criticism of the FCH stems from the fact that no clear predictions follow from it regarding: (a) the relative frequency of different extension behaviors that early words may exhibit; and (b) the correspondence between child intension and adult intension of the same terms. The main difficulty here is that Nelson and her colleagues (Nelson *et al.*, 1978) argue that early uses of words do not reflect underlying meanings. Since words are always linked to already existing concepts that do not undergo change, overextensions are perceived as statements of analogy (see p. 43 above). The hypothesis that a child's misuse of the word *ball* or the words *tick tock* should be read as "look, it's round" or "it sounds like a clock ticking" (1978:965) requires much stronger evidence than is available today. I question Nelson's conclusion that children overextend early words only when they try to comment on similarities between referents. In fact, Anglin's (1977) and Bowerman's (1978) data clearly indicate that both in comprehension and in production children attach the same names to completely dissimilar referents. As reported in Chapter 3, children often use action terms for both actions and objects (e.g., Gentner, 1982). How would the analogy explanation account for such a phenomenon?

Finally, the distinction between overextension and association, or overextension and the metaphoric use of terms (Winner, 1979), cannot be clearly deduced from Nelson, who neglects this issue altogether. One way of studying such differences might be through a comprehensive follow-up of how the same terms are misused over time. In such an analysis one could identify words which are recorded in a number of communicative contexts, not only while the child is attempting to make a statement, and thus reflect true overextensions. This could also reveal how consistent the child was in misusing a specific word. Infrequent misuses might indicate that the child was trying to analogize or to extend an existing word to convey meanings for which he had not yet acquired the appropriate word, while consistent misuses might reflect categorical overextensions.

The Prototype Model – M. Bowerman

A basic assumption of both Clark's and Nelson's models of word-meaning is that children attach words to a number of referents only if these referents share one or more perceptual or functional attributes. Bowerman (1978, 1980) was one of the first researchers to question the generality of this premise. Some words acquired by Bowerman's daughters, Christy and Eva, were extended to referents that apparently did not share any attributes with each other. Bowerman examined the several uses of each word and concluded that they showed a "complexive" extensional behavior that was very similar to what Vygotsky (1962) describes as an "associative" complex. In an "associative" complex, each member of the class is related to another member of the same class by means of one or more shared properties. However, all the members of the class do not share one or more attributes with each other. According to Bowerman, the complexive use of a word is characterized by an extension pattern of the following type: the word is extended to a number of referents that do not necessarily share attributes with each other, but there is one referent, or a group of similar referents, with which each shares one or more attributes (1978:283).

Bowerman's description of "complexive" uses of words is compatible with a theoretical framework that has recently attracted much attention in cognitive psychology (e.g., Anglin, 1977; Brown, 1977, 1979; Carey, 1982; Fillmore,

1975, 1978; Rosch, 1975, 1977; Rosch and Mervis, 1975). This theoretical model, termed the Prototype Model (PM), has been developed to account for human categorization behaviors. The PM proposes that the membership of an entity in a category is a matter of degree. This contrasts with a basic premise of the classical view of concept structure, according to which category membership is a matter of all-or-none, i.e., an entity either is a member of the set or is not, and there is no question of degree of membership.

In the PM, in contrast to the classical view, category membership can be rated. It is suggested that each category is centered around one member which is the "best exemplar" of that category. The "best exemplar", i.e., the prototype, is the core of the category and it is "surrounded by" other members that are not as representative for the category. However, these members share attributes with the "best exemplar". The members of a category that are furthest from the core are termed peripheral members, since they share the least with the "best exemplar". In sum, the claim of the Prototype Model is that it is possible to measure degree of membership in a category by calculating the number of attributes that an entity shares with the prototype.

Bowerman (1978, 1980) hypothesized that words that show complexive behaviors are initially identified with one referent or a group of closely related referents. This referent (i.e., the "best exemplar") is usually the referent to which an adult has most frequently applied the word. After a period in which use of the word is restricted to one or to a set of "best exemplars", it is extended to several referents that share one or more features with it. One then observes a complexive usage that is the result of the prototype structure of the underlying concept to which the word is attached.

The Prototype Model of word-meaning, as Bowerman adapts it from Rosch and her colleagues and applies it to child language, predicts quite a complicated pattern of extension. It attributes to the child the mental capacity to carry out detailed, systematic analyses of word-meanings. According to this model, the child performs decomposition and novel recompositions of semantic features that he or she has extracted from the underlying representation of the "best exemplar". The model presupposes that children are capable of performing such fine analyses from at least an age close to the onset of verbal production.

Bowerman views complexive uses of words as strong evidence of the child's application of highly systematic procedures during the early phases of language development. She challenges Bloom's (1973) and Vygotsky's (1962) suggestion that complexive uses of words stem from instability in categorization behaviors. According to Bowerman, complexive uses of words suggest that young children's categorization behaviors are relatively sophisticated, since they appear to reflect the same basic procedures that Rosch has argued are central to *adult* categorization.

The PM in its original formulation has been compared with the SFH and the FCH. Bowerman did not offer it as a self-sufficient alternative to these earlier models, however, nor did she argue that it was applicable to all children's words. Rather, she developed the notion of prototypes to account for the behavior of particular words. Although Bowerman herself did not offer the Prototype Model as a comprehensive theory of the development of word-meaning, it has since been accepted as such by other researchers (e.g., Anglin, 1977; Barrett, 1986; Kuczaj, 1982).

The main predictions of the PM are that children will initially attach words to a specific referent (i.e., the prototype) or to a restrictive set of referents that resemble each other and the prototype. Children's first applications of a new word thus take the form either of underextension or of regular extension. Since the meaning of each word consists of a mental representation of the set of abstracted principal perceptual or functional features of the prototype, subsequent applications of words take complex forms. Children will extend words deliberately even to extremely dissimilar exemplars, across adult grammatical categories, and to novel instances that barely resemble any member of the class on any recognizable measure. Bowerman's model also predicts that the role of parental input would be significant at two distinct levels: firstly, children would tend to learn those words earliest which were modeled to them frequently in identical non-linguistic contexts; and secondly, initial uses of a newly acquired word would be restricted to the naming of a referent salient in that context and frequently named by the parent with the same term.

An empirical test of the above predictions (which do not coincide with those of either Clark or Nelson) is needed in order to determine the scope of applicability of the PM. A rich data base which would allow for longitudinal analyses, comparisons among different words and the various contexts in which they were learned, as well as detailed information about parental input, are the necessary conditions for verifying this model and evaluating it in comparison to other models. Chapter 11 below reports on analyses of this kind which I conducted on the Hebrew data and considers the appropriateness of the PM in explaining these findings.

The Word-Referent Pairing Model – I. M. Schlesinger

Schlesinger's model of word-meaning acquisition is presented at length in his 1982 publication *Steps to language*. In two chapters of his book (5 and 6) the author explains how, in his view, lexical learning progresses, and how meanings are established in the child's mental lexicon. Schlesinger's Word-Referent Pairing (WRP) Model is radically different from other explanations of how children learn the conventional meanings of words. This fact stems from two basic assumptions that Schlesinger makes. The first assumption is related to Schlesinger's general philosophy of language acquisition. The second is more specific to the issue at hand, namely, the relationship between words and underlying concepts.

In Schlesinger's opinion, learning processes – and possibly very complex ones that have not yet been identified – can explain how the language-learning child infers underlying structures and rules of the language from the input data (a position much closer to behaviorism than to nativism). Moreover, unlike other researchers, Schlesinger does not assume that the child learns words as labels for previously existing non-linguistic concepts or categories. In his view, children form concepts and word-meanings concomitantly in an interactive process which is both lengthy and bidirectional.

The WRP Model is based on the old Augustinian paradigm of learning words, which is clearly a behavioral one. The basic notion of pairing a word with a single referent is a central feature of that approach, which has been further extended to explain not only a single word-referent pairing, but a more complicated process of matching a word with a set of referents and a series of psychological cues. Schlesinger proposes that initially all words (for objects, actions and relationships) are paired with single referents. As the result of that pairing, the word is stored in the memory alongside an internal representation of the referent. At this stage, the word does not stand for a concept, but is associated with a particular instance of that concept. To the question of how the child picks the particular referent for each new word, Schlesinger provides psychological explanations. He argues that young infants attend to wholes rather than parts of objects, to the most salient aspects of complex situations, and to those stimuli that are shown to them by pointing or verbal direction (e.g., "look at that x", "this is a . . . "). Gradually, through repeated experiences with word-referent pairings, some involving the pairing of the same word with several referents, the child discerns similarities between the referents which are paired with the same word.

The move from the simple strategy of naming specific entities to the more generalized behavior of denoting a category is, of course, a crucial transition. To explain this transition, Schlesinger invokes two psychological operations: (a) discrimination learning; and (b) positive cue extraction. Discrimination learning is the result of a conflict between adult-model language and the child's underlying assumptions about the meaning of a particular word. If, for example, the child encounters an object which reminds him of a paired referent, and concurrently the adult provides a new name for that object, the child is induced to perceive salient distinctions between the new object and his internalized representation of the paired referent. This salient distinction, which might be either perceptual or functional, will then become a *negative cue* for one word and a *positive cue* for another. For example, the perceptual distinction of "mane" for "horses" and not "dogs" will become a *negative cue* for the word *doggie*, and a *positive cue* for the word *horse*.

Unlike Clark or Nelson, Schlesinger believes that during the early phases of language acquisition, children will not attend to specific features or distinguish between unidimensional components. Rather, a number of complexly interrelated dimensions and global configurations will constitute psychological cues for category membership.

The process of positive cue extraction complements that termed above "discrimination learning". This process is enhanced by repeated uses of the same word to name a number of related referents. When the child perceives a new instance of a category, and the adult names it, the name recalls (or invokes) previously experienced paired referents, which are then compared with the new instance. Via such comparisons, the child identifies repeated properties which are similar across referents. Those properties then become positive cues for the word in question.

The underlying category of a word is termed by Schlesinger a "protoverbal element". The generation of a protoverbal element is the direct consequence of repeated exposures to the language that is spoken to and around the child. As stated earlier, the child does not come to the language-acquisition task pre-equipped with certain concepts for which he has yet to find names. On the contrary, the protoverbal elements develop concurrently with the words the child learns. According to this proposal, words enhance the conceptual development of the child.

Protoverbal elements function in both comprehension and production. In production, the child assigns the intended referent to a protoverbal element, and then conducts a lexical search to find the word associated with this element. In comprehension, a word is first assigned to its protoverbal element, thus enabling the lexical message to carry meaning for the listener. The protoverbal elements, then, are mediators between words and their referents.

As might be assumed, protoverbal elements develop with time. In their mature form they consist of: (1) the internal representation of previously encountered paired referent(s); and (2) a set of cues that are isolated through experience with the word and its paired referents. Throughout development, protoverbal elements may take the form of either (1) or (2). Thus, it is possible that early in the process of lexical learning, a protoverbal element may consist of only a paired referent, and then later, when cues are isolated, cues and referents will operate jointly in the assignment of instances.

A final clarification called for here is that cues in Schlesinger's account are not restricted to single words. The same cue is often associated with a number of categories or words. Cues may also vary in degree of association. The values of cues are not constant and are related to the frequency of their occurrence (in the different instances of that category) and the relative degree of their saliency for the child. It is assumed that a specific word is elicited in a given situation as a result of the sum total of the values of all of the cues. Schlesinger proposes that the underlying organization of each protoverbal element is hierarchical. He believes that the internal representation of a paired referent is located at the top of a hierarchy which is surrounded by cues varying in their degree of membership (i.e., their values). The lower you go, the finer the discriminations that you can make. The following example illustrates this point:

> A bushy tail may have become a cue for a "fox", but when it later turns out that animals called by other names have bushy tails, discrimination learning may set in. That is, the child will note properties that distinguish the different kinds of bushy tails – those that are cues for "fox" and those that are not. (1982:127)

The above explanation coincides very well with recent proposals about the prototypical structure of human categories. It accords with the view that the membership of an exemplar in a category is not a matter of all-or-nothing, but rather a matter of degree (e.g., Anglin, 1977; Bowerman, 1978, 1980; Brown, 1979; Rosch, 1977; Rosch and Mervis, 1975).

Schlesinger himself makes no explicit statements about the empirical predictions of his model. However, a number of such predictions follow directly from his theoretical discussion. It is clear that the nature of linguistic input plays a predominant role in predicting the course of meaning development. Frequently modeled words, and those which are ostensively defined, would be candidates for correct mapping. Therefore, the acquisition of object words might precede the acquisition of words for actions and relations. Also, basic-level terms (Brown, 1957) would be learned prior to superordinate or subordinate terms. Deictic terms would constitute a late-emerging subset of the lexicon, which is also a difficult subset of words to learn (see Schlesinger, 1982: Chapter 6, for a discussion of how these meanings are assumed to be learned mainly through linguistic experiences). It must be recalled that in Schlesinger's terms the linguistic input is not perceived as a simple model for imitation. Rather, the assumption is that it plays a crucial role in enhancing or suppressing the child's active processes of analysis.

The second clear prediction of the WRP Model is that word-meanings would develop from the specific to the general. Underextensions would predictably be a rather early and frequent phenomenon, and late generalization the rule rather than the exception. Misuses of new words might be recorded and would be the direct result of mistakenly perceived similarity and/or mispairing of a word with its referent. Schlesinger suggests that early misuses may evolve from wrong generalizations on the basis of contiguity. This could also be the result of a failure to link a word with one specific aspect of the situation (1982:113). The assumption that category formation is a lengthy process leads to the conclusion that overextensions of the type described by either Clark or Bowerman would be recorded at a late stage. Only after the child had acquired the two necessary constituents of a protoverbal element would he be able to extend a known word to an unnamed referent on the basis of observed similarity of cues.

Schlesinger's WRP Model calls for empirical verification. A number of questions deserve answers which could emerge from an experimental or observational study. Do mothers truly provide help in identifying words' referents? How do they do this? Is it the rule that each new word is initially underextended either in comprehension or in production? Another issue that is not at all clear is how and when children "decide" to generate a new protoverbal element. Does every new word heard by the child open the way for a new concept? How does the child decide whether a newly encountered referent is a member of an existing protoverbal element or not?

A descriptive study designed to provide detailed longitudinal information about the course of the use of first words would help to explore the extent of the generality of this new model.

Revisions and extensions of the original proposals

In recent publications, Clark (1983a, b, 1985), Nelson and Lucariello (1985), and Barrett (1986) have responded to the major criticisms directed against the SFH, the FCH, and the PM, by suggesting a number of radical revisions and new extensions. To the best of my knowledge, the new proposals have not yet been empirically tested. In Chapter 12 some of the claims presented in this section will be examined against the findings of my investigation.[1]

Clark (1983a, b) responded to the major criticisms against the SFH by replacing it with a new and independent theory of lexical meaning which she termed the Lexical Contrast Theory (LCT). In her "fresh look" (1983a:820) at the problem of lexical acquisition, Clark admits that this process is simpler than she had previously hypothesized. Clark argues that lexical learning is explained primarily by two principles: contrast and conventionality. The first principle, which is also the higher-level one, represents the idea that every two words in a given language contrast with each other or flag different conceptual categories (1983a:825). The second principle is based on the premise that linguistic devices are arbitrary so that each meaning is encoded in a given language by an agreed-upon (i.e., conventional) symbol. Clark argues that from the very first steps of language learning, children realize that languages utilize conventional means to express meaning, and therefore learn those means in order to become successful code users.

> I will argue that the acquisition and growth of the lexicon is much like the construction of a dictionary: What is continually being added are conventional meanings that contrast with those meanings already available. (1983b:67)

Clark's new theory is much more general than her SFH model. In her relevant publications, Clark does not directly treat the question of how early

[1] It should be noted that when designing, conducting, and summing up the results of the present research, I was not aware of the new theoretical proposals which had not then been published. Nevertheless, I decided to incorporate the new models into the present chapter in order to provide an updated review of the literature, and also because my analyses show that a number of the claims made by these authors are correct and can be supported by empirical evidence.

meanings are represented or stored in the child's mind. Clark seems, however, to admit that adjunct theories (of the kind that young children entertain) about what words can be used for, how meanings relate to each other, and how non-linguistic and linguistic input are integrated, may explain the course of early semantic development.

The main implications of Clark's new position are that the conceptual development of the child precedes and governs the acquisition of words. It is argued that children will acquire words only for existing and well-established concepts. Furthermore, words are treated in the model as labels that are picked up by the child mainly for communicative purposes. The second implication is exemplified in Clark's new explanation of overextension, according to which words are sometimes misused by the child in production in an attempt to extend them to cover unnamed categories. Overextension, then, is not the result of misclassification, partial representation, or the identification of similarities between underlying semantic features. Rather, it is a reflection of initial attempts to communicate verbally, with a limited lexicon at one's disposal. Clark's new explanation of overextension is thus strikingly similar to Nelson's (1974) original claim that words' intensions cannot be inferred from the way in which the words are extended.

To my mind, the LCT cannot be treated as a new comprehensive model for word-meaning because it is much less specific than such a model would have to be (see also Merriman, in press). The description of the structure of the lexicon which it provides is both too general and too limited, and its terms are too vague. In the present formulation, the model predicts that only conventional words in adult speech will enter children's early vocabularies, that early lexicons will consist of words that belong to completely different real-world contents, and that semantic fields will develop gradually by continuing differentiation. These predictions can be tested empirically, and I will report on such an attempt in Chapter 12. As even Clark admits, the LCT cannot work independently. This is primarily due to the fact that the developmental issue of changes over time in the child's conceptual and linguistic processing abilities is completely ignored, as well as the result of the assumption that words' intensions cannot be identified through the analysis of their repeated uses in different contexts.

A revised and somewhat elaborated model of word-meaning has recently been published by Nelson and Lucariello (1985). While maintaining Nelson's original claim that words are always attached to underlying existing concepts, Nelson now argues that since children's conceptual abilities change over time, words will have different meanings at different times in development. Ironically, Nelson now grants relatively more significance than does Clark to the role of early communicative experiences and the linguistic input to the child. The two researchers still differ with regard to the question of whether well-established concepts are a necessary condition for the learning of new words. While today Clark argues that new words are learned only for well-defined categories, Nelson now suggests that early words do not initially signify object concepts, but are, rather, attached to unpartitioned event representations.

Early cognitive structures, argue Nelson and Lucariello, are undifferentiated mental units that consist of relations belonging to the same event representation. Thus, for example, when the child initially utters the word *dog*, it is not a term of reference denoting one member in the collection of dogs, but rather a term for a set of relations in which dogs play a part (1985:37). Through repeated experience with objects, children generate concepts which consist of their knowledge about actions, functions, relations between objects, and their perceptual properties.

In support of her new claims, Nelson cites a number of researchers who argue that early word forms are not referential (e.g., Carter, 1979; Dore, 1975; Halliday, 1975). She contends that since several researchers have shown that during the early phases of production children utter word-like forms which have no internal representation beyond their conditions of use, these must be pre-lexical rather than lexical terms. She adds that true lexical expressions enter the child's lexicon only after he is able to partition event representations into their main non-linguistic components. According to Nelson and Lucariello, this is achieved towards the second half of the second year and is exhibited by a number of linguistic manifestations (some early words drop out of the lexicon, others are learned with a clear object denotation, multi-word expressions emerge, etc.).

Nelson is not very specific as to the processes by which words change their meanings. She does not state whether this occurs suddenly or gradually, and most surprisingly, she completely neglects the question of whether or not, in her present treatment, words' extensions do reflect their intensions. The theoretical claim that words change their meanings over time clearly makes sense and has never been explicitly stated only because it is a built-in assumption of every theory of meaning acquisition. What does seem to require empirical support, however, is the suggestion that early productions are situation-based and holistic. In point of fact, evidence that this is indeed the case has begun to appear in recent years.

I have argued elsewhere (Dromi, 1982, 1984) that my analyses of an entire one-word lexicon of a Hebrew-acquiring child show that early words sometimes exhibit extension patterns which cannot be explained by any componential model of meaning. These words, in my opinion, are situation-based and I maintain that they are invoked by the realization of the contexts to which they belong. In my previous writings I have proposed that the phenomenon of uttering words as cover terms for whole situations is explained by a *word-context production strategy* that operates during the early phases of lexical development (see Chapters 11 and 12 for an elaboration of this claim). My study also reveals that, as predicted by Nelson and Lucariello, the one-word period is indeed divided into two phases: a preparatory phase and a phase of consolidation. The differences between these two phases are described in detail in Chapter 9 of this book.

Independent support for the claim that meanings evolve from representations of whole situations can be found in Barrett's recent writings (1982, 1986) in which he presents a revised version of Bowerman's PM of word-meaning acquisition. In a diary follow-up of the early semantic development of his own son (an English-acquiring subject), Barrett identified initial word productions that were event-bound and non-referential. Barrett argues that early words encode holistic representations of routine events which are fairly limited in scope and consist of a single person, a single action scheme and a single object (e.g., a bath-taking situation). Barrett provides quite a detailed explanation of how a number of words which were initially event-bound were later attached to their more referential conventional meanings.

Barrett reports that he observed a gradual process by which the child learned to appreciate major constituents in the general event scheme. He suggests the term "decontextualization" for referring to the process of disembedding one component of the scheme and attaching a word to designate it. Barrett contends that only when words are attached to prototypical referents does the child start to use them to denote novel referents. This transition occurs when one or more features shared by novel referents and the prototype are recognized. The establishment of a prototypical exemplar for a word is not, however, the end of the semantic specification process. Once lexical development is in progress, the child generates semantic fields and carries out comparisons among prototypes. Thus, he identifies and adds contrastive features to the underlying representations of words that express closely related meanings.

Barrett's elaboration of the PM explanation incorporates two new notions, early holistic representation and abstructed contrastive features, to explain how related words (i.e., names of objects and actions) become mutually exclusive semantically. Barrett's treatment of contrasts is far more specific than Clark's (1983a, b) and, in fact, evolves from his earlier criticisms of the SFH (see Barrett, 1978; and previous sections of this chapter). The extended PM theory, which now takes a modular form, accounts for the numerous extension patterns of early words. The theory predicts that the time, or "age", of the word (and/or the child) will have a strong impact on the course of linguistic performance. The model predicts that a wide variety of pathways to meaning will be identified even within a single lexicon (see also Carey, 1982), a prediction which is strongly supported by my finding that 58 different extension combinations or profiles were identified in one subject's lexicon of 337 Hebrew words (see Dromi, 1983 and Chapter 12). The more specific prediction of the extended PM, that overextensions would be recorded relatively late during lexical development, is also confirmed by my analyses, which clearly indicate that overextensions are not recorded during the first phase of the one-word period (see Chapters 9, 11 and 12).

Summary

We have reviewed competing theoretical models of word-meaning acquisition, focusing mainly on the predictions of each model in regard to extension behaviors of early words. We have seen that the models differ in structure, content, and predictive power. Researchers vary in their treatment of:

(a)   the interrelationships between concept formation and the acquisition of words (compare Clark, Nelson and Schlesinger);

(b)   the relative significance of linguistic input and early communicative experiences (compare Barrett, Clark, Nelson and Schlesinger);

(c)   the different types of word extensions and their implications for word intensions (compare Clark, Bowerman, Nelson and Schlesinger); and

(d)   the explanation of why early words show certain extension patterns (compare Barrett's, Bowerman's, Nelson's and Schlesinger's accounts of why children misuse words or extend them for whole situations).

The study reported in Chapters 7 to 11 was designed with the aim of evaluating the proposed models by testing the validity of their predictions as manifested in early lexical development of one child. The disciplined case-study was designed in such a way as to enable a close follow-up of words' extensional behaviors to be carried out. The following chapter will consider the basic philosophy behind this research technique.

6   Case-study methodology: justification and outline of principles[1]

Longitudinal naturalistic studies of very small groups of subjects have traditionally been associated with the study of language development. Diary reports of parents, as well as transcriptions of audio- or video-recordings of single subjects interacting with their peers or family members, are quite frequently cited in the literature as the main source of evidence for particular theoretical claims. Yet, even though naturalistic studies are so commonly conducted within developmental psycholinguistics, they are rarely accepted as powerful methodological tools outside our field. Readers very often regard naturalistic studies as merely a collection of anecdotal observations which may serve only for initial piloting or preliminary theorizing. As a result, some researchers avoid the application of naturalistic paradigms. Moreover, since social scientists typically employ quantitative research methods, graduate students and even experienced researchers quite often become much more familiar with the basic principles of experimentation than with the philosophical foundations of qualitative research. This state of affairs reduces the likelihood of introducing scientific advances to naturalistic methodology, which, theoretically speaking, can be still further developed. The study which is reported in Chapters 7 through 11 of this book was designed within the theoretical framework of qualitative research. The present chapter is therefore devoted to a concise presentation of the underlying ideology of this scientific approach.[2]

The ideology of qualitative-research paradigms

A number of distinct philosophical assumptions underlie quantitative- and qualitative-research approaches. While quantitative research is based on the assumption that a theory must be constructed with a strong linkage to experimentation, qualitative approaches completely deny the possibility of

[1] A previous version of this chapter was circulated as a paper entitled: Case-study methodology: An artistic portrait or a scientific investigation? This paper was critically reviewed by Ruth Berman, Annette Karmiloff-Smith, and Sidney Strauss. I have learned from all of them, and I wish to thank them for their invaluable comments. Special gratitude is extended to Annette Karmiloff-Smith who pointed out a number of unconvincing arguments and loose reasonings. Her constructive intention and encouraging reaction to my earlier paper persuaded me to rework some ideas and to include the present chapter in this book.

[2] While I was planning and actually running my case-study research I was unaware of the need to explain the methodological issues I raise below. It was only later and through my attempts to present my findings and conclusions that it became evident to me that it is crucial to consider the underlying ideology of qualitative research. I strongly believe that without this background it is hard to evaluate the results of a case-study and to judge their generality.

conducting strict and clean experimentation on questions that are related to human functioning in social environments (Guba and Lincoln, 1981). Where the quantitative approach maintains that scientific knowledge progresses only by testing specific and well-motivated hypotheses, qualitative researchers argue that behaviors can be understood by a trustworthy analysis of a given process occurring in its natural context (Rist, 1977; Sanders, 1981). The verification of what is learnt from specific experimentation in relation to the general population is an important goal for a quantitative researcher. Accordingly, within this research tradition great efforts are directed towards the development of statistical means for deriving correct inferences about the real world from the laboratory results (Hamilton, 1981). The scientist who conducts a qualitative study, on the other hand, usually strives for a complete and highly detailed picture of the phenomena he wishes to understand. Therefore, within this framework, the major effort is devoted to the incorporation of as much evidence as possible, while concurrently testing competing hypotheses as to the underlying rules that may explain observed behaviors. In qualitative thinking, statistical measures are less significant because an attempt is made to understand a process in its unique complexity. Only after patterns of general significance are revealed from first-hand evidence can such patterns be tested for broader generality by means of comparisons with the results of other studies.

Qualitative studies, like quantitative ones, are not conducted in a vacuum. In both frameworks of research the investigation emerges from a well-defined concern or a set of specific problems. While in the experimental world specific hypotheses must be stated prior to the planning of the research design, in a naturalistic approach research begins with a set of open questions which seem to require systematic exploration. The set of research questions guides the choice of data collection procedures, the type of data analysis, and the boundaries of research (i.e., for how long it will be conducted, in which settings, by what means of data collection, etc.).

Case-study methodology

One of the most popular types of naturalistic research is the case-study, first used in the field of clinical psychology. At the beginning of this century, clinical case-studies were widely employed by psychologists to describe the effects of particular interventions on individual patients. Such case-studies were usually written in a literary, anecdotal style and often did not include enough details to allow for successful verification (Kratochwill, 1978). The scientific value of case-studies was often questioned by experimental psychologists who, at most, agreed to accept this tool as a preliminary method for generating scientific hypotheses (Stake, 1978).

It is only lately that case-studies have begun to attract renewed attention. A number of researchers have recently advocated this approach for studying very complex, context-bounded, and highly dynamic processes (e.g., Rist, 1977; Shallice, 1979; Stake 1978, 1981). Stake argues, for example, that case-studies are very powerful tools for the educational evaluation of closed systems such as individuals, institutions, specific programs or specific populations. Denny (1978) and Leean (1981) hold that case-studies should be viewed as intensive or complete examinations of an issue, facet or domain which constantly changes over time.

Two characteristics of early speech make case-study methodology the suitable choice for a research paradigm in this realm: (a) during the early periods of production the linguistic knowledge of the child changes quickly and constantly (e.g., Braunwald, 1978; Nelson and Lucariello, 1985); and (b) it has been shown that early verbal productions are strongly dependent on their linguistic and non-linguistic contexts (e.g., Bates, 1976; Clark, 1982; Peters, 1983).

Peters (1983:87) and Clark (1982) have shown that experimental conditions are overly constraining for very young children, since they contain tasks which are too simplified and too isolated from the regular experiences of toddlers. Young children tend to show high levels of stress during testing and sometimes manifest low performance because they are restricted by the questions and the instructions, with which they do not always want to comply.

As noted by Iwamura (in Peters, 1983), the normal drive of young children to communicate in their own environments sometimes triggers newly acquired linguistic constructs which cannot be elicited in laboratory conditions (see also Bowerman, 1976; Karmiloff-Smith, 1979, for a discussion of this experimental dilemma). Since early words are often phonological modifications of conventional forms and a child's expressions are so telegraphic, a close familiarity with the subject and his or her non-linguistic experiences is a necessary condition for correct interpretation (see Rodgon, 1976; Braunwald and Brislin, 1979).

A case-study investigation of early speech must be distinct from a mere collection of anecdotes about specific speech events. Selective descriptions of specific speech events are often used by researchers to support a given claim, but they must be treated with great caution. When a child is observed selectively and/or randomly, transient and short-lived phenomena can be noted and mistakenly interpreted as representative of a typical and regularly occurring linguistic behavior. In a selective method of data collection, the examples noted may be irregular or limited only to those which best accord with the researcher's hypothesis. Anglin's (1977) criticisms of old diaries, which were too biased towards the inclusion of overextensions, is a good example of this problem (see also Barrett's, 1978, criticisms of the SFH).

The researcher undertaking a case-study must commit himself to an ongoing and intensive data-collection process. Close and continuous familiarity with the subject and the contexts of study is the only guarantee for distinguishing between accidental, transient, or atypical behaviors and characteristic features of the phenomenon under investigation. Since case-studies are not based on one-off experimental testing, their internal validity is a direct function of the continuous effort that is invested in an active and daily process of data collection. The inclusion of various means for collecting the information is also recommended in order to establish a broad-spectrum record. When data are gathered by various means, the drawbacks inherent in each method are counterbalanced by the existence of an additional source. When specific rules for data collection are followed and these are known prior to the actual gathering of information, the difficulty of validating the data is greatly minimized (see Braunwald and Brislin, 1979; Guba and Lincoln, 1981; and the following section).

Meeting tests of rigor

Case-studies are open to criticism for subjectivity and the relatively limited scope of their generality. When a case-study of early language development is conducted by a mother-investigator, this problem is even more obvious, since the mother is intimately linked with the subject and therefore may overcredit him with knowledge which he does not yet have. In my opinion, it is a task of the mother-researcher to prove that her analysis is as objective as possible and her description scientific rather than artistic.

A number of methodological principles can be followed in order to minimize biases and increase the level of objectivity and generality of case-study results. The best means of validating data is to incorporate a number of independent methods for data collection. Not only do various sources compensate for the drawbacks of each individual one, but the identification of links between sources is a necessary condition for proving validity (Guba and Lincoln, 1981). An explicit statement of the rules for data collection and analysis is also required to increase trust in case-study results. If the data are collected continuously in a manner faithful to a set of known rules, there is no danger that only partial evidence will be recorded.

When the criteria for data inclusion and exclusion are given, readers can evaluate the data and their general level of detail. They can also judge the plausibility of the conclusions drawn from the study. The researcher's decisions are open to critical review only if the definitions that were used during data analyses are provided. Such definitions are also helpful when a need to replicate the study with other subjects arises, or when researchers wish to compare their findings with the reported results of other studies. Since case-studies are so intensive, they are usually carried out with a small number of subjects. It is thus frequently desirable to compare the results of a given case-study with those from studies of a different nature or conducted by a different researcher.

It is highly advisable to carry out inter-judge reliability measures on case-study data and analyses. These procedures minimize the unlikely possibility that the case-study report might be based on a one-sided interpretation of a specific interaction between one subject and one observer. Parallel observations, double coding, and independent application of the classification systems by a second scorer are all very useful. Since parallel analyses are extremely time-consuming (and also very expensive), it is generally agreed that only ten per cent of the data be double scored.

Limitations of the case-study methodology

Like all other methodologies, case-study investigation has its limitations. It is important to consider these limitations prior to the selection of the research tool. Case-studies require a highly labour-intensive effort, and as Braunwald and Brislin (1979) report, the need continuously to record all the available information concerning the linguistic development of a single child is an extremely demanding task. Moreover, such a study is an invasion of privacy for the whole family. An honest record should follow the child and the family into the most private and embarrassing moments of their personal life. In addition, the effect of writing down whatever the child says is to place a value on the child's productions that even he or she notices from a very young age.[3]

In case-study research, working hypotheses and theoretical concepts very often arise during data collection and analysis. This fact begets an obvious conflict. On the one hand, the researcher wishes to carry out all procedures as initially planned, but on the other hand it is sometimes necessary to modify definitions or decisions to avoid superimposing constraints on the naturalistic nature of the data. It is important to be aware of this possibility and to remain flexible and attentive to the phenomena observed when establishing boundaries or limitations on the inquiry. In devising categories for the analysis of case-study data, researchers should also proceed in a similar manner. The categories must be functional and appropriate for describing the data at a desired level of specificity. Categories should be selected so as to cover most of the evidence, keeping to a minimum unassignable or ambiguous information. At the same time, the categories should be general enough to enable application to other data as well. If this is

---

[3] It is debatable whether diarists' children are affected by the mere fact that their language becomes the focus of interest for their mothers. I completely agree with Braunwald and Brislin (1979) who report that, towards the end of the second year of life, subjects notice that their speech is being recorded. Keren started to react overtly to my taking constant notes about her speech at the end of the one-word stage. Like Braunwald's subject, J, Keren used to remind me to write down her words or sentences when I didn't do so. In my opinion, the fact that Keren's linguistic development was followed so closely generated a high degree of linguistic awareness in her. Even to this day, when Keren is 7:6 years old, I am often surprised by how conscious she is of her own speech and the verbal expressions of others. The quotation at the beginning of Chapter 2 illustrates how critical Keren is about the speech of other children.

ņot done, the analysis will be too particular and the conclusions drawn from it too specific.

Case-study results are always very complex. Straightforward answers to specific well-defined questions will rarely be derived from a case-study investigation. Researchers who select case-study methodology should be prepared for repeated attempts to examine their findings so that they will be able to make the best sense of their results. The conclusions of case-study research will never allow generalization beyond a specific point. General outlines of development, or norms about large populations, can never be inferred from this type of analysis.

Since they are naturalistic in principle, case-studies do not allow for an examination of specific causal-effect links between behaviors or for the direct testing of underlying covert knowledge. For example, the comprehension abilities of young children cannot be traced in a case-study design. In an intensive study that spans weeks or months, the investigator cannot introduce repeated and controlled comprehension tests, since such intervention would clearly constrain the subject's naturalistic interactions with the observer, and hence could substantially affect the regular course of language acquisition.

A final point to consider in regard to case-studies is their relatively small publication output. Case-study results do not lend themselves to publication as a set of short articles which address specific issues. In most cases they appear as books or long monographs, publications which are not always as readily available to readers as are journal articles.

7 A disciplined case-study of early lexical development

Chapter 6 presented the rationale for conducting a disciplined case-study and the main theoretical principles involved in it. The present chapter is devoted to the description of my own case-study investigation of the linguistic development of one subject throughout the one-word period. The emphasis in this description is laid on the data-collection procedures and the measures of reliability and validity, primarily for the following reasons:

(a)   it is these aspects of the methodology which make it distinct from anecdotal observations and/or other types of naturalistic methods,

(b)   during the execution of my research program I encountered specific problems that were unique to the content of early speech. The solutions I adopted for such problems are presented here in the hope that they may guide other researchers.

The subject and the settings

The subject of this investigation is my daughter Keren – a first and only child. Keren was born in the United States while her Israeli parents were graduate students. During the first four months of Keren's life we (her Hebrew-speaking parents) were her primary caretakers. During that period she was exposed to only a little English when an American woman babysat for her, or when our friends played with her. When Keren was four months old we moved back to Israel. Since then Keren has been exposed only to Hebrew, which is her parents' native tongue and a fluent language for her grand-parents. When Keren was six months old, a non-native Hebrew speaker – a professional caretaker (*metapelet* in Hebrew) – began to take care of her four times a week for six hours each time. The *metapelet* spoke Hebrew fluently, but some morphological and syntactic deviations could be identified in her speech. She sometimes confused gender markings on verbs and nouns, and she often substituted the dative marker *le-* for the direct definite marker *et ha-* which is obligatory in Hebrew. In general, her dialect was typical of Eastern-European immigrants to Israel and included several baby words which are not conventional in the language and were not used by us or by our parents. For example, she would say *ham* when feeding the baby and *hita* when taking the baby for a walk outside. The effects of the *metapelet*'s speech on Keren's lexical development are discussed in the following chapters. Keren was 10(12) (ten months and twelve days) at the beginning of data collection. On this particular day I identified her first comprehensible word:[1] *haw*, which she uttered in the course of our walk outside when we passed a little white dog which was barking at us. Keren was pointing to the dog when she said *haw*. On the last day of recording, Keren was 17(23). This cut-off point was selected seven days after I had realized that Keren was frequently producing two- and multi-word utterances. Keren's transition from one-word to multi-word productions was quite sharp. When she was 17(16) I noted in her diary: "Today it becomes evident to me that Keren does not face 'programming-span' limitations or other constraints of production any longer. Most of her new expressions are two- and multi-word utterances. It happened quite suddenly." Out of the 39 speech events that were recorded in Keren's diary on the day that she was 17(16), 17 were novel productions of two-word utterances. On the same date, during 30 minutes of audio-recording, Keren produced a total of 279 utterances, 36 per cent of which were multi-word expressions.

The natural speech data were collected when Keren was playing alone or in the course of spontaneous interactions with other people. I was the only observer–recorder of data, and therefore my own interactions with the child are described frequently. Most of the data were collected in our home, which is a typical Israeli apartment, located on the second floor of an apartment building and decorated in Western style. Some of the data were recorded outside in the yard, in a public playground, while out for a walk, or during shopping or social activities with friends and relatives. The following sections describe the specific procedures employed in collecting the data.

The handwritten diary[2]

The diary record of Keren's linguistic development constitutes the main source of data in the present investigation. The diary includes extensive information about Keren's linguistic behavior throughout a total period of 32 weeks (seven months and twelve days). During this period most of Keren's comprehensible utterances were noted down, accompanied by detailed and systematic descriptions of the non-linguistic contexts in which they were produced.

For inclusion in the diary, an utterance had to satisfy the following

---

[1] For an operative definition of a child's comprehensible word, see p. 70 below.

[2] Many practical issues considered here also appear in Braunwald and Brislin's (1979) discussion of the modern techniques for conducting a diary study. Unfortunately, I was completely unaware of this publication at the time of planning my study. I wish to thank Dr. K. Ruder and Dr. J. Wright from the University of Kansas who helped me to overcome many problems and to deal with a number of questions, while giving me insightful methodological suggestions.

definition of a "comprehensible word": any utterance that carries some underlying meaning as judged by the listener who is familiar with the child (see Veneziano, 1981 and Chapter 2 for a justification of the interactive approach). A word may answer this definition without our being able to understand it. It is sometimes obvious that the child is trying to convey meaning or communicative intentions and yet these cannot be interpreted. As the following rules for considering identifiable repeated phonological constructs in various contexts (i.e., comprehensible words) indicate, the assignment of such constructs to the diary can be made if one or more of the following criteria are met: (a) phonological resemblance to an adult word; (b) repeated productions of the same phonological construct in similar contexts; (c) gestures used by the child to indicate the referent for the utterance; (d) intonation patterns and repetitions which indicate that the child is looking for an adult response to an utterance and/or is not satisfied with a given adult's response and therefore keeps producing the same construct again and again. (See Table 12 below for examples of words which initially were uninterpretable.)

Words imitated from the speech of others and all spontaneously produced words were recorded in the diary. Special attention was paid to the various linguistic and non-linguistic contexts of production. Finally, interactions among old and new words were noted on separate columns of the diary page so that processes of extension and differentiation of meaning could subsequently be evaluated. All the data were entered on pre-planned recording sheets with five vertical columns. These sheets were placed around the house, ready to be filled in at any moment.

The data were entered on the recording sheets from right to left according to the direction of the Hebrew writing system. Consistent notational rules were followed in entering the data: the child's utterances were transcribed phonetically (see Appendix D for a description of the phonetic notations used); notes on the non-linguistic contexts of each utterance were written in Hebrew orthography; names of family members were abbreviated; the age of the child was noted in months and days, along with the full date. In the fifth column to the right, the mother's interpretational comments were entered. The comments included glosses of the child's utterances and several types of interpretative comments such as: overextension; used as dative; first emergent structure; causative verb; sequential one-word utterances; prototype; non-conventional usage; masculine plural ending, etc. The wide variety of comment types reflects my aim to be uninfluenced as far as possible by any specific theory or model of thinking while collecting the data. My goal was to establish a broad-spectrum record that would enable me to address several different theoretical issues related to the early lexical development of the child. In Table 1 below, a typical recording page from Keren's diary appears in English translation.

Table 1. A typical page from Keren's diary

Date/Age	Place	Event	Child's utterances	Mother's comments
Dec. 31,1980 16(3)	K's room	In the A.M. K wakes up with a cold. M gives her an aspirin and says: Keren, kxi kadur/ 'Keren, take a pill!' K stretches out her hand, takes the pill, puts it in her mouth, and says:	adur/adur/ '(a) pill'	adur - (kadur) which is a homonym in Hebrew used also for '(a) ball'. K says adur only for pills. Her word for ball is hupa.
		K sees a lollipop on the counter. She says: When she is asked: mi kana lax?/ 'Who bought it for you?' she answers:	ukara/urara/ '(a) sweet' (175) nira/	grandmother's name

Table 1. Continued

Date/Age	Place	Event	Child's utterances	Mother's comments
Dec. 31, 1980 16(3)	In the kitchen	K is sitting on her chair. She asks M to sit on another chair, While banging her hands on the chair K says: (Yesterday K asked M in the same way to sit on the ground in the garden.)	ima ev/sev/ 'mother sit, sit'	K says the verb in masculine although she is addressing me. This is the first time she says sev in relation to a chair. The word is accompanied with the same gesture as when sitting on the rug. Sev = performative?
	Parents' room	K wants to pass through the space between the wall and the double bed. She pushes herself to the wall and says: (This event already occurred three weeks ago. I thought it was accidental then.)	nes/ 'to enter'	K says 'to enter' instead of 'to go through'. This is an overextension of a verb form.
	Parents' room	K sees M putting on some make-up. She says again and again: M doesn't understand. She tries to give K all kinds of things from the drawer. K doesn't want them and says: Finally, M lets K choose for herself. K takes M's plastic eyeshadow brush and sticks it in her ear.	onez/onez/ 'ear' (176) lo/ 'no'	Does K mean 'to put to the ear' or '(a) stick' ? This example is ambiguous between overextension and association.

Table 1. Continued

Date/Age	Place	Event	Child's utterances	Mother's comments
	In K's room	After M has turned on the heater, she takes some items out of the closet to change K's clothes. M says: nikax bgadim lasalon ki sam xam/ 'Let us take some clothes to the living room, because it is warm there.' K picks up several items of clothing while saying: She goes to the living room. On the way she drops a diaper. M asks: ma kara?/'What happened?'	xam/xam/ 'warm,warm'	A delayed imitation.
		K answers:	tul/tul/ '(a) diaper, (a) diaper'	K names the object and not the action although she sometimes uses the word ala (nafla) 'fell down' when she drops things.
Dec. 31, 1980 16(3)	Living room	K notices M's coat on the couch in the living room. She says:	ima/meil ima/ 'Mother, coat-mother' (177)	

Note: Child's words which are numbered in parentheses were recorded here for the th time. The number is the actual number of the word in Keren's cumulative lexicon. S glossary for explanation of notational symbols.

I kept the diary myself, and collected data continuously at all times and in all the places in which I could observe and record my daughter's linguistic behavior. Three sampling criteria were applied in selecting the data to be entered each day:

(a) Mainly new comprehensible utterances were recorded in the diary.
This selection rule was chosen for both practical and theoretical reasons. When data are collected continuously, one must be selective. It is impossible to record everything the child says unless the period of investigation is limited to a few days (e.g., Bowerman, 1973, on Kendall). Since the goal of

the present investigation was to describe developmental processes of change, special attention was given to the following types of phenomena:

(1)   the several first productions of a newly acquired phonological construct that seemed to be comprehensible;
(2)   the accumulation and differentiation of the contexts in which a previously acquired comprehensible word was uttered;
(3)   unusual usages of new and old comprehensible words;
(4)   disappearances of regularly occurring comprehensible words;
(5)   modifications in the phonological or morphological characteristics of all comprehensible words already productive in the child's lexicon.

A newly acquired comprehensible word was recorded at least three times in each context of occurrence, or whenever its morphological or phonological manifestations changed. When a recognizable construct was heard in the same context for the fourth time or more, it was not again recorded in that context.

(b) Data was entered at the time of production or immediately afterward.
This rule is very important. It greatly increases the validity of the data base, since no reconstruction from memory is attempted. It is true that I frequently had to interrupt whatever I was doing in order to enter data into the diary. One way to minimize the amount of interruption was to record only new comprehensible words or old words in new contexts. For the first few months of the study, new comprehensible words emerged at a slow rate, and quite regularly Keren produced a word repeatedly in very similar contexts. Therefore, it was possible for me to ignore a specific production if I felt that the interaction should not be interrupted.

During the first five months of the study, Keren never expressed signs of dissatisfaction with the fact that I was always writing down what she was saying. Only during the last two and a half months did difficulties begin to emerge. At that point, the data started to accumulate very rapidly, and it became obvious that Keren began to be aware that her mother was always busy with other things while she was playing with her. Keren used to ask for my pencils and papers, and on several occasions attempted to interfere with my writing. My solution to this problem was to note only Keren's exact words in column four, and to use shorthand notation for the description of the contexts. I also started to carry around a microcassette recorder and to record exact imitations of Keren's utterances and short descriptions of the contexts of occurrence.

Keren responded well to my verbal imitations of her childish speech. On many occasions she herself repeated a new construction several times, and so it was recorded directly on the tape. Admittedly, the overt process of reinforcing Keren's new utterances may have contributed to the rate and course of her linguistic development. This possibility is not central here, however, since this study is neither a comparative nor a normative one. The problem of building a reinforcement system into any intensive observation of a child's development is inherent in the design. I agree with Scollon (1976), and Braunwald and Brislin (1979), who argue that the very fact that a child is being studied places a value on his or her verbalizations that even a young child can appreciate (this point was discussed in Chapter 6).

(c) Keren's mother is the only observer and recorder of data.
It is important to consider this final selection rule because it dictated a time-sampling limitation on the process of data collection. All my judgments were based on the information I gathered through the direct observation of my child. During the period of data collection I stayed at home with Keren for three full days and four afternoons each week. When Keren's *metapelet* (caretaker) or her grandparents (who took care of her when I was absent) told me about new words, I would note them down in parentheses. This information was not considered as primary data for analysis.

During the total period of investigation, 3,518 entries were recorded in Keren's diary. These entries included information about the different uses of 337 words that were acquired by the subject over a period of seven months and twelve days. Keren's complete cumulative lexicon is presented in Appendix A. In order to determine the rate and order of acquisition of new words, a criterion of three recordings in spontaneous production was invoked. A new word was entered into the cumulative lexicon on the date of its third recording in the diary.

The audio-recordings

In order to compensate for the fact that a considerable amount of the data were collected by hand at the time of production or immediately following it, nine audio-recordings served as supplementary sources of evidence. The recorded samples ranged in length from 55 to 180 minutes, with an average length of 83 minutes. These data were collected in order to compensate for the drawbacks of the procedures that are typical for the recording of selective examples by pre-planned criteria. The speech samples were recorded no more than three weeks apart, and they provided a representative picture of Keren's ordinary speech in specific blocks of time. Recordings started when Keren was 13(26) because earlier than that the rate of production was so slow that in the course of one hour of taping very few comprehensible words could be identified. The set of recordings served the following purposes:

(a)   They constituted a permanent record that could be listened to repeatedly. They served as the main source of evidence for phonological and morphological changes over time.

(b)   They provided an excellent data base for conducting external validity and

Table 2. A summary of the audio-recordings

Recording number	Date	Child's age	Duration in minutes	Total no. of child's utterances	People present
1	Oct. 24, 1980	13(26)	55	208	Mother, Father Keren
2	Nov. 18, 1980	14(21)	90	358	Mother, Keren
3	Dec. 3, 1980	15(5)	55	362	Mother, Father Keren
4	Dec. 18, 1980	15(20)	100	500	Mother, Keren
5	Dec. 26, 1980	15(28)	60	855	Mother, Keren
6	Dec. 30, 1980	16(3)	55	749	Mother, Father Keren
7	Jan. 14, 1981	16(17)	180	911	Mother, Father Keren
8	Feb. 6, 1981	17(9)	90	490	Mother, Keren
9	Feb. 13, 1981	17(16)	90	701	Mother, Keren

reliability measures on the diary record (see pp. 84–9 below and Appendix B).

(c)   They provided a rich source of data on the characteristics of the mother's linguistic input to the child and the patterns of interaction between the mother and the child. Such patterns (some of which were routinized interactions) could have been identified only in the process of real-time sampling, and they turned out to be crucial for understanding the processes studied here.

The tape-recorded sessions took place in our home. I followed a strict rule of not interrupting a recording after it was begun. Some tapes contained long intervals of silence, and some recorded occasional phone calls or unexpected visits.

The recording equipment used was a Panasonic microcassette recorder model RN–166. It was inserted into the front pocket of a vest, which I sewed especially for the purpose of recording.[3] Keren wore her green vest on top of any shirt, so her mobility was not at all affected, and she only very rarely paid attention to the recording equipment itself. At the end of a full hour of recording I took the recorder out for a few minutes in order to turn over the cassettes. During all the recording sessions I kept notes on the non-linguistic contexts of each verbal production, many aspects of which were inaudible. It

[3] I wish to thank Dr K. Ruder for the idea of using a microcassette recorder, and Mrs. C. Ruder for the model and sewing instructions for the vest.

was very easy to record spoken notes directly onto the tape at the time of recording. The spoken notes were short and I tried to use a formal speech register so that the contextual notes could easily be distinguished from my verbal interactions with the child.

The quality of the audio-recordings was surprisingly good. The microcassette recorder turned out to be very sensitive, and since it was placed so close to the subject's mouth the signal-to-noise ratio obtained was highly efficient. For purposes of later transcription and the establishment of a permanent file, I copied each microcassette onto a regular cassette tape using a professional deck recorder. Table 2 summarizes characteristics of the recording sessions in detail.

The total amount of data collected by the audio-recording procedure is quite impressive. As shown in Table 2, the number of utterances produced by the child in the span of one audio-sample increased as she grew older. A total number of 5,134 utterances were recorded during 13 hours of audio-taping; 223 different words appeared in the transcripts at least once.

The transcriptions of the audio-tapes

The audio-recorded sessions were transcribed for further analysis. All the speech productions of Keren and the other participants were transcribed phonetically. Only the short contextual notes were written in Hebrew orthography. The symbols used in transcribing the tapes were largely those of the International Phonetic Alphabet. Intervocalic consonants and vowels that were slightly deviant from conventional adult articulations were transcribed using the closest IPA symbol, and then circled. Whenever agreement could not be reached as to the quality of a vowel, it was transcribed as a schwa.

Ochs's (1979) general guidelines for displaying verbal and non-verbal contexts on a transcript were followed. Each transcription page was divided into two columns, one for each participant. The non-verbal context and the verbal data for each participant were displayed in separate locations in each column. Superscripts were used to indicate discourse variables such as initiation of a conversation, overlap between two speakers, and turn-taking. The notation of intonation and other prosodic information was basically adapted from Ochs (1979) as well. Appendix D presents the English translation of the guidelines developed for transcribing the Hebrew data, and a short example of a transcribed event.

An enormous amount of time was involved in transcribing the Hebrew tapes. A second-year linguistics student was the primary transcriber.[4] After several hours of practice, the average time required to transcribe one hour of tape was twenty hours. For purposes of assessing reliability, two tapes (the first and the last) were transcribed by a second independent transcriber who was unfamiliar with either the subject or other details of the present research.

Table 3.   A summary of the video-recordings

Recording number	Date	Child's age	Duration in minutes	Total no. of child's utterances	People present
1	Nov. 1, 1980	14(4)	30	123	Mother, Father Keren
2	Nov. 28,1980	15(0)	28	132	Mother, Father Keren, Merav
3	Jan. 10,1981	16(13)	28	75	Mother, Father Keren
4	Feb. 21,1981	17(24)	25	160	Mother, Father Keren

The video-recording

Four thirty-minute play sessions of Keren with one of her parents were video-recorded. This was initially planned as an additional source of primary data that would document not only the audible components of situations but also their visual aspects. Portable video-tape recording equipment (Sony AVC–3400) was placed in our living room for the total period of the thirty-two weeks of the study. Nevertheless, Keren never regarded it as a natural part of her surroundings. She talked very little and often ran away from the camera. After the third attempt I decided to stop bothering her by trying to video-record her natural behavior and I video-recorded only pre-planned play sessions. Four sessions were recorded, as listed in Table 3.

The data obtained through the video-recording sessions were not used as supplementary primary data. They served exclusively for reliability and validity measures of context description (the measures of reliability are described below).

The organization of the data for analysis

The preparation of the data for further analysis required initial organization. This organization involved the construction of working tables, the aim of which was to present all the relevant data for each word in one table so that the history of the word could be readily traced.

Each entry in Keren's diary was assigned to one or more working tables (depending on the number of comprehensible words recorded in the entry). The entry itself was copied, including all comments and descriptions of the

Table 4. A working table for the word *ev-evet* (*laševet*) 'to sit down'

Diary Page no.	Date/Age	Event	Transcript Date/Age	Event
44	Dec. 22, 1980 15(24)	In the living room. K pulls grandfather Moshe to the living room. She bangs her hand on the couch and says: <u>sev</u>/ 'to sit'.		
week no. 24				
			Dec. 26, 1980 15(28)	K says: <u>?ima/?ima</u> 'mother, mother' and bangs her hand on the rug. She is trying to show M that she wants M to sit beside her. Later on, K says: <u>ab</u>/ '?', and then: <u>?ima</u>/ 'mother'. M asks once more: <u>ma?</u>/ 'what?' and K answers: <u>?av/?av</u>/ 'sit sit'.
			Dec. 30, 1980 16(2)	K says: <u>ima</u>/ 'mother' and bangs her hand on the rug. She is trying to invite M to sit on the rug beside her. M says: <u>ken/ani rak avi li et hasveder</u>/ 'yes, I'll just get my sweater'. Later K says: <u>sifa</u>/ '?' M asks: <u>ma?</u> 'what?' and K responds: <u>saf ?ima</u>/ 'sit mother'. M says: <u>hine ani ešev po, tov?</u>/ 'here, I'll sit here, O.K.?'

Table 4. Continued

Diary			Transcript	
Page no.	Date/Age	Event	Date/Age	Event
			Dec. 30, 1980 16(2)	K says: ?ima/ 'mother' a few times, and bangs her hand on the rug. Each time, M responds: ma?/ 'what?' Finally K says: sev /'sit down'. M says in response: sev?/ at roca še?ima tešev? 'sit, do you want mother to sit?' Then M sits down.
51	Dec. 31, 1980 16(3)	In the kitchen. K is sitting on her (high) chair. She asks M to sit on another chair in the kitchen. While banging her hands on the chair, K says: ima ev/sev/ 'mother sit, sit'. (Yesterday K asked M in the same way to sit on the sand in the garden.)		
week no. 25				

Table 4. Continued

Diary			Transcript	
Page no.	Date/Age	Event	Date/Age	Event
53	Jan. 1, 1981 16(4)	K is riding her bicycle. When she sees M she says: sev/sev/'sit, sit', and bangs her hand against the seat.		
56	Jan. 3, 1981 16(6)	In the living room K asks F to get up from his chair, and says: kumi/'get up'. Then she asks F to put her on his chair. She says: sev sev/ 'sit, sit'.		
63	Jan. 7, 1981 16(10)	In K's room. K is playing with her toy furniture and her doll. She calls the couch: hupa/'?' and tells the doll: sev buba/ 'sit doll'. When K herself wants to sit on the couch she says: sev areni/ 'sit Kereni'!		

week no. 26

			Jan. 14, 1981 16(17)	M and K are looking at a picture book. M says: hine naftali yošev al hasir/ gam keren yoševet al hasir/naxon?/ 'here is Naftali sitting on his potty, Keren also sits on her potty, right?' K says: efet/tiyax/ 'to sit, rug'. (K prefers to sit on the rug.) M responds: ševet/ šatiax/tov beseder švi al hašatiax/ 'to sit, rug, all right, sit on the rug...'

Table 4. Continued

Diary			Transcript	
Page no.	Date/Age	Event	Date/Age	Event
			Jan. 14, 1981 16(17)	K says: uca/'I want'. M asks: ma kereni/'what Kereni'. K answers: avat/'to sit'. M asks: laševet?/ ?eifo at roca laševet?/'to sit? Where do you want to sit?'
week no. 27				
77	Jan. 15, 1981 16(18)	In the living room. K wants F to sit next to her and tell her the story about the baby. She says: evet aba/ 'to sit daddy'.		
week no. 28				
87	Jan. 22, 1981 16(25)	K is alone in the bathroom. She is sitting in the bathtub and play-ing with her little plastic teddy bear. From outside M and F hear her saying: sev tanuax/ 'sit rest'. They see K trying to put the teddy bear on a butter-fly sticker, which is attached to the bottom of the bathtub.		
week no. 29				

Table 4. Continued

Diary			Transcript	
Page no.	Date/Age	Event	Date/Age	Event
107	Feb. 6, 1981 17(9)	In K's room. M suggests that K sit in the sun and warm up. K says: <u>evet semsa</u>/<u>evet semsam</u>/'sit sun' 'sit sun'. She repeats it several times.	Feb. 6, 1981 17(9)	K and M are playing with some play-dough. M says: <u>kama harbe plastelina</u>/ <u>ma at roca šenaase?</u>/ 'look how much play-dough (we have), what do you want us to make?' K says: <u>dod</u>/ 'an uncle'. Later on, M says: <u>?ima crixa lakum al hara-glaim bišvil šeyiye la koax laasot lax dod yafe/naxon?</u>/ 'Mommy has to get up on her feet, so that she can make you a nice uncle, right?'K says: <u>kumi/?avat</u>/ 'get up, sit down'. M says: <u>hine hapanim šel hadod</u>/ 'here is the uncle's face'. At the same time K says: <u>?evet</u>/'to sit down'. <u>?avat</u>/ 'to sit down'. M says in response: <u>hine ima yoševet</u>/'here, mummy is sitting down'.
	Feb. 7, 1981 17(10)	In the kitchen. K wants to sit on M's lap. She says: <u>ima sevet alyi</u>/ 'Mother, sit on me'.		

week no. 31

Note: Throughout this table the verb 'sit down' is recorded in either imperative masculine form: <u>ev</u> (<u>šev</u>)! 'sit down', or in its infinitive form: <u>evet</u> (<u>lasevet</u>) 'to sit down'. An obligatory feminine inflection for the contexts of addressing M, or when speaking about her own intentions to sit down, is consistently deleted by the child.

non-linguistic contexts. All the phonological approximations and the morphological modifications of the same lexical item, as well as all the entries that described uses of the same lexical item in different contexts, were entered onto the same table.[4] The entries were copied onto the table in chronological order of occurrence in the course of data collection.

The audio-recorded transcriptions were also sorted and all the occurrences of meaningful words, accompanied by short descriptions of the adult input to the child within the same communicative act, were copied onto the relevant working table at the appropriate chronological points. In Table 4, one such table is presented. This is the working table of the word *ev-evet* (*laševet*) 'to sit' (133).[5] It was chosen to illustrate how the two primary sources of data – the diary and the audio-recordings – were integrated to provide a complete picture of the child's use of one lexical item over a long period of time.

A total of 337 working tables were constructed. The number of entries in each table varied depending on the number of recordings of the word in the child's diary. The shortest tables included only three entries (since no phonological, morphological, or contextual changes were observed for that word from its emergence till the end of the study). The longest table (for the word *ima* 'mother' (053)) included 163 entries. Horizontal lines were drawn on each working table to represent the thirty-two weeks of investigation. This was done in order to conduct a week-by-week evaluation of the processes of change observed.

Reliability and validity measures

Several different measures of reliability and validity were conducted in order to assess the data, the form of their presentation, and the analysis.

1. What is a comprehensible word?

The criteria used for deciding whether an utterance was comprehensible or not were given above. In order to find out whether these criteria were functional, and whether observers other than the mother could follow them and make similar judgments about comprehensible words, the following measures were conducted:

(a) *Comprehensible words in the transcript*   Two independent judges – Judge A and Judge B – were separately trained to identify comprehensible words in the phonetic transcriptions of the child's speech. It was thoroughly explained

---

[4] The procedure of assigning data to specific working tables was carried out manually. Obviously, however, with today's computerized technologies the same procedure could be followed with great ease by any commercial package for text analysis, and hence even be performed much more efficiently.

[5] Numbers in parenthess indicate the word number in Keren's cumulative lexicon.

to each that repetitions, intonation patterns, gestures (reported in the contextual notes), and repeated uses of the same forms in similar contexts might help in identifying comprehensible utterances. It was also stated that some words were idiosyncratic forms for the child. The judges were asked not to consider the mother's immediate responses to the child's speech. Following a short period of training, each judge was asked to identify comprehensible words in all nine audio-recordings. In the total set of transcripts, Judge A identified 243 words, while Judge B identified 230 different words. The inter-judge reliability between the two scorers was 95 per cent.[6]

(b) Mother's recording of comprehensible words The mother's sensitivity to the occurrences of comprehensible words in Keren's ordinary speech was assessed as follows. A comparison was carried out between the mother's immediate verbal response as recorded in the transcript and the judgments of Judge B with respect to the first occurrences of each of the 230 productions that were identified as words. The mother's responses to the same occurrences indicated the following:

i.   She considered 224 words to be comprehensible productions, and interpreted them in the same way as Judge B.
ii.   She considered three words as comprehensible but interpreted them differently from Judge B.
iii.   She could not make up her mind whether six words were comprehensible or not.
iv.   She failed to respond to five words as comprehensible, even though the same words were identified by Judge B as such.

The level of agreement between the mother and Judge B on the identification of comprehensible words ranged from 95 per cent to 98 per cent, with a mean of 96 per cent.

2. The description of contexts

The video-taped recordings were used in order to assess the mother's abilities in describing the contexts of each utterance. Video-recording No. 4 was selected for viewing by Judge B, who was instructed to select six communicative situations for a video-presentation of normal language development in a lecture. Judge B was instructed to view the situations very carefully and to prepare a script of each situation including intonation, gestures, repetitions and timing of the verbal production.

In the course of a lecture on the one-word stage, four of the six situations were presented to the class. I was also present, along with my research

---

[6] The primary transcriber and Judge A was Mrs. S. Eilata, my research assistant, to whom I wish to convey my deepest appreciation and gratitude. The second transcriber and Judge B was Mrs. M. Schleifer, a graduate student in Education, who was not informed of the details of this study. I wish to extend my thanks to both of them for their significant role in conducting the different reliability and validity measures.

assistant Judge A. Judge B showed two situations twice and gave to the students a copy of her written description of each scene. The two remaining situations were then shown, and the students were asked to write a detailed description of each. I (the investigator) and my research assistant (Judge A) wrote descriptions of the situations at the same time as they were being shown to the students. For the two of us, as for the students, this was the first viewing of the tape.

The following three analyses were carried out as separate tests of the mother's precision in describing the contexts of the speech events.

(a) A comparison between the mother-investigator and Judge B   The mother's descriptions of the two situations were compared to the original descriptions written by Judge B in lab conditions with no limit on the number of viewings. A component-by-component comparison was performed between the two descriptions and scores ranging from 0–2 were assigned to each component of the mother's descriptions. (In this scoring system, 0 = missing information, 1 = incomplete information, 2 = identical information.) For her description of the first situation, the mother received a total score of 18 points out of 20. For her description of the second situation, which included many more speech events, the mother received 19 points out of 22. (See Appendix D for the description of situations and scoring procedures.)

The agreement between the mother and the observer who viewed the tapes under lab conditions ranged from 86 per cent to 90 per cent, with a mean of 88 per cent. This score was obtained despite considerable differences in the conditions under which the context descriptions were prepared.

(b) A comparison between the mother-investigator and nine other observers   Out of 35 students' descriptions of the two situations, the nine most detailed descriptions were selected and scored according to the same scoring model used above.

The average scores of the nine observers were calculated for situations I and II; these were 16 and 11 points, respectively. The scores of the mother (18 and 19 points, respectively) were thus higher for both situations. The differences between the scores of the students as a group and those of the mother can be attributed to the different weight of the verbal component in each situation. In situation I the non-verbal context was richer than in situation II. In situation II most of the information was contained in the verbal interaction. These results show the significant role of training in documenting verbal interactions. They clearly indicate that the performance of trained observers in documenting early speech is considerably better than that of untrained observers.

(c) A comparison between the mother-investigator and Judge A   This comparison was carried out as an inter-observer reliability measure. The two observers had formal training in child language. Both were highly familiar with Keren's linguistic system. Finally, both transcribed the contexts under the same viewing conditions. A point-to-point comparison revealed a high level of agreement, ranging from 80 to 100 per cent with a mean of 90 per cent. Two points of disagreement were recorded for situation I. The mother omitted from her description one verbal response of the father, who repeated the word *af '(a) nose'* twice. In the second case the mother transcribed the child's verbal response as *is* while Judge A transcribed the same response as *as*.

3. The phonetic transcriptions
The following procedures were followed in order to establish confidence in the written transcriptions. As indicated above, the first and last audio-recordings were independently transcribed by Judge A and Judge B. (Both used the same guidelines for transcription described in Appendix C.) Any discrepancies between the two were discussed together with the investigator until some agreement was reached. In the few cases in which agreement could not be reached, two versions of the transcriptions were included in the final transcript. The proportion of agreement between the two judges was 98 per cent for the first audio-recorded session, and 99 per cent for the last audio-recorded session.

4. The reconstructed lexicon
As explained earlier, the two judges listed the comprehensible words that Keren produced during the 13 hours of recording. A content comparison between the two lists was carried out, and a new third list was generated. This list included 223 words that were considered comprehensible by both judges. The third list is presented in Appendix B. Words appear in this list (i.e., the reconstructed lexicon) in their order of emergence in the audio-recordings. Several comparisons were conducted between the original lexicon and the reconstructed lexicon that now included all of the words that were audio-recorded throughout the period of study.

(a) Quantitative information   Sixty-six per cent of the words that were acquired by the subject during the one-word stage were recorded at least once in one of the nine audio-recordings. Since all the measurements that are reported below are based on a comparison between the hand-recorded data base and the audio-recorded sample, the results obtained manifest a high level of validity since two thirds of the data were obtained from two independent sources of information.

(b) Qualitative measures
i. A comparison between the reconstructed lexicon and the original lexicon

(which is based on diary data) revealed that out of the 223 words listed in the reconstructed lexicon, 202 were entered into the cumulative lexicon on the basis of three occurrences in the handwritten diary (i.e., 91 per cent of agreement on the number of comprehensible words). Of the 21 words that were not recorded by the mother in the diary but were judged to be comprehensible words in the audio-recordings, 16 were classified by the two judges as imitations, possibly meaningful, or occurred only in one context (while a word had to occur three times before it was entered into the cumulative lexicon). Thus, when these 16 words were excluded from the reconstructed lexicon, the percentage of agreement between the judges and the mother on the recording of new words rose to 98 per cent. These findings indicate that although the mother had to make judgments constantly and for a long period of time, and despite the different criteria for selecting the data, she was highly successful in making accurate decisions about the emergence of new words or new contexts for the use of old words.

ii. A percentage agreement on the date of recording a new word in the original diary and in the reconstructed lexicon was also computed. Agreement was defined as: *first recorded in the diary either before the date of recording in the reconstructed lexicon, or within seven days following it.*[7] The agreement on date of acquisition was 91 per cent.

A closer look at the words that were not recorded in the diary soon after the date of recording in the reconstructed lexicon revealed that some occurred in the audio-recordings as imitation only, others were produced only once, and some were judged by either Judge A or B as only possibly comprehensible. When all questionable words were excluded from the reconstructed diary, the percentage agreement on the date of recording rose to 92 per cent.

The high percentage of agreement between the diary and the reconstructed lexicon indicates that the procedures of data collection applied in the present study were both reliable and valid. The finding that only 66 per cent of the total lexical repertoire of the child appeared in the audio-recordings indicates how powerful and appropriate a diary study is for documenting early lexical development. It would seem that even when intensive audio-recordings in natural settings are conducted by a mother who is also the investigator, only a sample of the child's lexical abilities is obtained.

5. *The categorization system*   In order to establish the reliability of the categorization system (which will be described in Chapter 8 below), an independent judge (Judge B, who was not deeply involved in the research project) categorized a randomly selected sample of 43 working tables (about

---

[7] The criterion of seven days was arbitrarily selected, since it was hypothesized that if an occurrence in the recording is a first occurrence of a new word, within a period of seven days, two more occurrences of this word are likely to be noted by the mother, and hence included in the diary.

13 per cent of all the data). This judge was trained in the application of the coding system before this measure was taken. A comparison was carried out between the judge's scoring and the investigator's scoring of the same words. Inter-scorer agreement on the complete set of analyses which were conducted for each word was 95 per cent.

8   *The categorization system: operative definitions*

The present case-study investigation addresses three distinct but related issues. First, it deals with quantitative aspects of the one-word period, with special reference to its status as a developmental stage. Second, it discusses the development of reference, and illuminates the problems of identifying the referents of early acquired words for purposes of classification. Finally, the study describes the course of meaning acquisition by examining the extension behaviors of words and how they change over time. The present chapter is devoted to the presentation of the categorization system, and to the description of its application in scoring the data.

The categorization system was developed in order to carry out a systematic analysis of the referential and extensional behaviors of early words. The set of working definitions was devised specifically for the analysis of the Hebrew single-word data.[1] The rules were developed over a period of pilot analysis which started six weeks after the completion of data collection. In the course of pilot application of the rules on a set of 30 working tables, certain rules were refined and others discarded. The code as presented here was strictly applied to all the data. During the period of data analysis (August to September 1981), no modifications were introduced into the code.

Two subsets of working rules for classifying words are presented below. Each set of rules operates at an independent level of analysis. At the first level of analysis, words are judged with respect to their reference. Each word is classified as belonging to one of five categories: object words, action words, modifiers, social words, and indeterminant words. The second level of analysis is performed to allow for the description of the scope of words' extensions. At this level of analysis, words are assigned to one of four categories of extension: underextension, regular extension, overextension, and unclassified. As will be illustrated below, each of the four categories of extension is defined relatively to the conventional meaning of the word in adult speech. For example, an object word that is a common noun in adult speech (e.g., *buba* 'a doll'), but which is used by the child as her name for one

---

[1] An attempt was made, however, to design a system that would be applicable to the analysis of single-word utterances in any language.

specific referent (e.g., her orange doll), is assigned to the referential category of object, and to the extension category of underextension.

The analyses at the level of reference and the level of extension are carried out sequentially. On each dimension, a word is scored at weekly intervals. Descriptions of all the different uses of a given word during one week are evaluated before the decision about how to classify the word is made. An isolated score of a word reflects its behavior on one dimension during one week only. Profiles that describe the changes over time in referential and extensional behaviors are generated by summing up isolated scores. A profile reflects the behavior of the word throughout the total period of investigation.

The complete set of explicit definitions, several justifications, and a few examples from Keren's data are given below with the following aims: (a) to illuminate the attempt to avoid the automatic assignment of the child's words to classes of reference only because of phonological similarities to adult words; (b) to encourage other researchers to replicate this analysis on case-study data of other subjects; and (c) to illustrate the detail of description in Keren's authentic diary.

In the last section of this chapter, the scoring system is explained and the code described together with a number of representative examples of scored words. These examples are given in order to show the form of scored data which was forwarded for computer analysis.

The categories of reference

The classification system consists of five classes. In order to assign a word to one of these classes, a decision must be made about the entity to which the word was applied. A distinction is made between words for (1) objects, (2) actions and states, (3) modifiers, (4) social words, and (5) words for which the reference cannot be determined. In making the final decision the scorer takes into consideration the form of the word, the linguistic and non-linguistic contexts of its occurrences, and any attempts the child has made to show what the referent of the word is. When a decision cannot be reached, either because the entries are incomplete or because the word could apply equally to more than one aspect of the situation, the word is classified as indeterminant. Since the analysis is based on a large number of successive judgments, the general picture of the word's reference is not distorted even if several indeterminant judgments are made along the way.

1. The category of object words

Words that are used by the child for single entities or "real things" in the situation

One of the following conditions must be met before a word can be included in this category:

(a)   The child is pointing to, touching, and/or showing an object when she utters the word. For example:

    (1) 16(6): In the bathroom; K is bathing and playing with bath toys. She points to a sticker of a butterfly on the bottom of the bath and says *papa* (*parpar*) '(a) butterfly'.[2]

    (2) 12(12): In the living room; F is lying down on the couch. K is sitting on the floor and looking at a picture book. Suddenly she gets up, approaches F, and shows him her book and says in a demanding tone *bu* (*buba*) '(a) doll'. (This book contains pictures of different kinds of dolls, with a picture of a doll on the cover as well.)

(b)   The child produces a word repeatedly in order to get an object. She is contented and stops her attempts to produce the word once she gets the object.

    (3) 16(4): In K's room; F and M are eating dinner. K leaves the kitchen and goes to her room. M hears her saying repeatedly in a whining voice *oto/x/x/* '(a) car'. M enters K's room. K stands near her closet waiting for M to give her a toy. When M gives her one of her car toys she stops whining.

(c)   The child produces the word in the course of an event and she chooses to encode verbally the object and not the action, even though the action word is included in her lexicon and is therefore also available.[3]

    (4) 17(2): In the kitchen; K is eating breakfast and playing with her teaspoon. It falls on the floor and she says *apit* (*kapit*) 'a teaspoon'. (It is judged that K is talking about the object rather than the action because in the past she has produced the words *al* (*nafal*) 'fell down', *?ein* 'no more' 'all gone', and *nili* (*tnili*) 'give me' in similar situations.)

(d)   The child produces a sequence of different words such that the identification of the referent of one word provides clues to the referents of others.

    (5) 15(10): In K's room; M undresses K and plans to take her to the bath. On the way K says *nes/x/x/* (*lehikanes*) 'to enter'. M does not understand what K means and she asks *maze nes?* 'what is nes?' K says *nes/abab/mayi/* (*heikanes*), (*ambatya*), (*mayim*), 'to enter', 'bath', 'water'. (Since the word *mayi* is known to me from past usage as K's word for water, I decide that *nes* is an action word and *abab* is her new word for the object bath.)

2. The category of action/state words

Words that are used by the child for encoding actions or states of objects

No distinction is made here between actions and states because the distinction among predicate classes is rather fluid and very difficult to make when dealing with single-word expressions (see Greenfield and Smith, 1976). In the present study, only modifiers are treated as a separate subclass of

---

[2] This example and all the following ones are English translations of entries in Keren's diary.

[3] I assume that when the child's lexicon is limited to only a few words, she is not likely to learn more than one word for the same referent. In other words, it seems to me unlikely that synonyms will be used by the child in the earliest phases of lexical development (see also Clark, 1983a, b).

predicate terms. For inclusion in this category the word must be used in one of the following ways:

(a) The utterance coincides in time with an action other than pointing or showing.

(6) 16(18): In K's room; M is sitting on the floor with K who is eating potato chips. She hands M a chip and says *ki* (*kxi*) 'take' (feminine imperative).

(b) The listener performs an action immediately after and as the direct result of a child's verbal request. Prior shared experiences of the child and her interlocutor indicate that the child is aware that her word is associated with an action or state.

(7) 17(2): In the living room; F is eating cake. K watches him very carefully and says *tuda* (*toda*) 'thank you'. F gives her a piece of cake and she appears to be very happy. (Since all the first occurrences of *tuda* share the context of the child's asking for something, it seems that the word is an action word that means something like 'give me'.)

(c) Words that are produced in response to adults' questions about actions or states; for example, "What is x doing?"

(8) 16(2): In the kitchen; M is eating lunch and K is looking at one of her picture books. M asks K *ma yip yip ose?*/ 'what is yip-yip doing?' K stands up, jumps, and says *hupa* (her word for jumping). (The picture shows a dog (yip-yip) who is jumping high in the air.)

(d) The word is produced in a new situation when it is clear that the child encodes the action and not the object because the object name has been acquired and used productively before. (The assumption that the child is not likely to learn synonyms at such an early phase of production is relevant here as well.)

(9) 16(18): In the living room; M, who has just returned from work, takes off her shoes and K puts M's shoes on and walks around in them saying *alax* (*halax*) 'went' (past, masc. singular). (It is the first time I have heard this word in this context. Since K knows the word *naal* 'shoe' and produces it very often, I assume that the new word is her word for 'walking'. It is interesting to note that she chose the masculine past tense form of the verb which is inappropriate in this context. I suspect that this form is learned from *aba halax laavoda*/ 'daddy went to work' which is often said to K when she seems to be looking for her father.)

(e) The word is produced in a sequence of single-word utterances – the identification of the referents of other words in the sequence indicate that this specific word is an action/state word. See example (5) above of the sequence *nes/abab/mayi* 'to enter', 'bath', 'water'.

3. The category of modifiers

Words that refer to properties and qualities of things and events

A varied set of contexts is needed in order to conclude that the child is speaking about some property and not about the object or the action itself. In some cases the scorer needs to examine the complete updated lexicon of the child in order to find out whether the child has a name for the object, and how she has used the word in question earlier.

> (10) 15(25): In the kitchen; M takes a loaf of bread out of the freezer. K touches it and says *?am* (*xam*) 'hot'. (K has used the word *pita* ('pita bread') several times before in similar contexts; moreover, this is the 8th recording of the word *?am*. In previous contexts K produced the word while touching or pointing to our heater, when it was turned either on or off. Until now I have interpreted the word *?am* as an object word referring to our heater.)

4. The category of social words

> *Words that constitute part of a social interaction and that seem not to have referential value*

Most terms included in this category are assertions of agreement, social expressive words, or non-conventional attention-getters. Also included in this category are words that are probably meaningless for the child, and that she uses only as speech routines or as memorized sequences. Consider, for example, the following description:

> (11) 17(2): In the living room; F and K are sitting and watching television. M is in the kitchen; K sees M. F asks K 'where is M?' K says *ulayim* (*yerušal ayim*) 'Jerusalem'. (Several days before, I had gone to Jerusalem and had told K about it. Since then K sometimes produces the word in contexts similar to the one described here. K herself has never been to Jerusalem and she has never given any sign of understanding the abstract concept of places.)

5. The category of indeterminant

> *Words that cannot be classified as belonging to any single one of the above categories*

In this category are included words of three kinds:

(a)   Words for which there are few and incomplete descriptions of use. If the descriptions are not detailed enough and do not permit a decision as to the word's referent it is assigned for the week in question to the indeterminant category.

> (12) 15(17): Outside; K and M are walking on the sidewalk. M says: *hine oto, po xone oto/* 'here is (a) car, (a) car is parked here'. K immediately says *oto* '(a) car'. (Since K imitated M and the non-linguistic situation is not described in detail, a decision about the reference of the word could not be made.)

(b)   Words that are used ambiguously by the child, in the sense that there is more than one aspect of the situation to which the word could refer with equal probability.

> (13) 12(29): In the living room; F is watering the plants (he does not speak to K or play with her). K is standing nearby and watching him very

carefully. Suddenly she says: *mai* (*mayim*) 'water'. (It is not clear whether K is naming the entity water, its container, or the action of *watering* the plants.)

(c)   Words that are used during the same week in different contexts, some of which indicate that the word belongs to one category (e.g., a word for an object) and some of which clearly show that the word also belongs to another category (e.g., a word for an action).

(14) 13(8): In K's room; F and M are speaking about going out tonight. K seems not to be paying attention. She is running around with her ball. M draws a map of the town on a piece of paper and says to F, *?ani ?efgoš otxa po al yad hašaon šel yafo.*/ 'I will meet you right here near the Jaffa clock.' F looks at M's drawing. K comes closer to her parents and points to the piece of paper in F's hands. She says *tita* (her word for clock/jewelry?) 'tik tok'. (The drawing on the piece of paper is very schematic. I don't think that K recognizes any shape of clocks or articles of jewelry there. It seems to me that her word *tita* was elicited by our adult word *šaon* '(a) clock', which is the name of the central square in Jaffa.)

(15) 13(9): In the study; K is playing with M's pen. While taking my pen and putting it close to her ear (as if she is listening), K says *tita* 'tik tok'. (Since the pen does not make any noise, and since I recorded the word before in similar contexts when K performed the same action with other objects (e.g., my ring, my necklace, and broken digital watch), I conclude that in this context *tita* is an action word rather than an object word.)

The categories of extension

This system of classification was developed to characterize the extensional patterns shown by each lexical item. At this level of analysis four categories are distinguished: underextension, regular extension, overextension and unclassified. The categories are mutually exclusive. As was stated earlier, each word is scored repeatedly at weekly intervals. Each score reflects the actual range of application of the word during one week of study, relative to the meaning of that word in adult speech.

1. The category of underextension

The use of a word for one referent only or restricted to a subset of instances of the adult category corresponding to the same word

The identification of underextension is reinforced by several conditions:

(a)   Recorded information about other contexts in which the child had the opportunity to use a word she knew but did not do so.

(16) 12(7)–15(7): K produces the word *pi* (*pil*) 'an elephant' only in those contexts in which her white elephant toy is present. However, she fails to produce the word when she plays outside on a slide in the shape of

an elephant, or when I show her other elephant toys or pictures of elephants in a picture book.

(b)   Familiarity with the contexts in which the word is modeled to the child frequently. A new word which is recorded only in a context closely similar to the context in which it has been learned is assigned to the category of underextension. Consider the following example of K's early uses of the word *atan (katan)* 'small':

(17) 16(8): In the living room; M and K are drawing on a piece of paper. K says *myau* (her sound for a cat) and M draws a little cat. K says *an/x/ (katan)* 'small'. M draws a smaller cat. K seems delighted and points excitedly to the two drawings.

The first occurrence of this word in this particular context followed many prior occasions on which I had drawn cats in several sizes and shown K their relative size, saying *hine katan veze katan katan/* 'here (is a) small (one) and this one (is) even smaller'. Since this information is included in the diary, a decision can be made that *katan* is an underextension until it is generalized to new and different instances.

Several types of restrictions may operate on the child during the early phases of production. During the course of data collection I observed four different types of restrictions. I therefore decided to distinguish between the following four subclasses of underextension:

Restriction to a specific object

Examples in the literature include the use of the word 'kitty' only for one specific cat – the family pet (Clark and Clark, 1977). In K's vocabulary, *bubi (buba)* (008) and *pi (pil)* (007) (see example (16) above) were used as proper names for the orange doll and white elephant, respectively, for a period of a few weeks.

Restriction to a specific person

Among the examples cited in the literature, one could consider here the use of *shoe* for mother's shoes only (Reich, 1976). There were some words in K's early lexicon that were used only in connection with one actor. Consider the following entries:

(18) 16(15): In the living room; K puts on F's shoes. K walks around saying repeatedly *?alax/x (halax)* 'go' (past singular masc.). Later on she takes off one shoe, hands it to F, and says *kax/x* 'take' (imperative singular masc.). For a period of 15 days K produced the word *alax (halax)* 'go' (past singular masc.) only when she herself was walking and wearing her parents' shoes. The first recording of *alax* in a different context occurred when K was 16(30).

(19) 16(0)–17(2): So far the word *ul (gilgul)* '(a) somersault' has been used only in the course of a game with my sister (K's aunt). K fails to name the action when other people perform it, or when pictures of people in non-canonical positions are presented to her. K uses the word to

request that her aunt perform a somersault; she has never asked me or her father to do this for her. Sometimes when I mention my sister's name K says enthusiastically *ul/x/x/*.

Restriction to a specific occasion

I noticed this type of restriction while recording some of K's early action words. It was obvious that K produced the word in certain specific circumstances but failed to utter it in others. The word *tov* 'ok' (259) is one example of this. For a period of 18 days *tov* was used only as a contingent response to the adult's question *xam midai?/* '(is it) too hot?', either in the bathroom when K was put into the bath or when her bottle of milk was given to her.

Another example is the word *ede* (*laredet*) 'get down' (075), which was initially used only at the time of the action and never when K was about to perform the action or in a state when she wished that somebody would pick her up in order to help her get down from a high place.

> (20) 15(0): In K's room; K is sitting on M's lap. M shows K a picture book; suddenly K starts to scream and shout in a high-pitched voice. M understands that K wants something. M asks *ma ?at roca yalda?/* 'what do you want, my child?' K indicates with gestures that she wants to get down. M asks *?at roca laredet?/* 'do you want to get down?' while putting her on the floor. At the time of the action K says *ede* (*laredet*) 'get down' (imperative singular masc.).

Restriction to a specific place

Some words may initially be uttered in one place only. Bloom's (1973) example of Allison's early uses of *car* as she stood at the window and watched moving cars is a good illustration of this category. K's use of *or* 'light', 'electricity' (026) is another example. It was used first when K was 13 months old. She said it in her parents' room, either while she was lying down and watching the lights or when she turned the lights on or off. Although she liked to turn the lights on and off in other rooms she never said the word *or* while doing so.

2. The category of regular extension

> *A flexible use of a word for a class of equivalent referents that all belong to the corresponding adult category for the same word*

The term "regular extension" rather than "normal extension" is proposed here because it is assumed that the categories underlying the child's use of words are not identical with those of the adult. Thus, even if the child is relatively flexible in using a new word, her uses may still be restricted to a limited set of equivalent referents. In the present analysis, a word is classified as showing regular extension as long as it is used as a class name, regardless of the size of the class. That is, common names are assigned to the category of regular extension when it is clear that: (a) the child has generalized the word beyond a specific exemplar, time, place, etc.; and (b) the child does not use the word outside of its normal range of application in adult speech. Proper names are also assigned to the category of regular extension if they are used appropriately.

One of the following conditions must be met in order for a word to be classified in the regular extension category for a specific week.

(a)   Within that week the child has used the word in different contexts. For example, the word *oto* '(a) car' was recorded seven times in the first week of usage. The variability of contexts clearly indicates that it was a class name from the outset:

(21) 12(16): in K's room; K is lying in her bed while M is dressing her. Suddenly K says *oto* '(a) car'. M hears the noise of a car engine outside.

12(16): Outside, in front of our house; K and M stand and watch a group of children playing. When a car comes into sight K says *oto* '(a) car'.

12(17): In K's room; M and K are playing. M hears the engine of a car starting outside. K says *oto* '(a) car'.

12(17): On the stairway; K is playing with one of her toy cars (the red VW). F comes home, K shows him her toy and says *oto* '(a) car'.

12(17): Outside; K is playing with a toy car she has just received from one of her friends (called Gilad). She is moving the car back and forth and says *oto* '(a) car'.

12(18): In the living room; M and K are watching television; K is holding a car (her yellow pickup). Suddenly she shows it to me and says *oto* '(a) car'.

12(19): In parents' room; K is walking around swinging a large shopping bag. F asks *ma yes lax sam?/* 'what do you have there?' K comes closer to F, shows the bag to F, looks inside it, and says *oto* '(a) car'. F and M are puzzled; we look into the bag and realize that K was right. There is a toy car (the red VW) inside the bag.

(b)   Within a given week the child uses the word in one context only, but there is clear evidence that the child picked the referent on the basis of several different samples modeled to her. Sometimes the referent of the word is not unique (e.g., *apit* '(a) teaspoon' in example (22) below), and it is therefore assumed that the child uses the word as a class name rather than as a proper name. In other cases the fact that the child is naming a referent that was rarely (or never) named by the parents before indicates that the child has generalized the meaning of the word beyond one referent alone (e.g., *babuk* 'a bottle'; in example (23) below).

(22) 14(2): In the kitchen; M is eating yogurt. K is walking around with her doll. Suddenly she approaches M and says *pit/x/ (kapit)* '(a) teaspoon'. M stops eating, shows K her teaspoon, and asks *ma ze keren?/* 'what is this, Keren?' K says very happily *pit/x/ (kapit)* '(a) teaspoon'.

(23) 16(6): In K's room; M is standing on a chair. She is looking for something in the closet. M takes out several items and gives them to K, who is playing on the floor. One of the items is a hot water bottle which has not been used since K was born. M gives the bottle to K; K shows it

to F. When F takes the bottle K says *babuk (bak-buk)* '(a) bottle'. She repeats the word in a high-pitched voice and F returns it to her to play with. K tries to open the bottle; she says *uax (liftoax)* 'to open' and indicates to M that she wants the plug removed.

(c) Within a given week a word is recorded only once but in a new context that is different from earlier contexts of use for the same word.

Included in this category are words that were initially underextended by the child. The following example is the first recording of the word *tov* 'o.k.' (259) in regular extension.

(24) 16(22): In the living room; K is playing with a number of animal toys. M, who is reading a book, stops reading and asks K *at roca še ?avi lax gam ?et hakof?/* '(do) you want me to bring you your monkey too?' K stops playing with her teddy bear. She looks at M and says *tov* 'ok'. (This is the first occurrence of *tov* in the full confirmation sense. In all the previous recordings K said *tov* as a response to the question 'is it too hot?', either when she was bathing or when I handed her a bottle of hot milk.)

3. The category of overextension

The identification of overextensions in the speech of young children is far more complicated than the identification of either underextensions or regular extensions. The main difficulty is related to the fact that young children quite often use words irregularly, but irregular uses do not always or necessarily reflect overextensions. Judgments about the correct or incorrect application of a word are usually based on the adult's expectations as a listener. Such expectations come from knowledge of the conventional meaning of the word. Irregular uses of words – i.e., their production in unexpected contexts – may not always reflect an underlying overly broad category associated with the "misused" word. Consider the following examples. When K points to the black handbag of her cousin and says *aba* 'daddy', is she overextending the meaning of *aba* to include the referent handbag? Is she commenting on the fact that her father has a black handbag too? Or is she perhaps stating that this handbag is her father's? When the word *pe* '(a) mouth' is uttered repeatedly while searching through M's purse for a lipstick, is K using *pe* as a name for lipstick or is she commenting on the relationship she recognizes between the object lipstick and her mother's mouth? A third example of a misuse which may or may not be an overextension is the following. K is playing with a five-year-old girl. She names the girl several times *yada (yalda)* '(a) girl'. When the girl falls, gets hurt and starts to cry, K points to her, looks at me, and says *nok/x/x/ (tinok)* '(a) baby' (masc. sing.). Does K know the adult meaning of the word *tinok* '(a) baby', and is she now expressing her belief that the girl is behaving/crying like a baby (even though she isn't really a baby)? Or does K's semantic definition of 'baby' perhaps include the feature [+ crying], so that the application of the word is entirely appropriate? In the present study, overextension is defined as:

> *An overly-broad use of a word for a class of several referents, some of which fall outside the adult category for the same word*

The criteria presented below are used to help in identifying overextensions of meaning. The rules are designed to allow for the examination of many entries of each word. Before assigning a word to the category of overextension the scorer has to examine the complete record of a word. It is extremely important to consider the description of earlier uses of a word before making any decision. The rules presented here complement each other; they do not operate in isolation. Therefore, it is important to examine the data in the light of the complete set of criteria. If a definite decision about overextension cannot be reached, the word is assigned to the fourth category in this taxonomy, the category of unclassified which is defined below.

(a)   Incorrect applications of a word are recorded at least three times before the word is assigned to the category of overextensions. Repeated incorrect applications of a word show that its meaning is quite different from the conventional meaning known to the adult. The repeated recordings of incorrect applications may involve different irrelevant referents (i.e., none of which are members of the adult category for the word). Alternatively, they may involve a single irrelevant referent only. In either case, at least three recordings must be observed before the word is assigned to overextension. Consider the following entries that describe incorrect applications of the Hebrew word *matate* '(a) broom'.

(25) 16(17): In the kitchen; M is washing dishes. K is playing with one of the doors of a closet. M hears K saying *matate* '(a) broom'. She thinks that K sees a broom inside the closet. However, when M turns around to see what K is doing, she realizes that K is playing with a green funnel used for watering plants.

16(19): In the kitchen; K is walking around holding a dustpan and swinging it back and forth. M asks *maze?*/ 'what is this?' K says very confidently *matate* '(a) broom'.

17(11): In the kitchen; K is taking out of the closet several items including a dustpan and a funnel. M asks *maze?*/ 'what is this?' When she points to the funnel, K says immediately *matate* '(a) broom'.

The incorrect application of *matate* on the first occasion is very problematic for interpretation. It is not clear whether the child is wrongly naming the funnel, or whether she is commenting on some relationship (e.g., size, contiguity) between the funnel and a small broom that M keeps in the same closet. Only when the word is recorded repeatedly in connection with irrelevant referents does it become evident that the meaning of the word *matate* is extended by the child beyond its conventional limits.

(b)   A possible basis for the overextension is identified. In most cases of overextension a possible basis for the extension of the word beyond its conventional range is quite obvious. The basis for overextension might be perceptual, functional, or even affective (Rescorla, 1980). No attempt is made here to classify words according to different bases for overextension, but when such a basis is identified it strengthens the inference that the misuse is indeed an overextension and not, for example, the expression of an association or a mismatch. Consider the following two examples. In both cases the basis for the extension is clear.

(26) 16(22): In parents' room; M and F are still in bed. K is playing with her small chair. She tries to push the chair between the parents' bed and the wall. M asks K *ma' at roca keren?*/ 'what do you want, Keren?' and K says *nes/ines/* (*lehikanes*) 'to enter'. (The use of the word *nes* (*lehikanes*) 'to enter' in contexts where *la'avor* 'go through' was more appropriate persisted until the end of the one-word stage and even beyond.)

16(22): In the kitchen; F, M and K are eating breakfast. M takes an avocado from the refrigerator. When K sees it she says *apuz/x/x/* (*tapuz*) '(an) orange'.

(c) There are uses of the word in pragmatic functions other than statements. When a word is applied to an unusual referent in a statement it is always problematic and sometimes completely impossible to draw a distinction between overextension and association. When the word is uttered as a request, however, it becomes much more likely that it is an overextension. Compare the following two entries for the word *pica* (*peca*) '(a) wound/cut/sore' (039).

(27) 15(5): In the living room; M and K are sitting on the couch. M is sticking together a torn page in K's picture book. K points to the scotchtape and says *pica* (*peca*) '(a) sore/cut/wound'.

17(28): In the study; K is walking around saying repeatedly in a whining tone *pica/x/x/* (*peca*) '(a) wound'. M is speaking on the phone and does not respond. K is looking for something. She opens the drawer and seems disappointed. Finally she sees the scotchtape on one of the bookshelves. She stretches her hand and says *pica* (*peca*) '(a) sore/cut/wound' and picks it up. Later on, K is playing with the scotchtape on the floor. She shows it to M and says again *pica/* (*peca*) '(a) sore/cut/wound'.

It seems much more likely to me that K's utterance *pica*, used as a request, means something like *I want x*, rather than *I want y, which is somehow related to x*. For this reason I would argue that the word *peca* 'wound' is overextended to refer to the object scotchtape rather than used to indicate an association between an absent referent (a wound) and the object at hand (the scotchtape).

(d) Overextended words persist in the child's lexicon for long periods of time, and they show high resistance to change. When the child uses a word in an unexpected context the adult very often corrects her and supplies the more appropriate word. It is interesting to note that, despite many corrections, some words are used incorrectly for quite a long time. The more the child resists correction, the more likely it seems that she is overextending the meaning of the misused word rather than using it associatively. K used the word *pica* (*peca*) '(a) sore/cut/wound' as her word for scotchtape for a period of seven months, well into the multi-word period. Consider the following examples from a tape recording made when K was 19(17):

(28) 19(17): In the study; M is sitting by her desk and K is playing quietly on the floor. Suddenly she says:

K: *ima hine peca/*
   Mommy here (a) sore
   'Mommy, here is a sore'

M: *?eifo yeš lax peca kereni?/*
   Where have you (a) sore Kereni
   'Where do you have a sore, Kereni?'

(K hands a piece of scotchtape to M, who then realizes that K was playing with the scotchtape all that time.)

K: *kxi ima ze peca/*
   take Mommy this (a) sore
   'Take, Mommy, this is a sore'

M: *ze lo peca ze cellotape/*
   This not (a) sore this scotchtape
   'This is not a sore, this is scotchtape'

K: *roca peca ima, tni li peca/*
   want (a) sore Mommy, give me (a) sore
   'I want a sore, Mommy, give me a sore'

M: *kxi cellotape kereni, ze niyar-devek/*
   take scotchtape Kereni this is sticky paper
   'Take the scotchtape, Kereni, this is sticky paper'

(K takes the piece of scotchtape from M, sticks it on her arm, and shows it to M.)

Three subclasses of overextension

Bowerman (1978) distinguishes between two types of overextension: "classic" overextensions and "complexive" ones. In a "classic" overextension, a word is extended to a number of referents that share one or more attributes with each other. These attributes may be either functional or perceptual (Clark, 1973; Nelson, 1974). In "complexive" overextensions, on the other hand, a word is extended to a number of referents that do not all share one or more stable attributes (Bowerman, 1978, 1980). I myself noticed a third type of overextension in the course of data collection. Here, a word is repeatedly extended to only one irrelevant referent, i.e., a referent that is not a member of the adult's underlying category for the word.

In the present study, the distribution of the three types of overextension was determined by assigning each word that showed overextension to one of the three subclasses: (i) overextension to only one referent; (ii) classic overextension, as in Clark (1973) or Nelson (1974); and (iii) complexive overextension, as in Bowerman (1978). An example of a word assigned to the first class is K's word *pe* 'mouth' (054), which was extended to mother's lipstick and was never used for other irrelevant referents. An example of a classic overextension is K's uses of the word *tik* '(a) bag/handbag' (079) for all types of containers, such as plastic and paper sacks of all shapes and sizes, pockets, and a pail. The class of complexive overextensions includes words that started from an identifiable point and then were overextended complexively. K's uses of *peca* 'a wound' (039) for a wound on her arm, ink marks on a piece of paper, spots on mother's skirt, scotchtape, the action of falling down, knives and balloons, suggest that this word belonged to the subclass of complexive overextensions.

4. The category of unclassified extension

> *Words that are used ambiguously, and words for which entries are not informative enough to insure a clear decision as to their extension are assigned to the unclassified category.*

A distinction is made between five different types of unclassified words.

Unclassified – incomplete entry

Whenever a decision cannot be reached as to the referential status of a word because the context is inadequately described, the word is assigned to Unclassified – incomplete entry. Since judgments are based on evidence collected across the period of a week, it is only when all entries for a specific word during that week are incomplete that it is assigned to this subclass. Whenever there are enough complete descriptions of the uses of a word during the week to allow for a judgment, incomplete descriptions are disregarded.

Unclassified – association or overextension

Whenever a decision cannot be made between overextension or association the word is assigned to Unclassified – association or overextension. The following entry of the word *dod* '(an) uncle' (051), which is used in Hebrew (in speech addressed to babies) as the word for '(a) stranger' or '(a) man', is given to illustrate the dilemma.

(29) 14(10): In the kitchen; K is sitting on the floor eating fruit. M hears rhythmic sounds (coming from the kitchen of our neighbor). K stops eating, approaches M, and says *dod* '(an) uncle'. I respond *bumbum mišehu dofek baxuc/* 'bumbum somebody is knocking outside'. K says *dod* '(an) uncle'.

During this week the word *dod* was recorded several times. In some instances it was clear that K used it as her word for a stranger (e.g., saying it while watching T.V. and pointing to a female reporter). In other instances it seemed that *dod* was K's word for noises coming from outside. The word is assigned to the subclass of Unclassified – overextension or association because it is impossible to decide whether *dod* was K's word for noise (in which case it would be an overextension or a mismatch), or, alternatively, K's word for '(a) stranger', which she uttered in the context of hearing noises to express her belief that somebody (*an agent*) was making the noise.

Unclassified – ambiguous

A decision as to the extensional properties of a word involves a positive identification of the word's referent. In some cases there are two or more entities in the same context to which the word could refer with equal probability, e.g., both an object and an action: in fact, it is possible that the word applies to the whole undifferentiated situation. In such instances the word is classified as Unclassified – ambiguous. This subclass differs from the subclass of complexive overextensions in that there is no identifiable starting point for the meaning or referent of the word.

K's uses of the word *dio* 'giddi-up' were almost identical to Eva's uses of *gi* (Bowerman, 1978). In most cases it was unclear whether K was speaking about a horse, the action of riding, any bouncing motions, or just sitting on top of inanimate objects. A typical example of the ambiguous entry for *dio* is the following:

> (30) 12(23): In the playground; K and M are playing; K approaches a big rocking horse that she likes very much. She says *dio/x/* (this is the first time I have heard the word. It is not clear to me whether K is simply naming the horse or whether she is asking me to let her ride on it as she usually does).

The use of *dio* is ambiguous since it is equally likely that the word means '(a) horse', 'riding', or both. The word is assigned to the category of Unclassified – ambiguous until there is clear evidence for one meaning alone. (In the case of *dio*, when K acquired the word *sus* '(a) horse' she stopped producing *dio* when she saw horses and limited her further use of *dio* to riding only.)

Unclassified – empty words

Sometimes words are produced in contexts that are acceptable, although they do not reveal much about the meaning of the word for the child. The following correct use of the words *mudedet* (*yom-huledet*) '(a) birthday', in the course of an audio-recorded dialogue between K and myself, illustrates this category:

> (31) 17(12): In K's room; M and K are looking at one of K's favorite picture books. The picture shows a lady who is baking a birthday cake.
> M: *Keren ma ?ima osa po?/*
>   Keren what mommy do [feminine] here?
>   'Keren, what is mommy doing here?'
> K: *uga/*   *mudedet/*   *ababa/*
>   (a) cake (a) birthday barbaaba (a storybook hero)
>   'a cake,   a birthday,   Barbaaba'

Keren has never been to a birthday party. What she means by the word *mudedet* is unclear. Since she has never uttered the word in contexts other than the one described here, I assume that the word is empty and functions simply as part of a speech routine that is connected to this picture book which happens to describe a birthday party.

Unclassified – no conventional word

Many descriptions of early lexicons contain reports of the child's producing nursery words that do not correspond to conventional adult words in terms of either form or meaning (e.g., Bloom, 1973; Braunwald, 1978). The definitions of the three main classes of extension (underextension, regular extension, and overextension) presented earlier are based on comparisons of the child's uses of a word with the conventional range of meaning of the corresponding adult word. A nursery word is nevertheless sometimes meaningful (e.g., *haw* 'bow wow' for a dog, *tu* for a train, or *pipi* for urinating), and it is not difficult to determine its range of application. In the present classification, all of the child's non-conventional words for which a clear meaning can be identified are considered as Unclassified – no conventional word. When a nursery word is used ambiguously, or when it is impossible to determine its meaning, the word is assigned to one of the other subclasses of Unclassified.

K's use of the word *haw* 'bow wow' (001) exemplifies the difference between the subclass of No conventional word and the other subclasses of Unclassified. *Haw* was the first meaningful word in K's lexicon. For a period of 23 weeks she used it for both barking and dogs. Only after learning the adult word *kelev* 'a dog' (336) did K stop using *haw* for dogs and limit its usage to barking only. This change in the word's extension is reflected in the present code by the fact that the word was first assigned to the category Unclassified – ambiguous and later to the category Unclassified – no conventional word. The word was not assigned to the category of regular extension since *haw* is not a conventional word in Hebrew.

The scoring procedure

In the course of analysis, each of the subject's productive words was repeatedly scored on the dimensions of reference and extension. Coding started with an examination of the working tables that provided the complete set of relevant data points about the natural history of each word from the time of its emergence to the end of the one-word period. In order to allow documentation of the course of referential and extensional development throughout the period of data collection (July 10, 1980 to February 23, 1981), this period was divided into 32 weekly intervals. A one-week interval was chosen as the basic unit of measurement because it appeared to provide an optimal level of description for the dynamic developmental processes. It was important to select a basic unit that was long enough to contain several data points for each word, and yet short enough to remain sensitive to changes over time. For most working tables an interval of one week was neither too detailed nor too global. Therefore, scores were given to each word on the basis of all the behaviors it manifested over one week of study.

Each working table was divided by horizontal lines according to the calendar, starting on July 10, 1980 (an example is given in Table 4, p. 72). The fact that the calendar weeks were used is significant because it provides a clear indication of the real chronology. Since every change in the child's lexical development was identified in the framework of real time, it was possible to evaluate developmental processes across the child's entire lexicon, as well as to examine in detail the changes in the use of each word over time. In most cases judgments as to the category membership of a word for a specific week were based on several entries. Whenever conflicting evidence was encountered, the word was assigned to the categories of Unclassified or Indeterminant for that week. If during a single week only one entry was recorded for a word, this entry was taken as sufficient evidence for judgments to be made as to reference and extension.

In order to allow for the computer analysis of the data, all the information available about a given word was coded. The numerical code was designed to enable repeated measures to be documented with reference to identified time points throughout the one-word period. Information on the following five dimensions was coded for each word in the child's lexicon: word's sequential number; week of acquisition; adult part-of-speech; category of reference; and category of extension. Each word was scored for reference and for extension on the basis of the behaviors it manifested during the first week of use. Thereafter, any change in category membership was specified with reference to the time of the observed change. Just as the word's behavior was coded for the first week of its use, so it was coded for the last week of the study. The following example of the word *lopo* 'not here' (036) illustrates the coding of reference:

> *lopo*: 24 5; 25 2; 30 4; 32 4.
> The word was acquired during the 24th week of study, and was initially classified as indeterminant (5). During the following 5 weeks of study the word was used as an action word (2). In the 30th week of study (6 weeks after its emergence), the word changed its category of reference: the child started to use it as a social word (4). In the last week of study the word was still a member of the category of social words (4).
> (5 = indeterminant; 2 = action word; 4 = social word).

The coding of the word *yeled* '(a) boy' (094) is given as an example of the coding of extension.

> *yeled*: 23 13; 24 44; 25 22; 32 22.
> The word was initially restricted to a specific occasion: when K was pointing to a picture of a boy and a girl hanging on the wall in the course of a ritualized

game we used to play after K took her daily bath. This behavior lasted for two weeks. During the 24th week of study K uttered the word in vague contexts. It was impossible to decide whether the word was meaningful or not (44). The first evidence that *yeled* had become a class name was recorded during the 25th week of study. This usage persisted until the period of data collection was over.

(13 = underextension – specific occasion, 44 = unclassified incomplete, 22 = regular extension).

Judgments as to category membership and coding were carried out concurrently. The amount of time required for an analysis of one table ranged from 20 minutes to two hours, depending upon the number of entries in the table and the complexity of the behaviors described. As reported earlier, all words were analysed and scored by the principal investigator during a total period of two months. A subset of 43 randomly selected tables were independently analysed and scored by another scorer for inter-judge reliability (see Chapter 6 above). The second scorer reported that she could follow the rules with no difficulty.

9   *Measurement of vocabulary growth*

Chapter 2 offered speculative figures for the quantitative aspects of children's lexical development during the one-word period. These estimates were derived from the reports of a number of investigators who studied different children and various developmental questions. However, as noted in Chapter 2, collapsing evidence from diverse sources and speakers leaves too much room for speculation and inference. It is with this in mind that the following exact quantitative figures based on a direct and systematic measure of one subject's lexical development throughout the one-word period are presented below.

The acquisition of new comprehensible words

Keren's lexical development was carefully followed from the emergence of her first comprehensible word and until I encountered conclusive evidence that she was able to construct productive two- and multi-word combinations (see Chapter 7 for a detailed description of the data and the definition of a comprehensible word). Throughout the period of investigation, the subject's productions were limited to single-word utterances. This was manifested by suprasegmental features such as pauses, intonation contours, and repetition (Scollon, 1976). During the last two months of the study, sequences of single-word utterances were sometimes recorded. These sequences were similar to those observed by Bloom (1973) and termed "successive single word utterances". Keren's record also included a few unanalysed amalgams (MacWhinney, 1978). These expressions were routinized strings of words which were modeled as such to the child and were never broken up into their components or reconstructed in novel ways. Examples include: *mize* 'who is this' (092); *tnili* 'give me' (061); *abalada* 'Daddy went to work' (040); *xamidai* 'too hot' (071). The unanalysed amalgams are treated in the present study as single lexical terms.

During the period of investigation, phonological and morphological modifications of words were noted for many lexical items. These are treated in the present analysis as means of shaping the child's productions. In a synthetic language such as Hebrew, the addition of either prefixes or suffixes to a small number of stems is not sufficient evidence of morphological productivity (Berman, 1985; Dromi and Berman, 1982). Since I did not encounter clear evidence that a specific morpheme (e.g., number + gender) was applied productively across the child's lexicon at a specific point in time, I decided to treat morphological markings and phonological approximations analogously. (This subject will be considered more fully below.)

A new word was assigned to the child's cumulative lexicon only if the following *a priori* criterion had been met: a sequence of sounds must have been recorded repeatedly three times in various contexts before it was identified as a new comprehensible word. The date of the third recording was regarded as the day of acquisition for the new word. Both the diary record and the transcriptions of the audio-recordings served as the data base for identifying repeated occurrences of similar phonological constructs. Not all of the child's new comprehensible words were conventional words in Hebrew. Some non-conventional vocalizations were consistently produced by the child and hence functioned as comprehensible words, especially during the first months of study. No distinction is made in the present analysis between conventional and non-conventional Hebrew words. The assignment of a new word to the child's lexicon is also completely independent of the analyses of word meaning (i.e., reference and extension) which are discussed in Chapters 10 and 11 below.

Keren's first comprehensible word was recorded when she was 10(12). On this particular day I identified her word *haw* 'bow wow' (001), which she uttered while pointing to a little white dog which was barking at us. This event was recorded during a walk outside when we passed the dog (I was pushing Keren's stroller). It was the third time in which I noted that Keren said *haw* when she saw a real dog or when she heard it barking. The appearance of this first word was a novelty. It signified the first event in which the child uttered a specific sequence of sounds which she, the speaker, and I, the hearer, related to the same real-world referent. Prior to this day, I was never able to match Keren's infinite number of speech sounds with specific extra-linguistic referents. Therefore, I contend that the beginning of the one-word period can easily be identified if one is clear about what constitutes a comprehensible word.

The difference between a child who produces one comprehensible word and a child who utters a number of different unidentifiable speech sounds (i.e., sensorimotor morphemes in Carter's (1978a, b,) sense, or babbling in the more traditional interpretation) is a qualitative difference that is not simply a matter of degree. The growing ability of the child intentionally to produce similar sounds in repeated contexts makes it possible for him to communicate verbally with primary caretakers while referring to specific aspects in the non-verbal situation.

On the last day of my comprehensive recording, Keren was 17(23). This cut-off point was selected six days after I had noted in the child's diary that my subject had started productively to combine words. Keren's early word combinations proliferated suddenly, and as soon as she began to produce them they were noted in the diary very frequently. Thus, on the first day of the last week of the study (32), of the 39 speech events that were recorded in the diary, 17 were of productive multi-word expressions. On the last day of study, in an audio-recorded session of 30 minutes, Keren produced a total of 279 utterances, 36 per cent of which were multi-word expressions.

Keren's early word combinations conveyed basic semantic relations such as: existence (e.g., *hine kadur*/ 'here (is a) ball'), agent (e.g., *kereni oto*/ 'Kereni (is) playing with (a) car'), recurrence (e.g., *od buba*/ 'another doll'), location (e.g., *dubi kise*/ 'teddy bear (on the) chair'), etc. I completely agree with Schlesinger (1977, 1982) that the emergence of two- and multi-word constructions is the first linguistic evidence of the child's ability to encode semantic relations (see also Brown, 1973). According to this theory, combinatorial or relational meanings are not conveyed by single words. Rather, it is argued that single words function as linguistic labels that convey referential meaning only.

The one-word period, in Keren's case, spanned 32 weeks (seven months and twelve days). The period was distinct because it had identifiable boundaries and was characterized by the building up of a productive lexicon. My subject's complete cumulative lexicon of comprehensible words contained 337 entries. The full list of Keren's comprehensible words, the day of acquisition of each word, and English translations or glosses based on the meaning of the corresponding conventional word in colloquial Hebrew, are given in Appendix A.

The rate of lexical growth

In order to determine the rate of the subject's lexical development throughout the one-word period, I calculated the total number of words in the cumulative lexicon of the child at the end of each week of study. I also measured the number of new words acquired during each week. The interval of one week was selected as providing an optimal level of description, i.e., one that is neither too detailed nor too global to characterize the accumulation of new words throughout the one-word period.

Figure 1 shows the total number of words in the child's lexicon as measured for each week of study. The child's ages are given for the end of each week. Figure 2 presents the number of new words that were acquired during each week of study. This figure is plotted to show the slope of the acquisition curve of new words.

Figures 1 and 2 indicate that in the early phases of production new words entered the child's vocabulary very slowly. The rate increased gradually until it reached an average of about 18 new words per week between the 21st and

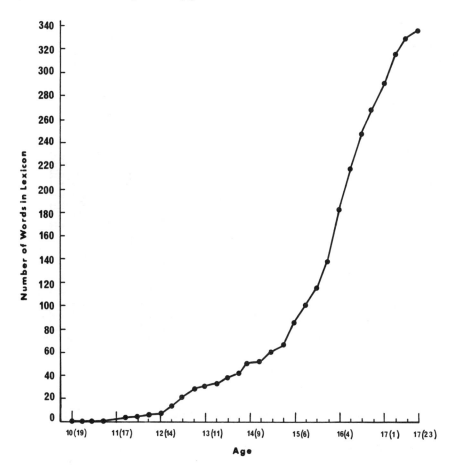

Figure 1.   Keren's cumulative lexicon of the one-word stage

24th weeks of study (ages 15(0)–15(26)). This average is lower than was predicted by Carey (1978), who estimated the average rate of learning new words during the first five years at about nine words a day (see similar and even larger estimates in Clark, 1983a:811; and Soja, Carey and Spelke, 1985).

During the 25th week of study, when Keren's age was 15(27)–16(3), I observed a striking increase in the number of new words that she acquired. A peak figure of 44 new words was recorded for that single week. This was at least twice as many words as had been recorded in any previous week, and also more than in any subsequent week. This higher rate persisted for the next two weeks. During this block of three successive weeks (25–27, ages 15(27)–16(17)) the child acquired a total of 111 new words which constituted one third of her productive lexicon. The sudden change in the rate of

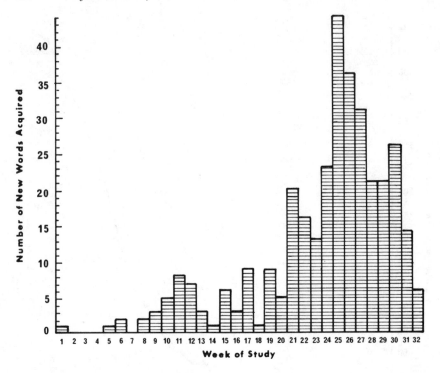

Figure 2.   The number of new words acquired, by week of study

acquisition was observed about eight weeks before Keren started to produce two- and multi-word utterances.

After three weeks of intensive learning, the rate of acquisition began to decline. During weeks 28, 29 and 30 (ages 16(18)–17(7)), the rate was similar to that observed for the weeks that preceded the sudden increase. During weeks 31 and 32 (ages 17(8)–17(23)), the last two weeks of the study, there was a further decline: the subject acquired only 14 and 6 new words, respectively. This corresponds to the point at which she started to combine words.

The rate at which Keren acquired new words was neither linear nor exponential, but rather curvilinear. Keren's continuous record provides strong evidence that a spurt in lexical behavior is indeed observed toward the end of the one-word period. In several previous studies on the one-word stage, researchers have noted anecdotally an increase in rate of lexical acquisition shortly before the onset of word combination (e.g., Bloom, 1973; Halliday, 1975; Nelson, 1973b). In two recent studies this increase in the number of words produced towards the end of the stage was measured directly during recorded experimental sessions (Corrigan, 1976; McShane, 1980).

My finding that towards the end of the one-word period the rate of word acquisition decreased is also of interest. It provides support for the contention that the one-word period is a distinct developmental stage with identifiable boundaries. One might argue that the low number of new words recorded in Keren's lexicon during the last few weeks of study is an artifact of measurement. For example, perhaps emerging new words were not included in the lexicon because they had not yet passed the productivity test. I doubt that this was the case, however, because during this time many more conversations than ever before were held between Keren and myself. In fact, during the last few weeks of study, the opportunities for Keren to utter known words and for me to record these uses increased significantly. Tables 3 and 4 in Chapter 7 clearly indicate that the amount of Keren's talking increased considerably towards the end of the study.

Since the observed slowdown in rate of word acquisition seems not to result from an artifact of measurement, we must consider whether it was idiosyncratic to the subject of this study. To the best of my knowledge, there is only one study in which the relationship between the growing lexicon of single words and the emergence of word combinations is considered.[1]

Anisfeld (1984:107–9) reports that in the case of five different English-speaking children who were studied by McCune-Nicolich (1981), as MLU values exceeded 1.0 morpheme per utterance, the rate at which new words were learned slowed down sharply. I hold that this slowdown in the learning of new words towards the end of the one-word period indicates that the stage, which has clear boundaries, is coming to an end. I suspect that other researchers have failed to document the slowdown which follows the lexical spurt mainly for methodological reasons. When the child's lexicon exceeds 50 or 100 different comprehensible words, it is extremely hard to observe it closely (Nelson, 1973b). Only in a study involving systematic daily recordings does one obtain the amount of information needed to generate an exact lexical curve.

A model of development which predicts that in the early phases of a stage new behaviors will be manifested infrequently, that later those behaviors will flourish, and that finally, at the time of consolidation, the behaviors will be recorded less often (e.g., Piaget's model (Flavell, 1963), but see also Chapter 2), closely represents the curve which was observed for Keren's lexical development. I suggest that following a prolonged period of the intensive learning of new words, the child spends time practicing the new forms and actively testing the range of their meanings and application.

In spite of the slowdown in Keren's acquisition of new vocabulary in the last few weeks of the study, I was still very busy collecting data for the diary. The new entries in the diary described the new uses of old words, their phonological improvements, and the acquisition of morphological markings. In other words, during this last phase of the stage the child was improving

[1] I wish to thank I. M. Schlesinger for bringing this discussion in Anisfeld's book to my attention.

her control over the words that already existed in her productive lexicon. It seemed that she was actively trying to explore the wide range of possibilities in which her words could be used in various communicative contexts. I hypothesize that the gradual decrease in the rate of lexical growth constituted the end of Keren's one-word stage of development and a prelude to her sharp transition into syntax.

Changes in word form

Throughout the period of investigation, all the overt changes in the form of a given word were noted. These changes are categorized as one of two types: (a) changes in the phonological manifestations of words; and (b) morphological markings on existing lexical items. Although I present phonological and morphological modifications in separate categories, I wish to note here that whereas the two classes are usually treated as distinct in adult grammars, they may not be so for the very young speakers. It is possible, as I have suggested, that for the child acquiring Hebrew as a first language, the addition of prefixes or suffixes onto a small number of stems is not sufficient evidence of morphological productivity.

In Hebrew, which is a synthetic language that employs rich bound morphology, even basic forms are inflected (see Berman, 1985, for a description of Hebrew morphology). Therefore, only clear evidence of alternation between forms can be used to test productivity. My data clearly show that most of Keren's verbs were initially acquired as imperatives and were inflected to either feminine or masculine. Alternations for gender markings started to emerge during week 25 of the study, at the beginning of the second phase of the one-word stage. Some verbs which had previously been used as masculine imperative forms regardless of the gender of the addressee (e.g., *kax* 'take' imperative, masculine) took on feminine inflections (e.g., *kxi* 'take' imperative, feminine). Other verbs which entered the lexicon as feminine imperatives (e.g., *zuzi* 'move' imperative, feminine) and were applied as such when Keren talked to her father and to boys, began to be used, in appropriate contexts, in the masculine form as well (e.g., *zuz* 'move' imperative, masculine). It should, however, be noted that Keren did not acquire the alternative forms for the various lexical items at the same time, and therefore we cannot confidently conclude that she suddenly appreciated the distinction of gender and applied it across the board.

Markings of tense in the verbal system were not noted frequently enough to be significant. Some verbs were always used in the past and others in the present. This finding is in accord with Berman and Dromi's (1984) report on an investigation of a larger sample of children acquiring Hebrew. This study found that productive verb alternations were not noted for one-word-stage speakers. During the second half of the stage, Keren started to use the plural forms of verbs, and also a limited number of person markings. Her initial attempts to inflect verbs to their plural and person forms were not consistent across all contexts or across the child's vocabulary. Thus, some verbs in some contexts were conjugated and others were not.

In the nominal system, which lexicalizes the distinctions of number, gender, and diminutive, I observed evidence of productivity mainly in the application of diminutive suffixes. Keren acquired the suffix -*le*, one of several options for encoding this meaning in Hebrew (see Dromi and Berman, 1982), during the 13th week of study. From that point she often addressed her parents and certain toys by saying -*imale, abale* and *dubile* ('little Mommy', 'little Daddy', 'little teddy bear').

The distinction between singular and plural nominal forms was recorded much more often than any other distinction. However, although Keren sometimes provided plural nouns when they were obligatory, she failed to provide them consistently. Plural markings were mainly recorded during the second half of the stage (starting in week 24), but even towards the final weeks of study I recorded examples that indicated that she did not supply the plural markings in all obligatory contexts. In the context of describing a picture book, Keren pointed to a picture of three cars and said: *hine/harbe/oto/* 'here, many, car'. This successive single-word expression clearly indicates that, although she appreciated that more than one car was depicted in the picture, Keren did not lexicalize this understanding by a plural noun form.

As figure 3 below indicates, my analysis shows that during the one-word period, phonological improvements and morphological processes are highly correlated. Therefore, it seems to me that both processes may function for the child as parallel means for shaping her own productions. This may be motivated by the growing communicative needs, as well as by the increasing awareness that words are conventional devices in any given language (Clark, 1983a, b).

Table 5 shows the distribution of 276 child words in three mutually exclusive classes of phonological forms by month of investigation.[2] In each column the distribution of the new words acquired in this particular month is presented. There are three classes of form: (a) conventional words; (b) phonological approximations; and (c) nursery words. While the first two classes refer to the child's attempts to produce conventional adult Hebrew words, the third category consists of non-conventional words, some of which are found in Hebrew "baby talk", others of which were idiosyncratic to my subject.

Of all the new words acquired by the child throughout the one-word period, 74 per cent were initially produced as phonological approximations of adult-input forms. Only 20 per cent of the words were articulated correctly from the outset. The group of nursery words was relatively small, and consisted of only 17 words (six per cent of all the words acquired).

During the first two months of study, nursery words constituted the major

---

[2] Sixty-one productive words were excluded from this sample because they were not recorded often enough to allow for repeated scoring, or analyses of changes over time (see also p. 121).

Table 5.   The distribution of phonological classes by the months of investigation

Word type	Month								Total no. of words
	First	Second	Third	Fourth	Fifth	Sixth	Seventh	Eighth	
Conventional words		1 (20)	2 (9)	2 (17)	6 (26)	8 (12)	20 (19)	17 (45)	56 (20)
Phonological approximation			16 (70)	10 (83)	16 (70)	54 (83)	86 (79)	21 (55)	203 (74)
Nursery words	1 (100)	4 (80)	5 (21)		1 (4)	3 (6)	3 (3)		17 (6)

Note: Numbers in parentheses indicate the relative frequency of the class in percentages.

category in the child's lexicon. The relative proportion of nursery words declined sharply towards the fourth month of study, and during the last month of study no nursery words were learned. The relative proportion of phonological approximations and conventional forms was constant throughout time. It was only during the last month of study that an increase was noticed for conventional forms, while a decrease was observed in the relative number of phonological approximations of new words. In general, then, it seems that the phonological form-class membership of a word (a, b, or c) is significantly related to age of acquisition ($X^2 = 148$, d.f. 54 <.001).

Since most of the child's words changed their phonological and morphological manifestations over time, it seemed desirable to measure the dynamic properties of the system. For this purpose the overall number of phonological changes of various types were recorded. These included: additions of previously omitted phonemes; modifications of consonants and/or vowels; substitution of a distorted phoneme by a more approximated one; and a complete replacement of baby words by conventional words. Morphological markings that were mainly inflections for number, gender, and diminutive on nouns, and number and gender on verbs, were also plotted for this analysis. Figure 3 presents the distribution of scores by week of study. Each bar in this figure represents the absolute number of words that underwent change during a particular week.

As mentioned earlier, there is a striking similarity between the rate of phonological and morphological acquisitions. The two parallel and fluctuating changes that are observed indicate that most phonological and morphological processes were recorded towards the end of the period, starting in the 21st week of study. The fluctuating rates of change during the second half of the period indicate that short periods of intensive modifications were followed by short periods of rest (compare, for example, weeks 24–27 to weeks 28–30). The last two weeks of study show an increase in the improvement of the system. This finding is significant, mainly because during this time the total number of new words acquired by the child

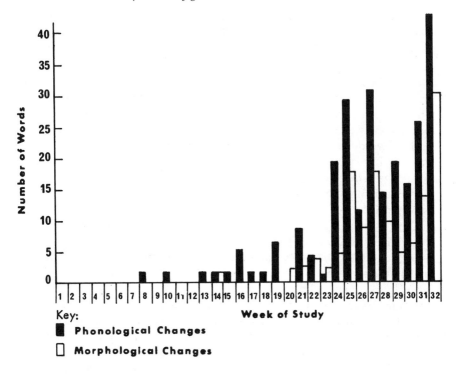

Key:

Phonological Changes

Morphological Changes

Figure 3.   The distribution of words which underwent phonological or morphological changes, by week of study

markedly decreased (see Figure 2). I therefore conclude here that the child's efforts to improve the form of her words was inversely related to the rate of her lexical acquisition. Towards the end of the one-word stage, the intelligibility of words improved considerably while the size of the lexicon remained more or less unchanged.

The contents of early words

The cumulative lexicon of the subject appears in Appendix A. Since the lexicon is so exhaustive, it is quite difficult to draw direct conclusions from it by a summary inspection alone. This section, therefore, considers the contents that Keren chose to lexicalize. As will be shown in the chapters that follow, a distinction must be made between the way a word is used conventionally and the way it is used by the child. The present analysis refers to adult semantic categories that are identified in the list of the child's words without going into detail about the underlying developmental processes that are reflected in the repeated uses of these words (see more in this regard in Dromi and Fishelzon, 1986).

Several semantic classes of words appeared in Keren's speech even before her lexicon reached the count of 52 different words. These categories, which at first included single or few representatives, were subsequently extended throughout the one-word stage by the addition of semantically related words. The initial list of classes includes words for: animals and the sounds they make; personal names; foods, drinks, and eating; toys, clothes, and other personal accessories (e.g., jewelry); furniture and typical home accessories; social words; and demonstratives. My analysis shows that among the earliest words we can identify are labels for objects and actions that are commonly encountered by the child in her close and familiar environment. It would seem that the words that are picked up by the child are those that are very frequently modeled to her in repeated contexts of everyday routinized experiences.

During the subsequent weeks of lexical development, new entries were successively added to existing categories. At the same time, new categories emerged. Keren started to name body parts during week 19. At approximately the same time, she began to denote qualities of objects and also to refer to the transfer of objects. Her verbs *kax* 'take' (062), and *tnili* 'give me' (061) emerged and replaced the earlier form *toda* 'thank you' (038) which was used to request objects. The first references to location: *amala (lemala)* 'up' (063), and to different positions of the body in space: *mod (la?amod)* 'stand up' (067) were recorded during weeks 20 and 21, respectively. Two weeks later, Keren started to refer verbally to the states of objects. When she saw broken toys or torn pages she said *ibar (nišbar)* '(is) broken' (115). Several personal names of family members entered Keren's lexicon during weeks 20 to 23. It is interesting that during these weeks she overextended her grandparents' personal names so that both the grandfather and grandmother on one side were called *nira*, the grandmother's name, and the grandparents of the other branch of the family were called *moše*, the grandfather's name.

As reported above, weeks 25, 26 and 27 were characterized by a spurt in lexical growth. Members of all the semantic categories entered the child's lexicon during this slice of time. It is clear, however, that the category of object words was enlarged and new kinds of object words, those denoting classes of instances, were introduced. Unlike earlier object words, which denoted very special objects that were familiar to the child from her immediate home environment, I now recorded generic terms that encoded representatives of non-specific instances or exemplars; for example: *piax (perax)* 'a flower' (129); *bayit* 'a house' (132); *even* 'a stone' (135); *erer (sefer)* 'a book' (187). During weeks 25 and 26, I also noted several new words for actions and change of location. Verb forms seemed to increase considerably. Among these were: *pes (lexapes)* 'to look for' (127); *ala (nafla)* 'fell down' (160); *gilgul* 'a somersault' (162), which was used to request the action; *uci (ruci)* 'run' (172); *nake (lenakot)* 'to clean up' (209). During week 24, I noted an obvious increase in the number of animal names and sounds. The proximity in time between the emergence of these words is interesting. A similar proximity in time in the emergence of words which are semantically related can be seen in regard to personal names, body parts, and clothes during week 26. Consider the following list: *onez* (*ozen*) 'ear' (176); *pupik* 'bellybutton' (178); *cici* 'breast' (179); *abis* (*lehalbiš*) 'to put on' (192); *gufiya* '(an) undershirt' (190); *taic* 'pantyhose' (198); *bayim* (*garbayim*) 'socks' (199). The names of Keren's cousins *efi* (202) and *iri* (203), and grandmothers *?ara?* (204) and *?axel* (205), which entered the lexicon successively, also illustrate the same phenomenon.

I recorded Keren's first attributes during weeks 28 and 29. The words *ola ola* (*gdola*) 'big' (256), *tov* 'good, ok' (259), and *atuva* (*retuva*) 'wet' (276) are the earliest examples. Keren acquired her first pronoun in its first-person inflected form at this time. This was the pronoun *iti* 'with me' (258). The general kinship terms *safa* (*savta*) 'grandmother' (269) and *saba* 'grandfather' were also learned relatively late. This happened towards the end of the study. Initially, the child never produced these terms without accompanying them with the grandparents' personal names.

During the last two weeks of study, I recorded two new categories in Keren's speech. The word *šeli* 'mine' was Keren's first possessive form, and the word *mipo* 'from here' (318) was the first lexical attempt to refer to direction. The last three words in Keren's lexicon are *para* 'a cow' (335), *kelev* 'a dog' (336), and *tiyul* 'a walk' (337). It is striking that all three words are the conventional Hebrew words for contents that Keren had previously named by non-conventional forms or nursery words. Those nursery words were amongst the earliest of the child's words and were used by her for a long time in different contexts. As we will see below, the substitution of conventional words for the nursery forms is not accidental. It signifies a change in the child's semantic system. I argue that only when Keren realized that the same words could not be used for actions and objects, or for an undifferentiated overall situation, did she acquire the grammatical forms (i.e., conventional words) that denote these contents in adult language.

Summary

In this chapter we have examined Keren's complete single-word lexicon from a quantitative and an adult semantic point of view. We have seen that the subject's cumulative lexicon contained 337 different Hebrew words. Keren acquired these words during eight months, between the ages of 10(12) and 17(23). The rate at which new words were added to the child's productive lexicon was not steady. Initially, Keren learned new words very slowly. After a period of 24 weeks characterized by a linear course of word acquisition (eight weeks before the one-word stage ended), the rate at which new words were learned changed radically. A lexical spurt during three successive weeks (25, 26 and 27) yielded the addition of over 100 new words to the child's lexicon. The intensive rate of word acquisition declined towards the end of the stage. During the last few weeks of study, rather than learning more words, the child improved existing words. Thus, she approximated the phonological forms of conventional Hebrew words, added morphemes to stems, and also examined the range of application, or the scope of conventional meanings, of already known words. During the last phase of the one-word stage, the subject substituted conventional words for non-conventional ones, and also ceased to use idiosyncratic forms.

The content analysis of Keren's data indicated that semantically related classes of words could be identified in the child's lexicon quite early. Several classes of words are represented in the first half of the one-word stage. During this period, the lexicon consisted of a number of classes each containing only a few members. During the second half of the stage, Keren added words to all of her categories at an increased rate. In some cases it was clear that words belonging to the same adult semantic fields entered the child's lexicon during the same week. During the second half of the stage, very few new categories of semantically related words were added to the child's lexicon.

Thus far we have considered Keren's data from an adult perspective. In the following chapters we shall examine the results of the qualitative analyses based on direct evidence from the child's actual repeated uses of her words in different contexts. Chapter 10 describes the underlying processes related to the evolution of word reference or word classes in Keren's speech, and Chapter 11 is devoted to the description of the development of word-meaning or extension.

One goal of the present study was to trace the development of word reference, and its correspondence to adult parts-of-speech. In Chapter 3 I discussed at length the difficulties in establishing whether a single-word utterance refers to an action, an object, or both. I also criticized the readiness of researchers to make such decisions without explicitly specifying the behavioral cues they are taking into account in classifying early words. I argued that it is erroneous to assign a child's words to different categories only on the basis of their resemblance to adult words that are used as nouns, verbs, adjectives, etc. Moreover, I claimed that only by looking at repeated uses of the same word in different contexts does it become possible to identify the specific element in a situation which is being verbally encoded by the child. Repeated scoring of the same word, reflecting changes over time, enables the researcher to examine the development of the referential properties of words. The present chapter reports the results of my analysis of Keren's lexicon. This was carried out by the application of the rules presented in detail in Chapter 8. In applying the system of rules, every effort was made to minimize the influence of the observer's knowledge of the referential properties of the same or similar words in adult speech. Scores were given to each of the child's words on a weekly basis, and a word could be assigned to different categories in successive weeks. Only 276 words out of the total of 337 were included in the following analyses. Sixty-one productive words were excluded from the sample of words because they manifested no changes in form, meaning, or use. These words were not recorded frequently enough to allow for their categorization. Sixteen of the words were personal names and the remaining 45 belong to a variety of adult parts-of-speech.

The distribution of child words in the various categories of reference

Each word in Keren's cumulative lexicon was assigned to one of five categories of reference: (1) object words; (2) action words; (3) modifiers; (4) social words; and (5) indeterminant words. Figure 4 shows how the words acquired

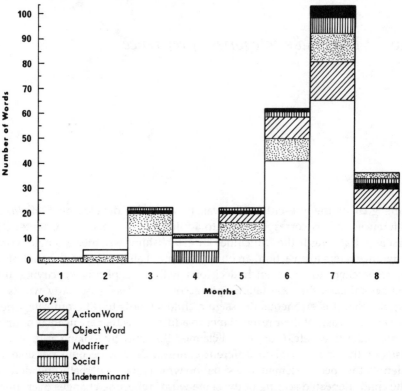

Figure 4.   The distribution of child's categories of reference, by month of study

by the subject during each month of the study were distributed in the different categories, according to the behaviors recorded during the first week of their use. The figure shows that all five categories were represented in the child's speech. Some words clearly designated either objects or actions. For example, *oto* 'a car' (011) was never used to point to non-object referents; *alax* 'walk' (226), on the other hand, referred to actions alone. Other words were used as social words: for example, *kuku* 'peekaboo' (034) produced while playing, or *ken* 'yes' (154) used as an acknowledgement. Still other words were modifiers: for example, *ol ol* (*gadol*) 'large' (173) to describe properties of objects or events. Finally, I identified a class of words which could not be assigned to any of the above mutually exclusive classes because they had multiple referential functions. For example, *xam* 'hot' (071) was used as the child's name for heaters and ovens, and at the same time was uttered in some contexts as a modifier denoting the property of being either hot or cold; *dio* 'giddi-up' (015) was used while pointing to pictures of animals as well as when pointing to the action of riding. Thus, in the present analysis, the indeterminant category was generated for words which manifested double- or multi-referential behaviors.

In the sample as a whole, the majority of words (59 per cent) were object words. The four other categories were far less well represented: indeterminant words constituted 16 per cent of the total lexicon, action words 14 per cent, social words seven per cent, and modifiers, the smallest category, only four per cent (eleven words). Object words were first recorded in Keren's lexicon when she was 11(16), during the second month of study. During all subsequent months (except for the fourth) they constituted the major class of new words learned. The first action word entered the subject's lexicon during the fourth month of study. This word was *toda* 'thank you' (038), and it was recorded during the 16th week as a verbal means of requesting desired objects. Starting with the fourth month, action words were learned continuously, and during the seventh month (weeks 25–8) they constituted the second largest group of new words acquired. Modifiers and social words first entered the child's lexicon during the third month of study, and showed a peak during the following month (weeks 13–16).

Of special interest to us is the category of indeterminant words used for both actions and objects or for objects and modifiers. During the first two months of study, most of the words acquired by the child were used for more than one function. Between the third and seventh months, five to ten words showed indeterminant behaviors. The relative number of words in this category declined significantly toward the beginning of the seventh month. During weeks 26, 28, 29 and 30, only one indeterminant word per week was recorded, and during the last two weeks of study Keren uttered no indeterminant words at all.

The results of the present analysis indicate that it is possible to determine the category of reference for many words that the child uses. The well-defined set of working rules applied, together with a systematic analysis of the contexts in which the words were produced, enables us to conclude that even in the early phases of production many words were used exclusively for object referents, and that several other words were used to refer to actions or as modifiers or social words. The category of indeterminant words comprised only 45 of the 276 words analysed. This category is important, however, mainly because it does not exist in adult language. It is interesting that some words were used by the child at a particular time in more than one way.

What kinds of words were initially used indeterminantly by Keren? My analysis reveals that some of them were nouns in adult speech, some were non-conventional forms (e.g., baby words made up by the child or borrowed nursery words learned from Keren's caretaker, who was not a native speaker of Hebrew), and the rest were adverbs and adjectives. What is common to all these words is the fact that they were modeled in opaque non-linguistic contexts, i.e., contexts in which it was difficult to identify the intended referent. For example, the contexts in which many modifiers are modeled are extremely varied (e.g., the word *wet* in connection with a wide range of objects). The difficulty involved in identifying the referent for a non-conventional word is also understandable. The words are not used by all the caretakers, and they may also be used differently by different people since there is no clear-cut agreement as to their meaning. Finally, many of the nouns that Keren used indeterminantly were learned from songs and rhymes, or were lifted out of speech routines. For example, the word *avoda* 'work' (040) was learned from the speech routine *aba ?alax la?avoda* 'Daddy went to work', said very often just after Keren's father had left for work.

As was shown in Figure 4, the classification of a word as indeterminant occurred more frequently in the early phases of the one-word stage than in the later phases. Moreover, early-acquired words that showed indeterminant behaviors seemed to remain in this category longer than later-acquired words. I hypothesize that as the overall linguistic experience of the child increases, her referential behavior improves, so that most words she acquires are used in only one referential function. In order to test whether linguistic experience and referential behaviors of words are related, the correlation between the child's age at acquiring a word and the length of time this word was used indeterminantly was calculated. A significant negative correlation was found ($r = -.50$, p. $< .001$). This result shows that as Keren got closer to the beginning of syntax, her linguistic system became more differentiated. In other words, she no longer used a word for referents falling into more than one category of reference – the mapping of words onto either object concepts or relational concepts was much sharper towards the end of the study than it was at the beginning of the one-word period.

The correspondence between the child's category of reference and adult parts-of-speech

Since adult part-of-speech membership has often been used by researchers as the main criterion for classifying children's words as referring to objects or actions (e.g., Bloom, 1973; Nelson, 1973b), and since it has been reported that children sometimes fail to identify the correct category of reference for the words they use (e.g., Griffiths and Atkinson, 1978; Braunwald, 1978), an attempt was made to determine the degree to which the child's categories of reference matched adult parts-of-speech.

Each word acquired by Keren was classified according to its grammatical category in modern Hebrew. Six categories were used: nouns, verbs, adjectives, adverbs, functors (prepositions, question words, social words and deictic terms), and non-conventional. This last category included words or sounds that were produced regularly and systematically by the child but that were not conventional words in adult Hebrew. The distribution of the 276 words in the six categories is presented for each month of the study in Table 6.

In order to measure the degree to which the child's categories of reference

Table 6. The distribution of words classified according to adult parts-of-speech, displayed by months of study

Parts-of-Speech	Month								Total no. of words
	First	Second	Third	Fourth	Fifth	Sixth	Seventh	Eighth	
Noun		2 (40)	13 (57)	6 (50)	14 (61)	44 (68)	71 (65)	26 (68)	176
Verb					4 (17)	7 (11)	18 (16)	6 (16)	35
Adjective						2 (3)	5 (5)	1 (3)	8
Adverb			1 (4)	2 (17)	1 (4)	1 (1)	3 (3)	2 (5)	10
Functor			1 (4)	3 (25)	2 (9)	4 (6)	5 (5)	3 (8)	18
Non-conventional	1 (100)	3 (60)	8 (35)	1 (8)	2 (9)	7 (11)	7 (6)		29

Note: Numbers in parenthese indicate the column percentages.

for words corresponded with the adult part-of-speech membership for the same words, the joint classification of each word at two different time points was tested. In Table 7 the category of reference assigned to each new word in the first week of its production is compared with the adult part-of-speech membership of the same word. Table 8 shows the same comparison for the last week of study.

The child's categories of reference correlate highly with adult part-of-speech categories at both periods of measurement. The correlation, which was initially high and significant ($r = .55$, $p. < .001$), increased slightly toward the end of the one-word stage ($r = .59$, $p. < .001$). This high correspondence is remarkable. As indicated in Tables 7 and 8, most words that were not classified "correctly" by the child were first used indeterminantly. As stated earlier, indeterminant behaviors were initially shown by nouns, non-conventional words, and adjectives or adverbs. Most of these words, however, were later used by the child according to a category of reference that corresponds to the "expected" adult part-of-speech.

In general, my findings suggest that children do not often completely misidentify the intended referent of adult words, despite occasional examples to the contrary, as reported in Griffiths and Atkinson (1978), of children using nouns as predicate terms. In the complete lexicon of 337 words, very few words (17 during the first week of use and ten during the last week of study) showed a complete mismatch of reference. Among the

Table 7.   Child's initial categories of reference and adult parts-of-speech

Parts-of-Speech	Child Category				
	Object	Action/State	Modifier	Social	Indeterminant
Noun	152	2	0	4	18
Verb	1	32	0	1	1
Adj.-Adv.	1	2	7	2	6
Functor	0	3	4	8	3
Nonconventional	9	0	0	3	17

Table 8.   Child's final categories of reference and adult parts-of-speech

Parts-of-speech	Child Category				
	Object	Action/State	Modifier	Social	Indeterminant
Noun	168	2	2	2	1
Verb	1	33	0	0	1
Adj.-Adv.	0	1	12	1	2
Functor	0	1	5	10	1
Nonconventional	12	8	0	3	3

Note: Words that stopped being produced by Keren during the study are excluded from this table.

words that did show a complete mismatch, most were nouns that were used as action words (a mismatch to which I will return); others were either verbs used as object words, or adjectives used as either object or action words.

I argue that when mismatch occurs it can usually be attributed to the context in which the word was learned. The following examples serve to illustrate this point. The adult noun *iga* (*rega*) '(a) moment' (052) was initially used by Keren as her word for the action of diapering. The following diary entries illustrate this quite clearly:

(1)   14(13): In K's room; K is playing in bed with some clothes and a diaper, which M has prepared for dressing her. K takes the teddy bear, puts it on the diaper and says: *iga* repeatedly. M doesn't understand and says: *rega . . . rega kereni ani axatel otax/* 'Just a minute Keren, . . . I'll diaper you in a minute'. K repeats after her: *iga* '(a) moment'.

(2) 14(17): In K's bed; after giving K a bath, M is getting ready to diaper her. K notices that M is folding the diaper. She jumps up and says: *iga buba/* '(a) moment doll'. She takes the teddy bear and tries to diaper it. When M interferes, she bursts into tears and goes on saying: *iga/ x/* '(a) moment'.

(3) 14(19): In the bathroom; K tries to get into the bathtub when F is in there. She says *iga/* '(a) moment'.

(4) 16(11): In the living room; on the couch. K is playing with a disposable diaper. She spreads it out and tries to get on it. She tries to diaper herself. She says: *iga/* '(a) moment' and looks at M.

(5) 17(3): In the kitchen; K is playing with a rubber band. She tries for a long time to wrap it around a honey jar. She lays the jar down, and tries to wrap it in many different ways. She says: *iga/das/dvaš/* '(a) moment', 'honey', 'honey'.

(6) 17(23): In the living room; K picks up her toy pig, and asks M again and again: *rega/maze?/* '(a) moment', 'what is this?'

I believe that Keren learned the word *rega* from my verbal expressions that she heard repeatedly in the context of being diapered. Keren was a very active baby and it was often quite difficult to diaper her. When Keren was restless I couldn't do so, and therefore I often asked her to quiet down for a moment. Note that in such a context I did not always supply the verb *lexatel* 'to diaper', and often I just said: *rega, kereni, lo lazuz rak rega bevakaša/* 'a moment, Kereni, don't move, just a moment please' (but see also example (1) above).

The adult verb *afa* 'fly' (past/present, singular, feminine) was used by Keren for the object bird for quite some time (following an initial period in which *cifcif* (a bird tweet) was used for this object). Note that Keren did not utter the infinitive form of the verb, which was her most common form of early verbs, but rather the past-tense form. The following example was recorded when Keren started to use *afa* 'fly' (past, feminine, singular) for 'a bird':

(7) 15(28): In parent's room; M and K are looking at a Chinese illustration of a tree and some flying birds. This illustration is hung on the wall.

K: *?ec/ac/*
  '(a) tree, (a) tree'
M: *?ec, ?efo ?at roa ?ec, keren?/*
  '(a) tree, where (do) you see (a) tree, Keren?'
K: *afa/*
  'fly' (past, feminine, singular)
M: *afa, cipor afa alyad ?a?ec!/*
  'fly, (a) bird is flying nearby the tree!'
K: *afa/*
  'fly' (past, feminine, singular)
  (while pointing to the picture of the bird)

Throughout the following eight weeks there was no indication that Keren was using *afa* as an action word. In the last week of the study, in exactly the same context as the one described above, Keren produced the word *afa* in a two-word utterance. This was the first occurrence of the word that could have indicated that *afa* was an action word. (It is not certain that *afa* means 'fly' in the following example, however, because occurrences of old words juxtaposed with new ones for the same referents were noted frequently in the data. See more on that phenomenon in Dromi and Fishelzon, 1986.)

(8)   17(16): In parents' room.
       M: *kereni ma ro?im šam batmuna?/*
          'Kereni what (do we) see there in the picture?'
       K: *afa/*
          'fly' (past, feminine, singular)
       M: *mi afa?/*
          'Who is flying?'
       K: *cipor afa/*
          '(a) bird (is) flying'

In conclusion, my findings show that there is a high degree of correspondence between the child's categories of reference and adult part-of-speech membership. In most cases the child carries out a successful analysis of the contexts in which new words are modeled for her, and only rarely fails to identify the adult's intended referent for a word. When she does fail, she uses the new word indeterminantly for a while, or extends it to unrelated referents which constitute components of the context in which she learned the word.

Further research is needed to determine the ideal conditions for learning new words. More specifically, the possibility that linguistic factors play an important role in establishing the match between a word and its intended referent must be tested. Below we consider some evidence that linguistic factors may help to establish a good match between adult parts-of-speech and child categories of reference.

Why are so many early words nouns or object words?

It has been reported that most of children's first words are nouns in adult speech (e.g., Farwell, 1976, 1977; Gentner, 1978, 1982; Goldin-Meadow, Seligman and Gelman, 1976). The proportion of nouns in Keren's corpus of one-word utterances was presented in Table 6 above. This table shows that although all six categories of adult parts-of-speech were represented in the child's lexicon, the majority of the words (61 per cent) were indeed nouns in the adult language. The other grammatical categories were far less well-represented in the lexicon: verbs (13 per cent); non-conventional (10 per cent); functors (6 per cent); adjectives (4 per cent); and adverbs (3 per cent). Figure 5 shows the distribution of nouns, verbs, and non-conventional words by the eight months of study.

There is a striking similarity between the distribution of categories in Keren's early Hebrew and the figures presented in Gentner (1982) for other

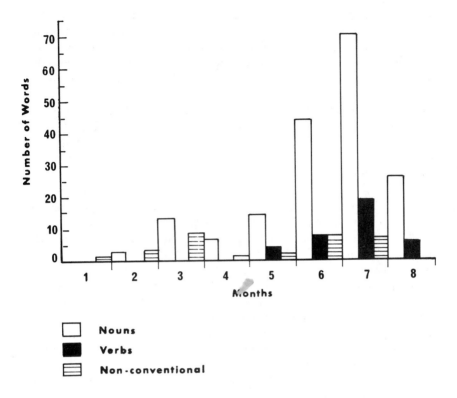

Figure 5.   The distribution of nouns, verbs and non-conventional words, by month of study

languages. In Hebrew, as in the other languages (i.e., English, Japanese, German, Kaluli and Turkish), nouns in adult speech constitute the largest category of words learned by the child, with the acquisition of verbs lagging behind. The nouns learned by Keren were, moreover, impressively similar to those reported to predominate in the early lexicons of children acquiring English: they related to animals, foods, names of individual people, body parts, toys, and other household accessories that can easily be manipulated (see the content analysis of the lexicon in Chapter 9 above).

The role of linguistic and cognitive factors and the interactions between them have commonly been invoked to explain why some forms are learned earlier than others (e.g., Brown, 1973; Carey, 1982; Dromi, 1979; Gentner, 1982; and Slobin, 1973). Gentner (1982) proposed that the fact that children acquire nouns before verbs reflects the relative importance of the conceptual complexity in determining the order in which new words are learned. She pointed out that objects, unlike actions, are concrete and tangible, and argued that this facilitates learning their names. In order to rule out the possibility that the earlier acquisition of object words is due to linguistic rather than cognitive factors, Gentner used cross-linguistic evidence. She argued that since languages differ with respect to the relative frequency with which nouns are used, the relative morphological transparency of nouns, word-order rules, and the teaching routines of parents, none of the above factors can account for the early emergence of nouns in all the languages studied.

I find Gentner's conclusion that cognitive rather than linguistic consider-ations explain the late acquisition of verb forms much too radical. I would argue, for example, that the strategy of dealing with each contributing factor one at a time is inadequate. In order to test the effects of contributing variables on the child's rate and pattern of learning new words, one should examine how these variables interact with each other in the learning contexts. The present study provides several grounds for questioning the suggestion that verbs are learned more slowly than nouns because of the child's cognitive difficulties in conceptualizing actions and identifying refer-ents for action terms. On the contrary, I found that Keren encoded action concepts early on, but she did so initially by using nominal terms in adult speech or words with double meaning. Thus, her first action term was, in fact, the social word *toda* 'thank you' (038) which she uttered when she wanted other people to transfer certain objects to her hands. The word *haw* 'bow-wow' (001) was used for barking and dogs; the word *pipi* 'urine' (009) was used for the potty, toilet, any undressed portion of the body, all kinds of wet or dirty objects and for the action of taking off clothes. In sum, words for actions were recorded in the diary from an early period of production, long before the first verb forms were acquired.

As soon as the first verbs entered Keren's vocabulary, they were used appropriately and consistently as words for actions. Tables 7 and 8 demon-strate that verbs showed a complete match with the category of action words. Linguistic rather than cognitive factors may explain the relative ease with which Keren mapped the Hebrew verbs onto their action referents. Most of the verbs used by the child as action words took the linguistic form of either imperative or infinitive. It is revealing that the child picked up the relatively complex morphological constructs first and did not prefer one of the tensed verb forms (Berman, 1985; Berman and Dromi, 1984). I hypothesize that the infinitive and imperative forms of the verbs, which were modeled to the child quite often (e.g., *at roca le?exol/lištot/lir?ot/lilboš/* '(Do) you want to eat', 'to drink', 'to see', 'to wear'; or: *kxi, tar?i, titni, xapsi*, 'take', 'show', 'give', 'look for' (all in feminine gender)) and which also took constant manifes-tations across various contexts, were easily learned because they all shared overt and consistent morphological markers (i.e., the prefix *li-* or the suffix *-i*). It is possible that the regular and repeated experiences of the child with a set of similar forms enhanced her realization that these forms encode actions rather than object concepts (see Schlesinger, 1982).

In order to test my hypothesis that, contrary to Gentner's (1982) pre-

Table 9. The number of changes in category of reference

Category	Number of Changes			
	No change	One change	Two changes	Three or more changes
Object	133	25	5	0
Action + Modifier	45	5	0	0
Social	12	4	2	0
Indeterminant	5	33	5	2

Note: This analysis is based on category membership assignment for the first week of use.

diction, action words were learned easily and were used consistently by the child throughout the period of investigation, a new score was computed for each word. This score reflects the number of changes that were recorded for the word throughout the period of investigation with respect to its membership in a given category of reference. Table 9 shows the results of this analysis. The two categories of action words and modifiers are combined into one category of "predicate terms" because they exhibited similar patterns of behavior.

A high dependency is observed between the type of word and the number of changes it underwent ($X^2 = 101.92$, d.f. = 9, p. < .001). As reported above, action words and modifiers showed the fewest changes. In fact, the vast majority of them (90 per cent) *never* changed their class membership, and the few words that did change category did so only once. In comparison, an average of 25 per cent of all object words, social, and indeterminant words changed their class membership. Most of these underwent a number of changes. This finding indicates that the mapping of action words was relatively easy for Keren.

In two studies, Tanouye (1979) and McCune-Nicolich (1981) reported that action words entered the lexicons of their subjects earlier than was expected. Tanouye, who studied Japanese children, found that nouns and verbs were acquired by the subjects at about the same time. McCune-Nicolich reported that many relational words entered the lexicons of her English-speaking subjects at the same time, and showed immediate and correct generalization to several contexts of use. These findings. together with my own observations on Hebrew, indicate that although verbs comprise a significantly smaller set of words in early lexicons, action concepts may be encoded early by forms other than verbs, and that when verb forms are acquired they are often used correctly from the outset.

Summary

Keren's vocabulary of single words consisted of words for objects, actions, and modifiers, as well as social words. It has been found that although most words showed distinct referential properties, some were initially used by Keren indeterminantly and referred to both objects and actions or objects and modifiers. This finding, which is unique to one-word-stage speakers, is highly significant. It shows that initially the child's linguistic system is not as differentiated as that of the adult. It also indicates that over time and with growing linguistic experience children grasp the basic distinctions that are grammaticalized in their language.

Keren's data clearly show that the structure of the linguistic input to the child and the process of matching a single form with a single aspect of the non-linguistic situation play a significant role in establishing reference. Keren reduced the size of the indeterminant category gradually, until during the last month of data collection it completely disappeared. Similarly, the clear-cut distinction between action words (verbs) and object words (nouns) was appreciated by the child during the last few weeks of research.

Very few complete mismatches of reference were noted in Keren's record. When, however, she used nouns in Hebrew as action words, the mismatch could be explained by looking at the non-linguistic contexts in which these words were modeled to the child. It is argued that when such contexts are opaque, the child may match a nominal term with a related action concept.

Keren's class of object words greatly exceeded other classes of words. The category of Hebrew verbs was considerably smaller in size than the class of Hebrew nouns. Moreover, this class emerged relatively late. I reported that prior to the acquisition of verb forms Keren used nouns or double-reference words to encode actions. When she acquired verb forms she initially expressed their infinitive or imperative forms even when tensed forms were required. Yet, although the category of verbs in Keren's speech was indeed much smaller than that of nouns, it should be noted that these forms were used correctly by the child from their outset.

Further studies are needed in order better to account for the striking differences in the relative proportion of nouns and verbs in the early productive lexicons of one-word-stage children. Closer analyses of the frequency of these forms in the linguistic input, detailed descriptions of the teaching routines of mothers and the non-linguistic contexts in which each word is learned (e.g. Braunwald, 1978; Ninio and Snow, in press) may bring us closer to the answers we seek. Detailed analyses of the processes involved in learning the meanings of new words can also reveal how elaborate the child's representation of a single word's meaning must be before this word is used productively. Experimental investigations in which novel names for objects and for actions are taught to very young subjects (e.g. Carey and Bartlett, 1978; Soja, Carey and Spelke, 1985) may reveal initial strategies that children apply in learning nouns and verbs. Such experimental evidence is needed in order to explore whether at the one-word stage the underlying semantic representations of these two classes of words are similar or not.

11 *The extension behaviors of early words*

A major goal of this case-study investigation was systematically to examine the question of how the young child matches words with their underlying meanings. I agree with Anglin (1977) that a clear distinction must be made between the intension and the extension of each term of reference. Since I strongly believe that the intensions of first words are untraceable (see the discussion in Chapter 4), I focused my analysis on extension behaviors.

A record was made of the initial extension of each new comprehensible word produced by my subject, and the changes in behaviors that were noted over time in repeated uses of each word. The entire lexicon of single words was broken down into four main categories of extension: underextension, regular extension, overextension, and unclassified. Each category was further divided into several subtypes (see the full set of operational definitions in Chapter 8 above).

An overview of the findings on extension types

The extension behaviors of 276 words in Keren's complete lexicon of 337 words were examined throughout the period of investigation. As stated in the previous chapter, 61 words were excluded from certain analyses because they were recorded only during the first week of their emergence, and therefore could not be subjected to comprehensive repeated analysis. Each of the 276 words was scored repeatedly, once for every week of the study. During any given week, a word could be assigned to any one of the four major classes of extension based on the descriptions of the different contexts in which the word was used during that week. The data for this procedure came from diary entries and transcribed audio-recorded utterances (see Table 4 for an illustration of how these two sources of information were co-ordinated).

Table 10 summarizes the findings on the relative distribution of the child's words in each of the four main categories of extension and each of the subcategories. The counts of relative frequency are based on the complete week-by-week record of coded data. When a single word exhibited more

Table 10.   Summary of extension types and their frequencies

Underextension		Regular extension	Overextension		Unclassified	
Object	42		Same referent	31	Incomplete	12
Person	20		Classic	36	Association	24
Time/context	17		Complexive	10	Ambiguity	28
Place	8				Empty words	39
					No referent	17
					Change – referent	2
Total no. of words	85	212	77		82	

Note: Numbers do not equal totals since each word could be assigned to more than a single category in different weeks.

than one pattern of behavior (during different weeks of study), it was counted more than once. This means that the total number of assignments to the categories of extension is greater than the number of words acquired by the child.

Each of the four categories of extension was represented in the sample of 276 different words. As indicated in the table, the largest group of words (75 per cent) exhibited regular range of use at one time or another during the one-word period. The other three categories were represented more or less equally, each covering 30 per cent of the total number of words analysed. That is to say, only about one third of the words acquired by Keren ever showed (during a single week or longer) underextension, unclassified behavior, or overextension. The breakdown of each category into its sub-types is, as expected, uneven. In the category of underextension we see that the majority of instances recorded were those which indicated a restriction to a single instance of a class of objects (e.g., *avizia* (*televizia*) 'television' (229) said only while pointing to our television set at home, and never when being asked about television in other places or while looking at picture books). Restrictions to person, context and time, and place were also noted for a number of words (e.g., *uci* (*ruci*) '(to) run' (172), said only when Keren was the agent; *?even* '(a) stone' (135), said only while throwing a stone; *yesena* (*yešena*) 'is sleeping' (307), used only when lying down in her own bed, and never on the sofa or in her parents' bed).

Forty per cent of the words that were ever overextended by Keren were classified as overextensions to the same referent only. These words were consistently recorded many times in relation to only one inappropriate referent. They were never overextended to other referents. Examples from this category are:

> *pe* '(a) mouth' (054), used for mouth and mother's lipstick;
> *mod (la?amod)* 'to stand' (067), used for standing and for climbing up;
> *na?al* '(a) shoe' (018), used also for socks;
> *mici* 'a cat's name' (206), extended to a tape recorder.

It is interesting to note that systematic overextensions to only one irrelevant referent have (to my knowledge) never been reported in the literature. One possible explanation for this is that the phenomenon was idiosyncratic to my subject. This seems unlikely, however, since 31 different action and object words were recorded as showing the same pattern of extension.

The second subcategory of overextension was the largest. Forty-seven per cent of the words showed "classic" overextension and were applied to different referents on the basis of one or a number of shared attributes. No attempt was made to define the basis for application, e.g., as perceptual, functional, or emotional (see Rescorla, 1980, on the different bases for application). Some examples of words that were classified in this category are:

> *mayim* 'water' (025), which was applied to all liquids;
> *?anuka (xanuka)*, 'the name of a Jewish holiday' (229), used for candles and
> other toys that are played with during this holiday in Israel;
> *ulam (sulam)* '(a) ladder' (269), used for all elevated places;
> *ses-ses (šeš)* 'the number six' (238), used for every typed figure on a page.

This subcategory of overextension is compatible with Clark's (1973, 1975) theory, which predicts that words will initially be used broadly, due to lexical entries that are only partially filled in.

The last class of overextension, "complexive", was also the smallest, containing only ten words (13 per cent of the words that were ever overextended). A word in this class was overextended to a variety of referents that did not necessarily share attributes with each other (cf. Bowerman, 1978). Examples taken from Keren's record include:

> *parpar* '(a) butterfly' (152), which was used for stickers, round objects,
> towels, and coloured spots on flat surfaces;
> *peca* '(a) sore/wound' (039), which was extended to knives, spots of dirt, and
> scotchtape;
> *avizia (televizia)* 'television' (229), which was extended to radios, electric
> outlets on the wall, the sound of people, and small electric appliances
> especially those used by her father.

The low frequency of "complexive" words in the present corpus may be related to the relatively early stage of production studied. Bowerman (1978) observed such uses in the speech of her two daughters only a few months after the beginning of the single-word stage. The fact that so few "complex-ive" overextensions were recorded in the early months of Keren's speech supports Bowerman's original claim that complexive uses of words are not necessarily signs of an immature linguistic behavior, rather they may reflect a quite developed pattern of word application which results from a detailed analysis of the word's underlying meaning.

The largest subcategory of unclassified words (48 per cent) consisted of empty words. These were produced by the child in more or less acceptable contexts, but it was impossible to conclude from the contexts of use that the child really knew even approximately what the words meant in adult speech. Some examples of empty words included:

?avoda 'work' (090);
kesef 'money/coins' (221);
?abaita 'to the home' (150);
nora nora 'very' (214);
atnudnik 'you (are a) nag' (174);
mipo 'from here' (318).

The word *kesef* 'money/coins', for example, was produced while playing with my purse. There was no evidence in the data to show that Keren used the word for either the coins or the purse itself. The word *?avoda* 'work' (090) was produced very often in acceptable contexts. Keren said the word after being asked about absent people, who in many cases were indeed at work. Note, however, that although the child used the word "appropriately", one could not conclude that she knew its adult meaning. The following conver-sation illustrates this point.

(1) 15(18): In K's room; K has just woken up from her afternoon nap. She is still playing in her crib. M has just returned from work. K does not know that her mother is at home waiting for her to wake up. M is sitting in the living room.
K: *miya!/x/x*
(the name of K's caretaker)
M: *šalom, kereni, ima babait!/*
'Hello, Kereni, Mother (is) at home'
(M is still out of K's sight)
K: *ima!/imi!/ ima le!/*
Mommy, mommy + diminutive
'Mommy, Mommy, Mommy!'
M: *?ifo: miryam, kereni?/*
'Where (is) Miryam, Kereni?'
(M enters K's room)
K: *?ein!/?avoda!/*
'allgone, work'

From conversations such as the above I could not reach a decision as to the meaning of the word *?avoda* for Keren. Was it her word for the concept "not here with me", was it an automatic unanalysed response to the question

"Where is X?" (e.g., Ruth Clark, 1976, 1978), or was it perhaps Keren's way of saying "has just left"?

Most of the empty words that were used by Keren share the property of having been modeled to the child quite frequently. Many come from speech routines, e.g., *aba ?alax la?avoda* 'Daddy went to work'; *hine higana ?abaita* 'here we are at home'; *?ani nora nora ?aiefa* 'I am very very tired'; or *kereni ?at-nudnik* 'Kereni, you are a nag'. I suspect that Keren picked up these words and started to use them long before she carried out any analysis of their exact meaning, and it is for this reason that they are included in the category of unclassified words.

The second largest subcategory of unclassified words (34 per cent) was that of ambiguous words. These were used by the child for actions and objects that were somehow related to each other. The difficulty in determining the meaning of these words stems from the fact that it was impossible to decide exactly to which aspect of the situation the word referred. The manner in which the child used the word indicated that she saw some general connection between a given word and several contextually related referents. For example, Keren's word *hita* (said very often by Keren's caretaker, usually while going out for the daily walk) (010) was used by Keren for a hat, a stroller, the motion of moving objects back and forth, the action of walking outside, and to indicate that somebody was going to leave the house. The word *pipi* 'urine' (009) was used for a potty, the toilet, wet diapers, the action of taking off clothes, when exposing covered parts of the body, while pointing to or touching undressed dolls or parents, and for water dropping from toys and water faucets. Another interesting example of a word that was used ambiguously for a long time was Keren's word *dio* 'giddi-up' (015), which was used for horses, the action of riding, any repetitive bouncing movement, and while sitting with two legs apart on a parent's lap, on toys, and on our heater.

The subclass of Unclassified – overextension or association included 24 words (29 per cent of all unclassified words). The main difficulty with the interpretation of these words was to determine whether the word was used in order to indicate that the child appreciated a relationship between her stable referent for the word and the entity indicated, or whether the word was overextended by the child as a *label* for the entity indicated. In some cases the word initially showed a period of regular extension, but at a certain point the child started to produce it in a new and "inappropriate" context. It was quite easy to identify the new entity in connection with which the word was used, but it was completely unclear whether the extensional meaning of the word included this entity as a new referent or not.

Let us consider some examples. Keren used the word *nad-ned* (said to Keren to accompany the motion of swinging) (023) for a period of three weeks only while she was swinging in the playground. When she started to use it when pointing to several pictures of swings in her picture book I could

Table 11. Some descriptions of contexts in which Keren used the word *dod* '(an) uncle' (051) (= any unfamiliar man)

---

(1) 14(7): On the stairway; M and K are climbing the steps; M hears loud voices of some neighbors who are conversing upstairs, out of sight. K says: dod/ '(an) uncle'.

(2) 14(10): In the kitchen; K is sitting on the floor eating fruit. M hears rhythmic sounds (coming from the kitchen of our neighbor). K stops eating, approaches M, and says: dod/ '(an) uncle'. M responds: bum bum mišehu dofek baxuc/ 'bum bum somebody is knocking outside'. K says: dod/ '(an) uncle'.

(3) 14(10): In the living room; K, F and M are watching television. When there is a closeup of a male face on the screen K says: dod/ '(an) uncle'.

(4) 15: In the living room; Merav (K's aunt) and two of her friends (a man and his son) have just left the house. M, K, and F are sitting on the couch. Immediately after the door is shut K says: dodim/ 'uncles' (it is the first recording of the plural masculine form of the word dod).

(5) 16(1): In K's room; K and M are playing on the rug. M hears the noise of a lawn mower coming from outside. K says: dod/ '(an) uncle'. M responds: dod, ken dod ose ra?aš ra?aš, naxon?/ '(an) uncle, yes, an uncle is making noise, noise, true?' K says: dod/ '(an) uncle'. She starts to whine. M asks: at roca lexapes et ?adod/ 'do you want to look for the uncle?' K says: dod/ '(an) uncle'. M opens the window. K does not come closer to it; she makes no attempt to look for the person.

(6) 16(11): On the porch; K and M are looking outside. K sees a car passing by with two people sitting in it. K says: oto/dod/aba/ '(a) car, (an) uncle, daddy'.

---

not decide whether she was saying 'a swing' (i.e., labeling the object) or 'for swinging' (i.e., predicating an action connected with the object). A similar example involved Keren's uses of the word *?inok* 'a baby' (064) when pointing to a crying child. It was very difficult to decide whether this word meant 'crying' or '(like) a baby'.

One of the best examples of this category is the word *dod* '(an) uncle' (051), which is used in the Hebrew addressed to young children as a label for a male stranger (= somebody whom you do not know). The two earliest recorded uses of the word *dod* occurred in imitation. We were looking at Keren's picture album and, while pointing to one of the pictures, I said *Kereni! hine dod/* 'Kereni here (is an) uncle'. Keren said *dod* just after me while pointing at the same picture. Table 11 presents several descriptions of subsequent contexts in which *dod* was recorded. On most of these occasions I could not determine whether the child was talking about the noises she heard or about the people who may have initiated these noises.

In summary, the subcategory of association or overextension included words that were likely to be either overextensions and/or associations. As was true for all other unclassified words, these words occurred frequently; nevertheless, their meanings could not be determined.

When and for how long in the history of a word is it misused?

The question of when in the history of a single word certain extension behaviors are recorded is of significance for two main reasons: (a) since

Table 12.   The timing of recording and the statistics on length of period in weeks for three extension categories

Extension type	First week of occurrence	Intermediate weeks	Last week of study	Mean	S.D.	Mode	Range
Under-extension	(77)	(11)	(15)	2	2	1	1–10
Over-extension	(22)	(55)	(24)	5	6	1	1–21
Unclass-ified	(52)	(30)	(36)	7	7	1	1–24

Note: Numbers in parentheses indicate number of words.

various theories on the acquisition of word-meaning make different predictions about the course of extension (i.e., whether meaning will develop from the general to the specific or vice versa), the empirical data can be used either to support or to refute opposing claims; and (b) the measurement of extension behaviors at different time points in the history of a single word may reflect the effect of time and the overall linguistic proficiency of the speaker in the use of a given word.

Table 12 presents the distribution of the major extension classes at three points in time: the first week in which the word was recorded; the time span from the second week of use to the one before last week of study (i.e., intermediate weeks); and finally, the last week of investigation, namely week number 32. The extension behaviors of words during intermediate weeks represent only those instances in which specific behavior was recorded in later weeks but not during the week in which the word was first produced. Again, since each word can enter different extension categories at different times (but not concurrently), the numbers do not add up to a total of 276 words. The length of time during which a word displayed a given behavior appears in the right-hand columns of the table. It is clear that there was great variability among the different classes and within each class with respect to this measure. Within-class variability was particularly noted in categories other than underextension, as can be seen by the relatively greater standard deviations compared to the values of the means.

Table 12 shows that many more underextensions were recorded during the initial uses of a word than during subsequent weeks. Moreover, a word was underextended in most cases for a short period of time (63 out of 85 underextended words exhibited this behavior for one week only). The longest period recorded for underextension was ten weeks, and only two words exhibited this irregular pattern.

These findings in regard to underextension support Anglin's (1977), and Kay and Anglin's (1982) claim that certain words are learned by the young child as labels for particular instances. This result also indicates that underextension can be detected even in the course of a natural investigation of early speech. Experimental designs do not seem, therefore, to be the exclusive tool for revealing underextension. The finding that it is a short-lived behavior may explain why underextension has received so little attention in naturalistic studies, and why it has mainly been noted by parent-diarists (e.g., Bloom, 1973; Bowerman, 1976; Reich, 1976).

The fact that only some words showed underextension in production, and that those that did were generalized to other referents quite quickly, is compatible with Reich's (1976) claim that underextension is primarily a phenomenon of comprehension rather than of production. However, Reich's (1976) argument that the meanings of almost all words develop from the specific to the general is more far-reaching than the evidence to date can support. It is a very complicated (and perhaps even impossible) task to measure systematically the development of comprehension in very young children. Given the lack of comprehensive empirical evidence, I am rather skeptical about the generality of Reich's model concerning the development of comprehension (see also Barrett, 1986).

The fact that underextension was recorded mainly during the first week of production is quite revealing. It shows that the strategy of pairing a word with a single referent might be an operative strategy that the child follows in acquiring meaning. Thus, my findings on underextension, coupled with the speculation that some words show it only in comprehension, provide strong support for the theoretical models of meaning which predict a developmental course of specific-to-general rather than the other way round. Of the models reviewed in Chapter 5 above, only Bowerman's and Schlesinger's make any explicit prediction that this will be the common pattern observed for newly acquired words.

In Clark's (1973, 1975) theory of the acquisition of word-meaning, the phenomenon of overextension is invoked to support the claim that meanings develop from the general to the specific. The present analyses show not only that in Keren's case only a subset of 77 words (28 per cent) ever showed this behavior, but that for most words it was recorded during the later weeks of use and almost never during the first week of a word's emergence.

The percentage of overextensions obtained in the present investigation is somewhat lower than the percentage of overextensions (33 per cent) computed for data pooled from six children in Rescorla (1980), and a little higher than the figure (20 per cent) given for two children in Gruendel (1977). These discrepancies may be ascribed to methodological differences. Rescorla (1980) computed percentages for the six children as a group, and did not report on individual differences. In addition, she defined overextensions more broadly than in the present study, and included in this category *all misuses of words* (e.g., unclassified associations (as I have termed them), or "predicate terms" in her terminology). Gruendel's report that overextensions were extremely rare in her sample was based on video-recorded data. I suspect that her methods of data collection, which involved filming children in one place for short periods of time, may have limited the number of opportunities the children had to use words inappropriately (see, for example, my discussions of Keren's restricted behavior during video-recordings in Chapter 7 above).

Most of Keren's overextensions (74 per cent) were recorded after an initial period of correct application. This finding shows that before extending a new word the child typically achieves a certain degree of familiarity with it. Contrary to Clark, then, very few words are initially used broadly and only later more narrowly defined until their meanings coincide with those of adults. Schlesinger's (1982) and Bowerman's (1978) theoretical models both predict the emergence of late overextensions. While in Schlesinger's model late overextensions are treated as empirical evidence for the transition from the initial phase of word-referent pairing to the more advanced level of labeling a class of instances, in Bowerman's conceptualization late overextensions reflect the child's tendency to decompose and recompose underlying elements in the representation of the prototypical examplar. As we shall see below, it is possible that both processes explain why overextensions are recorded rather late in the one-word stage.

The relatively high proportion of words which showed unclassified behaviors throughout the period of study (30 per cent of all the words in Keren's lexicon) is quite striking. Admittedly, this finding invites skepticism as to the precision of the classification system. That is, if so many words could not be assigned to one or another of the better-specified categories in the system, perhaps it was a poor system for classifying words according to their extensional behaviors.

The findings shown in Table 10 above indicate that only a minority of unclassified words were assigned to this class as the result of measurement difficulties. Twelve words were assigned to the category because the record of their use included one or more entries that were incomplete. In most cases a decision could not be reached only for the week in which an incomplete entry was the only one recorded for the word. Therefore, the word was assigned to the category only once. For a large body of information such as the one studied here, twelve words with an occasional incomplete entry (only 15 per cent of all unclassified words) is a very low proportion. Therefore, I argue that neither lack of information nor inadequacies of measurement can be invoked to explain why so many unclassified words were identified. Rather, I suggest that in most cases a word was assigned to the category of unclassified because it genuinely showed an inconsistent and complicated pattern of extension that was difficult to interpret.

Seventeen words, or 21 per cent of the category of unclassified words, were non-conventional. The relatively high proportion of words of this type is directly traceable to how decisions about the extensional behaviors of words were made. All the definitions of extensions (presented in Chapter 8 above) involve comparisons between adult and child usage. Therefore, the meanings of words in adult Hebrew had to be considered. Since non-conventional words lack an agreed-upon adult meaning, it was sometimes difficult to interpret their meaning for the child.

Let me illustrate this point with the following example. The word *ham* (said by the caretaker while feeding Keren) (009) was used by Keren for foods, for expressing her wish to eat, for describing the action of eating or inserting objects into her mouth, and for all kinds of dishes and pots. It was impossible to assign this word to the category of overextension because (a) the word has no conventional meaning in Hebrew, and (b) Keren herself never used the word in a more specific manner that would indicate that it had a primary meaning. In the absence of evidence for a conventional or primary meaning, it was impossible to argue that the child overextended the meaning of the word beyond its regular scope of reference. The following recorded conversations between Keren and myself show that I could generally tell that the word was related to food, mouth, and feeding. It was, however, impossible to determine the exact meaning of the word for the child and how the child's meaning was related to that of the adult.

(1)   15(20): In the living room.
        K: *?am/*
            ?
        M: *nelex sof sof lamitbax?/*
            we will go finally to the kitchen?
            '(Shall) we go finally to the kitchen?'
            ma ?at roca le?exol?/
            what you want to eat
            'What do you want to eat?'
        K: *?am/*
            ?
        M: *ma le?exol?/*
            what to eat
            'What (do you want) to eat?'

(2)   16(17): In K's room. K found M's lipstick on the floor. She is trying to open it. After she fails she hands it to M.
        K: *ima/pe/hape*
            'Mommy, mouth, the mouth'
        M: *naxon ze lape/ lapel hine ima sama le kereni sfaton/*
            true this for mouth, for the mouth, here mommy put to Keren lipstick
            'Correct, this is for the mouth, here Mommy puts lipstick on Kereni'
        K: *ima/*
            'Mommy'
        M: *ken sfaton/*
            'Yes, lipstick'
        K: *?am ?am/*
            ?   ?
            (K is playing with M's lipstick, bringing it closer to her lips.)

Only two non-conventional words that were initially used ambiguously by the child were subsequently used in a more restricted way. These were *haw* 'bow-wow' (001), which after the acquisition of the word *kelev* '(a) dog' (336) was said only for barking; and the word *?upa* '?' (010), which initially was used for round objects and abrupt contact with the floor, while Keren's word *?adur (kadur)* '(a) ball/(a) pill' (201) was used only for pills, and was subsequently used for jumping only when *adur (kadur)* took its conventional double meaning of both '(a) ball' and '(a) pill'. The fact that only two non-conventional words stopped being produced for a variety of different referents shows that the child's rules for applying these words were consistent. It seems that most non-conventional words were in fact used systematically by the child to refer to several different aspects of the same context.

The conclusion reached, then, is that the category "unclassified" was not an artifact of measurement. Most words were assigned to this category not because of lack of information, but rather because of difficulties in interpretation that were directly related to the child's tendency to use a single term for more than a single aspect or one constituent of the same situation.

Table 12 shows that, for most unclassified words, recording started with the initial uses of the word. Only in 30 instances were unclassified behaviors recorded during intermediate weeks for words which had previously been used "correctly" by the child. We see in Table 12 that in general the unclassified behavior of words decreased with time, but that for single words it persisted for a good number of weeks (mean score = seven weeks). Even during the last week of study, 36 words still showed unclassified behaviors. This figure, however, is very low compared to the figure of 197 words which was obtained for regular extension during the same week. The category of unclassified behavior is of significance to us since it reflects a linguistic behavior which is not observed for mature speakers. I will therefore return to a discussion of its implications in the last section of this chapter which examines the effect of time (or child's age) on the extension behaviors observed for new words. Space is also devoted to this topic in the next chapter which examines the generality of the unclassified phenomenon.

Extension profiles of the different words

The coding system used in the present investigation made it possible to generate (with the aid of a computer analysis) a closed set of all the extension profiles that were present in the data. Each profile is constructed of the combination of extension types and represents the various transitions that words underwent over time as manifested in the way they were used by the child. Table 13 shows the different extensions that were represented in the sample of 276 words, along with the relative frequencies of each. Each pattern is symbolized as a sequence of letters representing the different

Table 13. The frequencies of extension profiles of words

Initial under-extension		Initial regular extension		Initial over-extension		Initial unclass-ified	
Profile	Frequency	Profile	Frequency	Profile	Frequency	Profile	Frequency
D	13	R	98	O	8	U	17
DR	35	RO	1	OR	7	UR	10
DO	3	RS	1	OU	1	UO	1
DU	3	RDR	3	ORO	1	US	1
DRO	1	ROR	7	OUO	1	UDR	3
DRU	1	RUR	4	OROR	1	UDU	1
DRS	1	RUO	2	ORUR	1	URU	2
DOD	1	RORU	1	OUOU	1	UOR	2
DOR	3	RUOR	1	ORUROROR	1	UOU	7
DUD	1	ROROR	4			UOS	1
DUR	5	ROUOR	1			UROR	1
DROR	2	RUROR	1			UODO	1
DODR	1	RUROUR	1			UDROU	1
DODO	1					UROUR	1
DOUR	1					UOROR	1
DUOR	1					UOUOR	1
DUOU	1					UOUOUO	1
DOROR	2						
DURORO	1						

Note: Each extension profile represents the changes over time in the extension of a word. Capital letters represent the different categories of extension: D = underextension, R = regular extension, O = overextension, U = unclassified, S = stopped being produced. Thus, for example, the profile DRO represents the case of a word which was initially underextended, then regularly extended and finally overextended by the child.

categories of week-by-week extension behaviors, with left-to-right arrangement reflecting changes across time. Although each profile shows the sequence of changes in the category membership of a word, it does not show how long a word exhibited each extensional behavior. The results presented in Table 13 show that there were a great many different routes to meaning – 58 profiles in all.

The number of changes shown by the different words in the sample ranged from none to six. There were more words in the sample that showed consistent extension behavior than those which manifested changes. Additionally, most words that first showed underextended, overextended or unclassified behaviors were regularly extended immediately thereafter. A close examination of the transitions presented in Table 13 reveals that if underextension occurred beyond the initial phase of use for a new word, it commonly occurred after either regular extension or unclassified behavior and was very rarely recorded after a period of overextension. Conversely, a word that was initially underextended was rarely subsequently overextended. Words that were initially categorized as unclassified very frequently showed a period of overextension before being used regularly. The systematic patterns observed indicate that the categories devised for this analysis did indeed have psychological reality for the child. For example, the distinction made between the categories of underextension and unclassified is supported by the findings that: (a) a word that was initially attached to a specific referent very rarely showed subsequent unclassified behaviors, and (b) most unclassified behaviors were recorded for words only during initial use. This conclusion supports the view that extension behaviors of words do reflect the underlying structure of their meaning representation.

A surprisingly large number of words (98, or 35 per cent of the total number of words analysed) were classified as exhibiting regular extension from the very first week of their production and throughout the one-word stage. Two hundred and twelve words (75%) showed a regular range of application at one time or another. During the last week of study, 197 words (71 per cent of all words used by the child) were applied regularly (see also Table 12 above).

My attempts to look for regularities to explain the early extension behaviors of words were not very successful. I could not identify any consistent patterns that could explain why some words were used regularly and others were not. Consider these examples from the list of Keren's regularly extended words:

> *mina* '(a) tangerine' (110);
> *rak* 'only' (328);
> *vuv* (*zvuv*) '(a) fly' (101);
> *usi* (*kuši*) '(a) dog's name' (168);
> *tuki* '(a) parrot' (295);
> *evet* 'to sit' (133);
> *dai* 'no more' (36);
> *kaxa* 'like this' (070);
> *?apit* (*kapit*) '(a) spoon' (045).

This list contains early- and late-acquired words; action, object, and social words; words that were learned in the home and words that were learned outside; and, finally, words that were modeled frequently and others that were modeled very rarely.

It is interesting that the earliest word that was recorded as showing regular extension during the very first week of application was the relational word *dai* 'no more' (036). Bloom (1973) has argued that from an early phase in the one-word stage children verbally express the semantic notions of existence, disappearance, and recurrence. The words *hine* 'here' (016), *?ein* 'all gone' (017), and *dai* 'no more' (036) were all learned very early by the child. Note that from its first applications the word *dai* 'no more' (036) was used as a predicate term. This finding supports my previous claim that there is no evidence in my data that predicate terms are more complex for the child than object terms.

The observation that such a high proportion of words in the productive lexicon of my subject showed regular extension is strong evidence for the *tacit learning of meaning*. If so many words are used by the child correctly and flexibly right from the start, then an active process of establishing connections between words and non-linguistic cues must precede early productions. However, I agree with Carey (1982) that we are far from understanding how children go about matching words and concepts. This is obvious when we consider the fact that categories other than regular extension were also represented in my sample as a whole, and that altogether regular extensions constituted only 65 per cent of the cases. My interpretation of the above findings leads me to the conclusion that while, as some researchers have argued, certain words are learned as labels for existing concepts (e.g., Clark, 1983a; Nelson, 1974), others are used by the child long before a solid concept is formed. As Schlesinger (1982) argues, it is quite reasonable to assume that early concepts are being formed throughout the process of learning the lexical meanings of words.

What are the devices that help children to establish connections between words and meanings? Some researchers have hypothesized that syntactic knowledge helps the child in determining the possible meanings of words (e.g., Brown, 1957; Carey, 1982; Katz, Baker and Macnamara, 1974). Ninio (1980) and Ninio and Bruner (1978) have proposed that mothers make unconscious but very intensive and systematic attempts to indicate the referents of the new words they use, and that these efforts explain how children identify referents. Veneziano (1981) has argued that the mother's responses to the productions of the child determine the future range of application of these words. She presents many examples to show how mothers' interpretations of children's early words may serve as instructional devices for teaching the meanings of the words.

In this regard, the finding that 276 words of one child showed as many as 58 different patterns of extension is intriguing. It indicates that different words in the child's lexicon take different routes as their meanings develop. Several variables may contribute to the diversity of patterns. I would assume that intrinsic factors, such as the conceptual load of a term, the frequency with which it is modeled to the child, the characteristics of the linguistic and non-linguistic contexts for using the word in adult speech, the attempts of the mother ostensively to define the referent for the word, and finally the child's age and linguistic experience at the time of acquiring a new word, play significant roles in determining the initial and subsequent extension behavior of a new word.

The effect of time on strategies of meaning acquisition

The various analyses of the extension behaviors of first words (as manifested at different time points during the one-word period) call for a direct test of the

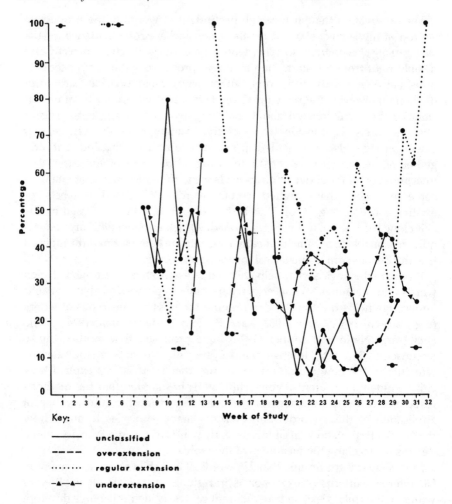

Figure 6.   The relative frequency of extension classes for new words, by week of study

effect of time (or age) on the general strategies of meaning acquisition. Does the child apply the same underlying rules for learning the meanings of words throughout the one-word period? Does the child alter his or her strategies at a specific point in time? If the child does change his or her way of treating the relationship between a word and its meaning, when does this change occur?

Data addressing these questions on the relationship between the calendaric time and the development of word-meaning are depicted in Figure 6. The relative proportion of underextended, overextended, regular extended, and unclassified words acquired by the subject in each of the 32 weeks of the study is presented, in reference only to newly acquired words for any given week.

A close inspection of Figure 6 reveals that during the one-word period the child does not employ a single strategy of meaning acquisition. It would seem that the span of time in question can be divided into two phases, each showing unique characteristics in regard to the mapping of words onto their meanings. During the first phase (weeks 1–18), the patterns of extension noted for new words are quite irregular: in some weeks all the words acquired were unclassified, in others most or all of them showed regular extension or underextension. This unpredictability, however, undergoes a change towards the 19th or 20th week of study. It becomes obvious that during the second phase of the single-word period (weeks 19–32), most new words learned (70 per cent and over) correspond somewhat to their conventional meanings. In the majority of cases, when the child started to produce a new word, it was either attached to a class of equivalent referents all belonging to the corresponding adult category for the same word (regular extension), or referred to a single referent which belonged to such a category (underextension).

The application of a new word to one correct referent or to a subset of correct referents clearly indicates that the child has succeeded in establishing a one-to-one relationship between a word and its conventional meaning. The move from underextension to regular use of a word depends on the child's generalization abilities, and, in fact, takes place in a relatively short time, as reported on the basis of the same data base in one of the earlier sections of this chapter. The tendency of new words to exhibit unclassified behaviors is significantly lower in the second phase of the stage than it is earlier. During the first phase there were several weeks in which only unclassified words were learned (e.g., 1st, 6th, and 18th weeks). This is not the case for the second phase. Between the 20th and 29th weeks of study, unclassified words constitute only 20 per cent of the new words learned. The relative proportion is even lower during the last five weeks of study.

The category of initial overextension emerges only in the second phase of study. This suggests that the application of a new word to referents that lie outside the adult category requires relatively mature processing abilities. It is plausible that only after having some experience with language can the child start to carry out detailed componential analyses of meaning. It is then that the child will extend the range of the application of a new word beyond its original scope to referents that share components with the standard referent (Bowerman, 1978). Another explanation might be that, after gaining some knowledge of the nature and function of words, children start to use existing words to express meanings for which they have not yet acquired more appropriate terms (Clark, 1983a). Given the amount of attention devoted to overextensions in the literature (e.g., Bowerman, 1978, 1980; Clark, 1973, 1975; Nelson, 1974; Rescorla, 1980, 1981), it is surprising that the relative proportion of initial overextension is so low, and that this category emerges so late.

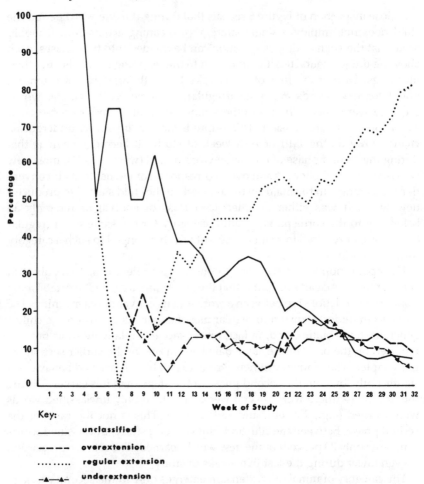

Figure 7.   The relative frequency of extension classes for all words, by week of study

The finding that three out of four extension behaviors persist across the two phases of the one-word period indicates that other factors, in addition to age, contribute in varying degrees to the observed extension behavior. Two candidates for such factors are: (a) the syntactic structure of the input to the child; and (b) mothers' practices of introducing new terms of reference. These factors will be discussed in Chapter 12.

The fact that words tend to change their extensional properties over time makes it necessary to examine not only new words, but also how all the words were used by the child in any given week. Figure 7 depicts the relative distribution of words in the four classes of extension by week of study.

The interrelationships among the four curves – representing the four classes of extension – are quite revealing. Throughout the 32 weeks of study (the one-word period), the two curves for underextension and overextension remain parallel and relatively low. In contrast, the curves for unclassified and regular extension cross each other and are negatively correlated. It is obvious that with time fewer and fewer words showed unclassified behaviors just as more and more words were used regularly by the child. The gradual and continuing increase in the number of regularly extended words is important. It clearly indicates that the child's linguistic system has undergone major change during the one-word period. It would seem that the more words that Keren learned, the more she became aware of their symbolic properties, their relationship to a class of referents (or an underlying category), and the overriding fact that they are used conventionally.

The move from the initial strategy of using words loosely to encode general intentions, inconsistent meanings, and personal experiences to the more conventional usage does not happen all at once. The child does not suddenly stop uttering unclassified words. As is shown in Figure 7, the relative number of unclassified words decreased constantly with time, whereas the number of regular extended words shows linear growth. The number of words applied regularly by the child increased considerably during the second half of the one-word period. In weeks 19–21 the number of regular extended words equals the sum of all the other three categories, and toward the end of the study it is even double or triple this number.

It seems to me that there is a great difference between the beginning and the end of the one-word period. Whereas at the beginning of the period each word is learned as a special case (and thus shows an idiosyncratic pattern of extension), at the end of the period most words that are learned are immediately attached to correct underlying categories (and thus are used flexibly in a variety of accepted contexts). During the final weeks of study, most words were used by the child in a manner quite similar to adult usage. On the basis of this finding, I conclude that the acquisition of lexical meaning is the most obvious, identifiable underlying developmental process in the one-word period. During this period, the child does not simply add words to his vocabulary. Rather, he seems to be actively involved in the exploration of the main property of words: the fact that they are associated with clear conventional meanings.

During the one-word period, the child learns how meanings are conveyed by words and which are the main principles to be followed in order to apply words correctly in the right contexts. I hypothesize that among these principles one could identify the following; (a) words convey consistent meanings; (b) words for objects are usually different from words for actions or relations; (c) words are conventional means in that they must correspond with adults' productions in both form and meaning; (d) words in most cases are associated with more than one specific referent; and (e) each pair of words in a person's productive lexicon contrast in meaning, unless these words are synonyms. My data show that the acquisition of these principles, and possibly others, is not instantaneous. Lexical meanings are learned in an ongoing developmental process which begins with the emergence of the first word and extends throughout the several months during which the child produces one word at a time.

12 *The generality of the case-study results and their*
    major theoretical implications

In the three preceding chapters we have examined in great detail the results
of my case-study investigation of the early lexical development of my own
daughter – Keren. We have considered three main aspects of early lexical
acquisition: (a) the quantitative aspect, relating to the subject's age at the
beginning and the end of the one-word period, the size of her lexicon, and
the rate at which she established it; (b) the development of word reference, or
the correspondence between words and real-world contents of objects,
actions, and relationships; and (c) the extension properties of early words as
reflected in the actual uses of these words in repeated contexts. The present
chapter surveys the major findings concerning Keren's lexical development,
tests their generalizability beyond the single subject who was studied so
extensively, and examines the various theoretical models of meaning in light
of these findings on early word use.

Summary of the findings

The entire lexicon of 337 productive words acquired by Keren, a Hebrew-
speaking child, between the ages of 10(12) and 17(23) – the one-word period –
constituted the data base for this investigation. A carefully controlled
case-study design was employed and utilized three sources of information:
handwritten diary notes, periodic audio-recordings, and video-recorded
sessions. This combination of data-collection procedures was planned to
compensate for the drawbacks inherent in each individual procedure. It also
provided the means for conducting five different measures of reliability and
validity on the data, and these factors were then found to be reasonably high.
The procedures of data analysis were all based on pre-planned, well-defined
codes, which were especially devised for measuring changes over time in the
child's overt linguistic behaviors. The referential and extensional behaviors
of each word in the child's productive lexicon were scored on a weekly basis.
The scores were then coded for further analysis by a computer.

   The results of the study provided information on a number of theoretical
issues. Evidence on the quantitative aspects of lexical acquisition was

evaluated with respect to its implications for the question of whether the one-word period is a distinct qualitative stage in language development. It was found that the one-word period has clear identifiable boundaries and an underlying characteristic – *the acquisition of lexical referential meanings*. The stage spanned about eight months during which new words were accumulated at a non-linear pace. The acquisition curve which best describes the rate of lexical growth throughout the stage is curvilinear. An abrupt change in the rate at which new words were accumulated was observed about two months before the child started to combine words productively. The lexical spurt was short, lasting for only three weeks. Following this spurt and until the end of the stage, the subject added only a few new words while improving existing lexical items in terms of both their form and their meaning. During the last few weeks of the one-word stage there was growing evidence of efficiency in establishing conventional meanings. During this period the child used most words correctly and in a wide range of contexts. She also substituted conventional Hebrew words for idiosyncratic forms.

Keren's data provide strong support for the claim that the one-word period is a distinct stage in language acquisition which manifests linguistic behaviors that are qualitatively different from those observed in the stages that precede and follow it. The stage is characterized by the acquisition of lexical meanings and the establishment of both reference and extension.

The theoretical question of whether it is possible to identify the referents of early words was also tested in this research. The code devised for the analysis of reference proved to be operative. Nearly all words could be assigned to one of four distinct categories – object words, action words, modifiers, and social words – on the basis of the description of the contexts in which they were uttered during any given week. The finding that some words, however, showed indeterminant behaviors, e.g., that they were used both as object and action words or as object words and modifiers, is significant. It shows that only with time and growing linguistic experience did the child acquire the universal distinction of verbs and nouns in her language. My results show that the linguistic distinction which is grammaticalized in all adult languages is not present at the beginning of the one-word stage, and is not acquired instantaneously. Increased experience with words and their use in repeated communicative contexts helps the child gradually appreciate this distinction and observe it.

A considerable overlap was found between child categories of reference and adult parts-of-speech (e.g., object words of the child were typically nouns in adult Hebrew). The majority of words that were learned by the subject (61 per cent) were nouns. Other grammatical categories were far less well represented in the lexicon (verbs: 13 per cent; non-conventional words: 10 per cent; functors: 6 per cent, adjectives: 4 per cent; adverbs: 3 per cent).

Although the acquisition of verbs lagged behind that of nouns, I question Gentner's (1982) explanation of this phenomenon solely on the basis of their relative conceptual complexity. My data show that Keren conceptualized actions and encoded them verbally long before she acquired her first verbs, sometimes using nouns of adult Hebrew and sometimes non-conventional words or social routine words such as "thank you". In some cases these words were classified as indeterminant, since they were used for both the action and an associated object (e.g., *ham*, used for 'to eat' and for 'food'). The results suggest that the mapping of verbs onto meanings is more precise than Gentner's model would predict. Compared to other parts-of-speech, verbs in the child's lexicon underwent the fewest changes in the category of reference to which they were assigned.

The main findings on early word extensions were as follows: four mutually exclusive categories of extension were unequally represented in the corpus. The majority of words (66 per cent) exhibited evidence of regular extension at one time or another during the one-word stage. One third of the sample of 276 words analysed showed underextended, overextended or unclassified behaviors. An analysis of when in the history of a single word it was misused by the subject revealed the following pattern: while underextensions were noted mainly during the first few weeks of production (mode = one week), the majority of overextensions were recorded during the later weeks of production and followed an initial period of under- or regular extension. Unclassified behaviors were observed for long periods of time with clear evidence of resistance to change. They were mostly recorded for early-acquired words which encoded routinized and repeated everyday experiences.

The category of unclassified, which has not been reported in earlier studies, covered about 33 per cent of all misused words. Its size was reduced considerably towards the last four weeks of study, and during the last two weeks none of the new words learned by Keren exhibited this non-conventional pattern of usage.

The analysis of changes over time in the extension behaviors of single words revealed 58 different profiles of extension for 276 words. Such a great variety of combinations strongly supports the position that different words follow various routes to conventional adult meaning (Carey, 1982). The subject's age and her growing linguistic experience had a strong effect on the extension behaviors of new and existing words. While during the early months of word learning the extension behaviors of new words were irregular and unpredictable, during the last months of study most new words were either used regularly or were initially underextended. This result indicates that the child's proficiency in mapping words onto conventional meanings greatly improved during the second half of the stage.

Keren's record strongly indicates that the one-word stage is divided into two developmental phases: a preparatory phase during which the child laboriously learns each word as a special case, and a phase of generalization during which the child manifests much more efficiency in symbolization, reflected by regular and conventional word extension. The last few weeks of the one-word stage seem to be devoted primarily to consolidation and equilibration. During these final weeks the child improves her repertoire of lexical items as a prelude to the sharp transition into syntax.

The generality of the case-study results

The information reviewed and discussed above is based on my close inspection of the within-stage developments of only a single child. In Chapter 6 I discussed at length the importance of verifying case-study results by comparing them with the findings of other investigations. Let us, therefore, compare Keren's early lexical development with what has been described for other children in the child-language literature.

Keren started to produce her first comprehensible words even before her first birthday. Novel multi-word constructions emerged in Keren's speech when she approached the second half of her second year. This result is compatible with a number of reports on early talkers (e.g., Bloom, 1973; Braunwald, 1978; Gillis and DeSchutter, 1984; Greenfield and Smith, 1976). The overall slice of time during which Keren produced single-word expressions was relatively long (i.e., 32 weeks). The exact measure is consistent with reports on other children (e.g., Braunwald, 1978; Halliday, 1975; Greenfield and Smith, 1976), and it confirms the claim that children utter "one word at a time" for a considerably long period of time. Such a measure of eight months is quite impressive, especially if one considers the relatively short span of time during which normal children achieve a full command of the basic forms, structures, and rules of their mother tongue (i.e., by about the age of 3:0 to 3:6).

Keren's accumulated lexicon of single words contained 337 entries. This figure greatly exceeded my expectations, which were based on Nelson's (1973b) count of about 50 different words in the lexicons of 18 English-speaking children of similar ages. However, the count is strikingly similar to that of 391 words which appears in Braunwald (1978), and is also in accord with Anisfeld's (1984) estimate that single-word lexicons include over 250 different words. In a recent study of early semantic categories (Dromi and Fishelzon, 1986), Keren's record was compared with that of three other Hebrew-speaking one-word-stage subjects. The size of two of the four vocabularies was almost exactly the same, and three exceeded 250 words (K = 337 words, M = 270 words, Y = 338 words). Only one boy in the sample, who started to talk late and produced single words for just five months, accumulated a productive lexicon of less than 250 words (G = 106 words).

The identification of a lexical spurt during the second half of the one-word stage (when Keren's age was 15(27)) confirms earlier references to this phenomenon (e.g., Bloom, 1973; Corrigan, 1976; Halliday, 1975; McShane,

1980). Bloom and Halliday both reported a sudden increase in the child's vocabulary between the ages of 16 and 18 months. Braunwald noticed this phenomenon when Laura was 17 months old. McCune-Nicolich (1981) documented it for five English-speaking subjects when they were 19 to 20 months old.

One might suspect that the low number of new words recorded in Keren's lexicon during the last few weeks of study is an artifact of measurement. I doubt that this was the case, since during this time many more conversations than ever before were held and recorded between Keren and myself. In spite of the slowdown in Keren's acquisition of new vocabulary in the last month of study, I was still very busy collecting new data for the diary. At that time new entries described new uses of old words, their phonological improvements, and a few acquisitions of morphological markings. As noted in Chapter 9, there is only one study in which the relationship between the growing lexicon of single words and the emergence of word combinations has been considered. McCune-Nicolich (1981) found that as MLU values exceeded 1.0 morpheme per utterance, the rate at which new words were learned slowed down sharply (cf. Anisfeld, 1984). I tend to think that this slowdown in the rate of learning is a much wider phenomenon than is known to date, and that it has never been reported only because researchers have failed to document it during periodical measurements (see also Chapters 3 and 9).

It has been reported that most of children's first words are nouns in adult speech (e.g., Farwell, 1976, 1977; Gentner, 1978, 1982; Goldin-Meadow, Seligman and Gelman, 1976; Griffiths and Atkinson, 1978; Huttenlocher, 1974; Nelson, 1973b). The proportion of nouns in Keren's corpus of one-word utterances was presented in Chapter 10. As we have seen, all six categories of adult parts-of-speech were represented in the child's lexicon. The majority of words (61 per cent) were indeed nouns in adult language, and the other grammatical categories were far less well represented in the lexicon. There is a striking similarity between the distribution of categories in Keren's Hebrew speech and the figures presented in Gentner (1982) for other languages. In Hebrew, as in other languages (e.g., English, Japanese, German, Kaluli and Turkish, as discussed by Gentner), nouns in adult speech constitute the largest category of words learned by the child, with the acquisition of verbs lagging behind.

In terms of their contents, the nouns learned by Keren were impressively similar to those reported to predominate in the early lexicons of children acquiring English. Keren's lexicon contained the names of individual people, animals, foods, body parts, vehicles, toys, and objects that can be manipulated (compare the list of nouns presented in Appendix A with reports of Nelson, 1973b; Braunwald, 1978; and Rescorla, 1980, 1981 on the early nouns of English-speaking children. See also Dromi and Fishelzon, 1986 for a comparison between Keren's and three other Hebrew-speaking children's early semantic categories).

Since very little is known about the behaviors of all the words that are included in one child's vocabulary, my quantitative findings on the extension of early words cannot readily be compared with available reports. Some measures and anecdotal descriptions of parent-researchers do, however, allow for a number of generalizations. Gruendel (1977) and Rescorla (1980) have reported that 25–30 per cent of the words learned by the young child are overextended in initial productions. Keren's figure of overextensions is slightly lower than reported earlier (see Figures 6 and 7). I suspect that this should be attributed to the difference in methodology. As I argued earlier, it is not advisable to compare the results of a day-by-day record with that of periodical sampling or indirect reports of naive observers (see also Fischer and Corrigan, 1981).

The data on underextension strongly support Anglin's (1977) and Kay and Anglin's (1982) claim that underextension in production is as prevalent as overextension. My results (presented in Figure 7), however, clearly indicate that Anglin's skepticism about the diary method appears to be unwarranted. It seems that a well-controlled diary study can provide rich evidence on the phenomenon of underextension.

Can a general conclusion be drawn from the many examples of the uses of words assigned to the category of unclassified? From a preliminary analysis of my findings, I conclude that:

(a)   Some words in Keren's lexicon showed a pattern of extension that could not be defined as overextension, underextension, or regular extension.

(b)   These words were mostly acquired early in the one-word period. (This conclusion is particularly true if the category of empty words is excluded.)

(c)   Many of the words that exhibited unclassified behaviors were non-conventional words in adult Hebrew.

(d)   Most words included in this category were modeled to the child very frequently in contexts that did not involve a clear indication of the referent of the word. That is, there was no evidence of ostensive definition in the behavior of the adult who modeled the word to the child (e.g., Ninio, 1980).

These properties, common to many unclassified words, convince me that a category of unclassified words actually existed in Keren's lexicon and did not merely result from the method of data collection or the procedures of data analysis.

It is possible that Keren's use of several words in an unclassified manner was an idiosyncratic behavior of one child. How general is the finding? Can it be compared with other reports on early uses of words by other children?

My descriptions of the early contents in which Keren said *dod* '(an) uncle' are remarkably similar to the early uses of the word *bow-wow* by Braunwald's daughter Laura. Braunwald described Laura's early uses of this word and concluded that it was:

> a multi-purpose word referring to the sound of barking, birds chirping, car and airplane engines or any noise audible in the house from the outside as well as to the sight of dogs and cars. (1978:520)

Braunwald argued that this lexical behavior resulted from a semantic mismatch: the child initially failed to identify the intended adult referent for the word and then subsequently matched the word with separate visual or auditory schemes that were based on her overall experiences with the word in different situational contexts.

I find Braunwald's explanation appealing, but I wish to extend it further. I suggest that when the young child fails to match a word with its conventional referent, he may initially associate this word with a holistic underlying representation of the global situation in which the word was regularly modeled to him. When early meanings are in fact non-differentiated, the child uses a word in appropriate contexts but without signaling to the hearer the specific meaning of the term. Keren's early uses of the word *dod* were unclassified because I could not decide whether she was referring to a person, to noises, or to both. In fact there were instances which supported each possibility and others which negated all of them. An analysis of the contexts for learning the word *dod* revealed that the child frequently heard this word during our walks outside. I often stopped for a short conversation with people whom I knew and Keren did not. In such cases I used to tell Keren immediately after completing my conversation:

> *ze haya dod at lo makira oto/*
> That was uncle you no know him
> 'That was somebody whom you don't know.

Such a context for learning a word is quite vague. It may explain why the word *dod* showed an unclassified pattern of extension, being used as a word for either people, noises or both.

Ferrier's (1978) descriptions of her child's use of the word *phew!* are strikingly similar to the observations of Keren's use of the word *pipi*. *Phew* was an exclamation used by the mother to express her feeling toward the unpleasant smell of wet diapers. Ferrier's subject learned the word and extended it to several referents that were somehow related to the routine of "nappy-changing". She subsequently used the term outside the nappy-changing situation to refer to nappies both clean and dirty, and finally to the nappy bucket which normally contained nappies but which on several occasions was empty (1978:306).

The third English study that can be compared with Keren's Hebrew record is the comprehensive diary record of Bowerman's daughters. Some of Bowerman's examples of early complexive uses of new words can be viewed as related to a general tendency of the child to use the same word for several aspects of the same situational context (Personal Communication, 1981). It is fascinating to compare Bowerman's descriptions of Eva's early uses of *gi* 'giddi-up' with my Hebrew examples of *dio* (used for 'horse' and 'riding'). The contexts in which the two children used the words are almost identical.

Some of Keren's early uses of unclassified words were similar to the early uses of certain words by Estonian-speaking children (Valsiner and Lasn, n.d.). These authors describe several contexts in which their subjects used the words for "thank you", "food", and "out to the yard". On the basis of their findings, they argue that a single phonetic form in the child's speech can carry a multiplicity of meanings which reflect the functions of the word in a given situational context. Their data indicate that initially the meaning of a word is the fuzzy set of contexts in which the word is uttered. By repeated use of the word, the child gradually restricts the number of contexts in which it is used. The authors conclude that the contextual differentiation of word-meaning that takes place during the early phases of linguistic develop- ment is an essential aspect of semantic development.

Barrett's (1986) descriptions of his own son's early uses of some words are the main source of evidence for the claim that repeated events are represented semantically very early. Barrett argues that during the initial phases of word use, meanings are event-bound. That is to suggest that children are dependent on the contexts of expression in establishing refer- ence. Barrett argues that first words are uttered in routinized ways and often while the infant is engaged in the actual performance of an action. Barrett's new proposal that meaning acquisition follows a step model is based entirely on examples which can be viewed as unclassified. Early meanings, according to the step model, are holistic and event-bound. Gradually they become decontextualized and are represented around prototypes and sets of criterial attributes or features. Only at a third step of symbolizing do children also start to abstruct contrasts which help them to generate the notions of semantic fields (see Chapter 5 and Barrett, 1986). Barrett's model explains the finding that unclassified words are early-acquired terms and that they are always associated with repeated everyday activities or situations. The fact that his model was developed independently of my earlier writings on this topic (e.g., Dromi, 1982, 1984) supports my contention that his son used early words in a manner closely similar to that of Keren.

An evaluation of the main models of word-meaning acquisition

An examination of the models of word-meaning, critically reviewed in Chapter 5 of this book, reveals that no model by itself is comprehensive enough to deal with the diversity of findings reported here. It must be noted, however, that some models seem to predict patterns of extension over time better than others, and some are more compatible with the findings, and are as such more satisfactory, than others. Clark's (1973) and Nelson's (1974) original models do not gain much support from the findings on the complete lexicon of one child. These models, which predict a course of word-meaning acquisition from the general to the specific, do not account for the high percentages of underextension and the late emergence of overextension. Bowerman's (1978, 1980) Prototype Model, and Schlesinger's (1982) Word-

Referent Model, which predict that most words will be used initially by the child as names of specific referents and will only later be generalized, better describe the overall pattern of my results than do the earlier models.

The Prototype Model was predictive in that it suggested diversity of extension patterns and complex combinations among them. Bowerman's prediction that overextensions will be noted after initial evidence of correct applications was found to be true. Two of Bowerman's basic assumptions, however, gained little empirical support. It was rarely the case that Keren's early uses of words were related to a prototypical event for the use of the word in adult language. Furthermore, very few cases of complexive–associative overextensions were identified in Keren's corpus (see Table 10). It is significant to note that those complexive uses which were recorded were for later-acquired words. It was mainly in the second half of the stage that I recorded complexive overextensions. In my opinion, this finding suggests that Bowerman's model, which attributes sophisticated abilities of decomposing and recomposing underlying features to the child, is incompatible with findings on the early periods of lexical acquisition. It would seem, however, that a categorical model of this type may well explain later phenomena which emerge as children gain more experience with words.

The prototype explanation is not satisfactory for unclassified behaviors. This is particularly true in cases where there is no evidence of initial correct use of the words prior to the unclassified extension. A number of examples (presented below) of the early applications of the word *niyar* 'paper' (051) (an unclassified word) will demonstrate that this word was never uttered by the child in contexts which could reveal that she knew the conventional meaning of the term in adult language.

Schlesinger's Word-Referent theory (1982) gains considerable support from the present empirical test. This model, which predicts that meaning will develop gradually and concurrently with the refinement of the underlying attached concepts, is compatible with the majority of my findings. It plausibly explains why so many words were initially underextended, and also accounts for the late emergence of overextensions. This is particularly true when we consider Schlesinger's proposal regarding the hypothetical structure of the protoverbal element. As stated in Chapter 5, Schlesinger believes that a set of cues are added to the underlying representation of the paired referent through repeated experience with the same word. As a consequence, it becomes clear that classical overextensions, which are based on the identification of shared underlying features, are not likely to occur early.

My finding that underextension was a short-lived phenomenon for most words, and that it was commonly followed by either regular extension or overextension, shows that a strategy of generalizing meaning from a limited set of examples is quite a simple one for the young word-learner. Recent experimental works strongly support this hypothesis on the ability of very young infants to generalize correct meaning on the basis of very few demonstrations (e.g., Golinkoff, Hirsch-Pasek, Badvini and Lavallee, 1985; Soja, Carey and Spelke, 1985).

The Word-Referent Model introduces a severe constraint on the process of word-meaning acquisition. This constraint is interactional in that it attributes significance to both the parents' modeling strategies and the child's ability to match words with non-linguistic referents. My results clearly indicate that the above constraint is indeed functional, and my unclassified behaviors were in fact the result of the child's failure to identify the correct referent of a word. In such cases the child started to produce the word in appropriate contexts and the word's underlying representation was of the whole scene or situation in which it was embedded. Only Schlesinger's model, which does not assume that well-defined concepts precede the emergence of new words, is compatible with this explanation.

My longitudinal follow-up of Keren's linguistic development throughout the one-word stage shows that with growing linguistic experience the child develops sharper distinctions. My results therefore support Schlesinger's claim that early words are not simply labels for pre-defined concepts. Schlesinger's emphasis on tacit learning via the activation of covert processes, in which positive and negative cues are accumulated, may explain the overwhelming number of initial regular extensions. Here, however, the theory runs into difficulty since such a hypothesis is neither testable nor is it falsifiable.

My finding that the majority of words are produced from the outset in regular and wide contexts is important. It must be predicted by a comprehensive theory of word-meaning. The main implication of this finding, in my opinion, is that it shows how closely linguistic and conceptual developments progress during the developmental period studied here. Further exploration of these ties are needed before more conclusive claims can be made.

Clark's (1983a, 1985) new theory of Lexical Contrasts does not make direct predictions of actual word extensions. As stated in Chapter 5, this theory is more lexical than semantic, and it does not treat overextensions as reflections of word-meaning. Clark's strong conviction that the two principles of conventionality and contrast are activated by the young child in the course of building a productive lexicon gains considerable empirical support. The content analysis of Keren's lexicon shows that with time she lexicalized finer and finer contrasts (see also Dromi and Fishelzon, 1986 in this regard). The findings on extension show that conventionality is a major and obligatory principle which children must follow from a very young age. As I have shown, however, there is little evidence that children start out on word acquisition well equipped with the principle of conventionality. Rather, while learning language they seem to acquire and subsequently to apply this principle. Only during the second half of the one-word period did conventional meanings predominate in Keren's lexicon, and only during this phase did she start to give up her non-conventional meanings and idiosyncratic forms.

The recent discussions on event-bound representations of meaning (Barrett, 1986), and of the "script" organization of early meaning (Nelson and Lucariello, 1985), are similar to my theoretical explanation of the unclassified phenomenon. In an earlier publication (Dromi, 1984) I presented my idea that early words are often associated with holistic representations of "scenes". My position, which has much in common with these other recent theories and yet was developed independently on the basis of the findings of the present research, is elaborated below and illustrated with a number of examples from Keren's record.

The underlying representation of situational words

The extension of a word to various objects and actions that constitute components of the same situational context may reflect a general cognitive procedure used by young children to organize their experiences. Among Keren's unclassified words I found many examples of words that were sometimes produced as cover terms for a whole situation and at other times used for separate elements of this situation. I term these words "situational words", and I argue that they were initially associated with Keren's schematic representations of early everyday experiences (e.g., Mandler, 1979, 1983; Schank and Abelson, 1977).

It has recently been suggested that the earliest form of organized knowledge revolves around "script-like" daily episodes. Nelson (1978), Nelson and Gruendel (1979, 1981), and Nelson and Lucariello (1985) have suggested that early generalized event representations are the basic building blocks of cognitive development. To my knowledge, there has been no research on the development of "scripts" in children as young as my subject. However, research on older children has shown that as early as two years of age, subjects show high sensitivity to interrelationships among different components or elements of the same representational "scheme", "frame", or "scene" (Schank and Abelson, 1977).

I suggest that Keren's situational words were words that she used before carrying out a detailed analysis of their meanings. I hypothesize that it was the knowledge of the appropriate context for using a word that elicited it at particular moments. Therefore, I propose that during the early phases of language acquisition a context-based production strategy is operating in the child (see Dromi, 1984 for an explicit account of this proposal).

The most obvious characteristic of situational words is that they are extended to several referents that do not share any attributes with each other. Furthermore, such a word is often uttered in an appropriate context, yet it is impossible to determine from this context which is the referent of the word, or to which specific element in the situation the word refers. Table 14

Table 14.   A selected set of descriptions of the contexts in which Keren used the word *niyar* 'paper' (050) (= a count noun)

---

(1) 14(5): In the kitchen; M is writing notes in K's diary; K observes M. Suddenly she starts to yell repeatedly: niyar/x/x/ 'paper'. M gives K a piece of paper. K continues to whine. She says again and again: niyar/x/x/ 'paper' and tries to catch M's hand. M gives K a pencil. K takes it happily. She sits down and draws on her piece of paper.

(2) 14(7): In the living room; M is writing in her diary. K pulls M's pencil, looks at it and says: niyar/ 'paper'. (K's tone is quite emphatic, I don't think that she meant verbally to request the pencil; rather, I think that she was naming it.)

(3) 14(10): In the kitchen; M is writing notes on a piece of paper which is attached to the refrigerator. K is sitting in her highchair; she says: niyar/ 'paper'. I confirm her utterance, saying: ken ani kotevat al niyar/ 'yes, I am writing on a piece of paper'. K seems satisfied.

(4) 15(7): In K's room; K is lying down on her back sucking her thumb. M enters the room. K gets up, picks up her little pillow, and shows it to M. She points to the applique of two birds on the cover of the pillow and says: niyar/ 'paper'.

(5) 15(17): Outside; M and K are walking on the sidewalk. Suddenly K stops, points to an arrow on the sidewalk (a chalk drawing from a children's game), and says: niyar/ 'paper'. M is very surprised. She says: ze ciyur/ 'it is a drawing'. Later on when we pass another arrow M stops, points at it and asks K: ma ze?/ 'what (is) this?' K says confidently: niyar/ 'paper'.

(6) 16(4): In the study; K takes out of my bag a pen, hands it to me and says: niyar/ 'paper'.

(7) 16(4): In the living room; K is playing with an empty plastic container of food. She sees a sticker on it with the name of the product. K gives the container to me and says with rising intonation: niyar?/ 'paper?'

---

presents the descriptions of a number of contexts in which the word *niyar* 'paper' (051) was recorded. Throughout the period of study it was never clear to me whether the word referred to pencils, paper, the action of writing and/or drawing, or the drawing itself. In retrospect, I believe that Keren used this word as a cover term for all of those referents and the interactions among them.

One could argue that the shifting referential behaviors described above for *niyar* and other unclassified words (e.g., *dod, hita, hupa, pipi*) show that they were associative complexes. Bowerman's (1978, 1980) model of meaning seems to be the only one that provides a plausible explanation for the behaviors noted. Nevertheless, I argue that these uses were not "pure" complexive overextensions. The main objection I had to classifying these words as complexive overextensions was the fact that they were never used either by the child or by the parents to label a "prototypical" referent. I find no evidence in my data that Keren initially associated the word with one referent (the "best exemplar") and only later extended it to other referents on the basis of shared properties she had identified.

The "ambiguous" unclassified words used by Keren were all applied to several referents that were somehow related to each other as different components of the same situational context. This observation leads me to the conclusion that these early productions do not involve the analysis of the features of a "prototype", as was postulated by Bowerman. I suggest that as it is global or holistic, the process observed is less differentiated and is therefore far less complex than Bowerman's model would indicate (see also Kemler-Nelson, 1984).

I argue that many of Keren's early misuses of words did not result from the featural analysis of an initial referent, followed by her application of the word to novel referents on the basis of featural similarities with the original referent. Such an assumption, which imputes a feature-based cognitive make-up to the child, is implicit in virtually all categorical accounts of early word-meanings. Rather, I argue that Keren produced some words in some contexts because they were attached to a complete, unanalysed representation of a "scheme", "frame", or "scene".

Mandler (1979) has distinguished between categorical and schematic organizations of knowledge. She argues that a scheme is a cognitive structure which is not based on similarity relationships between members of a class. Instead, the parts or components of a scheme are related to each other on the basis of contiguities of space or time. A similar distinction was recently made by Kemler-Nelson (1984), who demonstrated that under certain experimental conditions subjects made judgments about category membership on the basis of overall resemblance, while under other conditions category membership was determined by a systematic comparison of features. In a series of experimental studies, Kemler-Nelson has shown that young subjects tend to arrive at judgments on the basis of holistic rather than componential analysis of the stimuli. This finding led her to the conclusion that young children tend to process information more holistically than analytically. She claims that holistic processing is much simpler than is analytical processing.

In addition to providing an interpretation for most unclassified extensions, the notion of situational words or the assumption of a holistic non-componential underlying representation of meaning can account very well for several other extension behaviors that are observed during the early period of verbal production. Consider, for example, the early uses of the word *parpar* '(a) butterfly' (152) by Keren. This word was classified as showing a "complexive" pattern of overextension, since it was used for stickers, round objects, towels, and colored spots on flat surfaces. A close examination of the contexts in which Keren learned the word suggests that it was initially associated with the everyday experience of *taking a bath*. I frequently modeled *parpar* to Keren when she was in the bathtub, while pointing to a pink sticker of a butterfly. On the bottom of our bathtub were several other stickers of flowers, leaves, and red circles. I hypothesize that Keren failed to make a referent-word pairing between the specific sticker of a butterfly and the word *parpar*. As a result, she associated the word with the scene of taking a bath, and started to use it in contexts in which several referents associated with this "frame" or "scheme" were present: for example, stickers in general, circles, spots on surfaces, and towels.

Early overextensions of words to only one referent can also be explained by the "schematic" organization strategy. Take, for example, the word *na'al* '(a) shoe' (018), which was used for shoes and socks. It is true that an abstract feature such as [+ footwear] could be invoked to explain this overextension within a "categorical" framework, but note that Keren did not generalize the word 'shoe' for the referent slippers, as this approach would predict. Instead, she acquired the word *bayit* (*na'alei bayit*) 'slippers' (111) quite early, and used it regularly, while overextending the word *na'al* '(a) shoe' to the object socks. This extension behavior indicates that socks constituted an inseparable component of the scene of *putting on shoes*.

The argument becomes even stronger when we consider the application of the word *pe* 'mouth' to the object lipstick (*sfaton* in Hebrew). It is difficult to think of an abstract feature along the line of [+ four-legged] or [+ footwear] that is shared by mouths and lipsticks. It is therefore very plausible that the child overextended the word *pe* 'mouth' to lipstick because lipstick is an important component of the scheme of *mother putting on lipstick*.

The child's use of a situational word for the situation as a whole and for separate elements or components of this situation does not exclude the possibility that she may overextend it beyond the situation itself. My data include several examples of situational words that were overextended to referents which were somehow similar to one component of the situation. Keren's use of her situational word *niyar* 'paper' for the appliqué of two birds on her little pillow (see Table 14, example (4)) illustrates this behavior. Bowerman's (1978) description of Christy's use of the word *nightnight* for a tree being dragged away in a horizontal position is another example of an overextension based on a component of the situation in which the word had been modeled to the child and initially used by her. Keren's and Christy's examples of situational words that sometimes turn up outside their scheme are of great interest. They show that schematic and categorical principles of cognitive organization are compatible with each other, and may operate concurrently.

The underlying schematic organization of word-meaning provides an explanation for the behavior of most unclassified words in my data. It effectively explains the observation that the child sometimes used words that were semantically "empty" quite appropriately. It deals quite satisfactorily with ambiguous words and with words that could have been used by the child either as associations or as overextensions. This strategy also explains why instances of underextension typically last only a short period of time: after the establishment of a correct match, or pairing of a word with a single referent, the generalization of meaning is then quite easy for the child.

As we have seen, in addition to providing an interpretation for many or most unclassified and underextended word uses, the notion of situational words accounts quite nicely for several types of overextensions, particularly "complexive" overextensions and overextensions to one referent only.

Much more research is needed in order to understand fully why some words are learned by the child as cover terms for whole situations while others are not. It is also important to explore for how long a child may use words as cover terms for whole situations. When does the child realize that his usage is not conventional and how does he change it? Another direction for research would be to use language data to investigate cognitive organization. The early uses of situational words may help us define the elements and boundaries of the "scripts" in the mind of the young child. A close examination of all the uses of one situational word by the child may reveal the extent and the structure of the "script" associated with this word. Finally and most importantly, how are schematic and categorical analyses of experiences related to each other? Does schematic knowledge precede categorical knowledge? This might account for why many words that show situational behaviors are acquired early in the one-word period.

To conclude, the findings of the present study support the claim that categorical models of meaning do not provide a fully satisfactory explanation for the process involved in early semantic development. A featural model of the acquisition of word-meaning is neither flexible nor comprehensive enough to account for the great variability observed in the behaviors of early words. It also fails to explain the many different dynamic patterns that early words follow as they develop over time. I have argued that the words acquired during the one-word stage give evidence for the operation in the child of both schematic and categorical approaches to the organization of experiences. How the two cognitive strategies are related to each other must be the subject of future research. In any event, an adequate model of the acquisition of word-meaning must be broad-based and integrative enough to account for this diversity.

Epilogue

In concluding this book I will focus on two themes that emerged from the analysis of one child's complete one-word-stage lexicon. Both are related to the problem of how words are mapped onto their meanings. One of the most striking findings of this study is that 46 per cent of the words produced by the child showed regular extension (i.e., roughly adult-like usage) from the first week of use. This finding shows how successful the child usually is in discovering the underlying reference of a word. One should not ignore, however, the significant proportion of words which were initially used by the child irregularly. The question to be asked is, *what went wrong for those words that showed irregular extensions?*

A preliminary content analysis of Keren's words revealed that studying the contexts in which new words are learned is invaluable in our attempt to find answers to this question. For example, it was found that early words showing undifferentiated reference behaviors had typically been heard repeatedly by the child in contexts providing little opportunity for her to match the word with a specific referent (Keren's uses of *iga* 'a moment' (see Table 4) are relevant here).

Some of the repeated contexts may be important for the child for purely discourse reasons. For example, it may be of great consequence for a growing infant to learn what she should say in response to certain kinds of questions (e.g., "Where is Daddy?" "At work."). The context may be of special significance for the child for other reasons as well. Some contexts may be salient in terms of the non-linguistic experiences of the child, while others may be emotionally relevant for him. Thus, "the eating situation", "the bath situation" and "the diapering situation" share the properties of being frequently encountered and highly important for the child. It is therefore not surprising that words such as *ham* (for food, eating, dishes, and aprons); *parpar* '(a) butterfly' (for stickers, towels, spots of ink on pieces of paper, etc.) and *pipi* 'urine' (for diapers, taking off clothes, playing with body parts, the potty, and toilet, etc.) emerged early and showed undifferentiated meanings. Keren's early acquisition of the word *niyar* 'paper' (for everything included in "the writing situation" (see Table 14)) is quite understandable in view of the fact that she saw me writing all day and always while taking care of her. I claim that Keren learned this word so early and used it in such a global fashion because the situation was especially salient for her and because I had never stopped to show her what a piece of paper is.

A second explanation for the question of why some words are mapped correctly while others are not has been proposed by Brown (1957), Carey (1982), Schlesinger (1982), and Slobin (1973). These researchers emphasize the role of syntactic cues and other grammatical markers in directing the young child's attention to possibly significant aspects of the non-linguistic contexts in which words are learned. My natural production data provide additional support for this claim, which was originally formulated on the basis of comprehension studies with nonsense words (e.g., 'dax' vs. '(a) dax' or 'seb' vs. 'sebbing'; cf. Carey, 1982). I have argued (in Chapter 10) that Keren utilized the fact that all infinitive forms in Hebrew share the same grammatical marker (the prefix *li-*) in tracing the meaning of verbs. Slobin's (1973) claim that the relative complexity of linguistic devices can slow down or speed up the rate of language learning is thus supported even by data from a very young child.

I reported earlier that my situational words were words that are non-conventional in Hebrew. They therefore lack grammatical markers and are not usually embedded in syntactic contexts. For a non-conventional word there is no agreement as to a specific referent. The referent of such a word is thus never ostensively defined for the child by the mother or other care-takers. I argue that words such as *ham*, *hita*, *pipi*, *tita*, etc., were both salient and difficult at the same time. The child heard them (mainly from her babysitter) over and over again, but could not identify their reference. The fact that these words were usually modeled in isolation rather than in a syntactic context might have made them even more difficult for the child.

Much research is needed in order to verify my claims. I suggest that very detailed analyses of the linguistic and non-linguistic contexts in which words are learned should be carried out. Such analyses must include highly systematic evaluations of the modeling tendencies of parents, and whether they greet the child's first uses of new words with approval or disapproval (e.g., Veneziano, 1981). The present study dealt systematically and in great detail with the corpus of a single child. I suspect that subsequent research will prove that even this degree of detail is insufficient to explain the mysteries of early language acquisition.

Appendices

Appendix A. Keren's complete cumulative lexicon at the one-word stage

The subject's complete lexicon of single words consisted of 337 different entries, most of which were conventional Hebrew words. The following table lists these words in the order of their emergence. The two main sources of evidence – the handwritten diary and the phonetic transcriptions of the audio-recorded sessions – were combined for the purposes of the present analysis. A new word was numbered on the day of its third recording regardless of the time that had elapsed since its first appearance. The calendaric information is calculated on the basis of the date of acquisition, i.e., the day of the third recording. Weeks of study are the actual calendaric weeks of data collection starting on *July 10, 1980* (the day of the third recording of the word *haw* – the first word in Keren's lexicon) and ending on *February 20, 1981* (the date of the third recording of the word *tiyul* – word number 337 in the cumulative lexicon of the child). Child ages are given in months and days, thus 10(12) means that the subject's age was 10 months and 12 days on the day of acquisition of the first word *haw*. Child words are transcribed in their latest phonetic representation. Since the phonological forms of many words showed inconsistencies reflecting developmental trends of approximation to conventional forms, for each word the table lists the latest recorded form, which in many cases is also the most approximated one. The table also includes the conventional Hebrew forms, with a question mark in parentheses indicating that the word is not conventional. English translations are based on the meaning of the word in colloquial Hebrew. Comments are given for the non-conventional words.

Table A. Keren's complete lexicon at the one-word stage

Word no.	Week of study	Child's age	Child's word	Conventional form	English translation
1	1	10(12)	haw	(?)	a dog's bark
2	5	11(16)	?aba	(aba)	Father
3	6	11(17)	?imaima	(?)	--
4	6	11(18)	ham	(?)	said while feeding
5	8	12(3)	mu	(?)	a cow's moo
6	8	12(3)	?ia	(?)	a donkey's bray
7	9	12(8)	pil	(pil)	an elephant
8	9	12(11)	buba	(buba)	a doll
9	9	12(13)	pipi	(pipi)	urine
10	10	12(16)	hita	(?)	said while going out for a walk
11	10	12(16)	?oto	(?oto)	a car
12	10	12(18)	tiktak	(?)	the sound of a clock
13	10	12(19)	cifcif	(?)	a bird's tweet
14	10	12(20)	hupa	(?)	accompanying the perception of something making sudden contact with the ground
15	11	12(23)	dio	(dio)	giddi up
16	11	12(25)	hine	(hine)	here
17	11	12(25)	?ein	(?ein)	all gone
18	11	12(25)	na?al	(na?al)	a shoe
19	11	12(25)	myau	(?)	a cat's meow
20	11	12(25)	giad	(gil?ad)	a name
21	11	12(25)	miam	(miryam)	a name
22	11	12(27)	mor	(mor)	a name
23	12	12(28)	nadned	(nad-ned)	accompanying a swinging motion
24	12	12(28)	bamba	(bamba)	a type of snack
25	12	12(30)	mayim	(mayim)	water
26	12	13(0)	?or	(?or)	light
27	12	13(1)	?eti	(?eti)	mother's name
28	12	13(2)	?udi	(?udi)	father's name
29	12	13(2)	amir	(amir)	a name
30	13	13(6)	xor	(xor)	a hole
31	13	13(7)	ma	(ma)	what
32	13	13(7)	etze	(et-ze)	this (volition)
33	14	13(15)	pita	(pita)	a type of Arab bread
34	15	13(18)	kuku	(kuku)	peekaboo
35	15	13(18)	?ima	(?ima)	mother
36	15	13(18)	dai	(dai)	no more
37	15	13(22)	?od	(?od)	more
38	15	13(23)	toda	(toda)	thank you
39	15	13(23)	pica	(peca)	a sore/cut/wound
40	16	13(25)	avoda	(?avoda)	work
41	16	13(26)	tu-tu	(?)	the sound of a train
42	16	13(26)	?uga	(?uga)	a cake
43	17	14(2)	itot	(lištot)	drink (infinitive form)
44	17	14(2)	lav[1]	(xalav)	milk
45	17	14(2)	?apit	(kapit)	a spoon
46	17	14(3)	dli	(dli)	a pail
47	17	14(3)	puax	(tapuax)	an apple

Table A: continued

Word no.	Week of study	Child's age	Child's word	Conventional form	English translation
48	17	14(3)	?apci	(?)	sound made when sneezing
49	17	14(3)	tei	(tei)	tea
50	17	14(5)	niyar	(niyar)	paper
51	17	14(7)	dod	(dod)	an uncle
52	18	14(13)	iga	(rega)	a minute
53	19	14(17)	af	(?af)	nose
54	19	14(17)	pe	(pe)	mouth
55	19	14(19)	lala	(?)	produced when singing
56	19	14(19)	?et	(?et)	a pen
57	19	14(19)	?es	(?es)	fire
58	19	14(21)	cet	(lacet)	go/get out (infinitive form)
59	19	14(21)	ba?at	(taba?at)	a ring (finger ring)
60	19	14(21)	ze	(ze)	this
61	19	14(22)	tnili	(tni-li)	give me (imperative, feminine, singular)
62	20	14(23)	kax	(kax)	take (present, 2nd person, masculine, singular)
63	20	14(25)	?amala	(lemala)	up
64	20	14(25)	?inok	(tinok)	a baby
65	20	14(26)	kova	(kova)	a hat
66	20	14(27)	mic	(mic)	juice
67	21	15(0)	mod	(la?amod)	stand (infinitive form)
68	21	15(0)	?agala	(?agala)	a stroller
69	21	15(1)	boi-boily	(bo?i-?elai)	come, come to me (imperative, feminine, singular)
70	21	15(1)	kaxa	(kaxa)	like this, this way
71	21	15(1)	xam	(xam)	hot (masculine, singular)
72	21	15(1)	?eifo	(?eifo)	where
73	21	15(1)	meravi	(merav)	a name
74	21	15(2	urim	(kaftorim)	buttons
75	21	15(2)	?edet	(laredet)	get down (infinitive form)
76	21	15(2)	tiktak	(tik-tak)	a snap
77	21	15(2)	ul	(xitul)	a diaper
78	21	15(2)	ot	(maftexot)	keys
79	21	15(5)	tik	(tik)	a bag/handbag
80	21	15(5)	kaki	(kaki)	bowel movement
81	21	15(5)	nuf	(yansuf)	an owl
82	21	15(5)	tator	(traktor)	a tractor
83	21	15(5)	kof	(kof)	a monkey
84	21	15(5)	nira	(nira)	grandmother's name
85	21	15(5)	dubi	(dubi)	a teddy bear
86	22	15(8)	lo	(lo)	no
87	22	15(8)	on	(aviron)	an airplane

Table A: continued

Word no.	Week of study	Child's age	Child's word	Conventional form	English translation
88	22	15(8)	?ix	(?)	said in relation to a disgusting thing
89	22	15(8)	?uga-uga	(?)	taken from a children's song
90	22	15(8)	apuz	(tapuz)	an orange
91	22	15(8)	pax	(pax)	a trash-can
92	22	15(8)	mize	(mize)	who is this?
93	22	15(8)	nor	(sinor)	an apron
94	22	15(8)	yeled	(yeled)	a boy
95	22	15(8)	tova	(tova)	said while patting
96	22	15(9)	muse	(moše)	grandfather's name'
97	22	15(10)	ines	(lehikanes)	get/come in (infinitive form)
98	22	15(10)	abatia	(?ambatya)	a bath/bathtub/ bathroom
99	22	15(11)	mita	(mita)	a bed
100	22	15(11)	min	(binyamin)	a name
101	22	15(12)	vuv	(zvuv)	a fly
102	22	15(12)	kereni	(keren)	subject's name
103	23	15(14)	niti	(ronit)	a name
104	23	15(14)	?iti	(karit)	a pillow
105	23	15(14)	maraki	(marak)	soup
106	23	15(14)	puke	(pulke)	a drumstick
107	23	15(14)	fa	(trufa)	medicine
108	23	15(15)	deli	(dželi)	jelly
109	23	15(15)	magi	(pengi)	a dog's name
110	23	15(17)	mina	(klementina)	a tangerine
111	23	15(17)	bayit	(nalalei- bayit)	slippers
112	23	15(17)	maxe	(ma-ze)	what is this?
113	23	15(17)	?alai	(?alai)	on me
114	23	15(18)	fafa	(kfafa)	a glove/mitten
115	23	15(19)	ibar	(nišbar)	break (past, 3rd person, masculine, singular, passive)
116	24	15(20)	?ala[1]	(xala)	a type of bread
117	24	15(20)	gagaga	(?)	a duck's quack
118	24	15(20)	dag	(dag)	a fish
119	24	15(20)	yipyip	(yipyip)	a dog's name
120	24	15(20)	xalav	(xalav)	milk
121	24	15(20)	an	(šafan)	a rabbit
122	24	15(20)	kukiku	(ku ku?)	a rooster's crow
123	24	15(20)	beiga	(beigale)	a bagel
124	24	15(20)	teip	(teip)	a small tape recorder
125	24	15(20)	leidy	(leidy)	a dog's name
126	24	15(20)	poli	(poli)	a dog's name
127	24	15(23)	pes	(letapes)	climb (infinitive form)
128	24	15(23)	ipa	(ricpa)	a floor
129	24	15(24)	piax	(perax)	a flower
130	24	15(24)	mus	(beit šimuš)	the toilet

Table A: continued

Word no.	Week of study	Child's age	Child's word	Conventional form	English translation
131	24	15(24)	acic	(ʔacic)	a flower pot
132	24	15(24)	kis	(kis)	a pocket
133	24	15(24)	evet	(laševet)	sit (down) (infinitive form)
134	24	15(25)	mapayim	(miškafayim)	eye-glasses
135	24	15(25)	even	(ʔeven)	a stone
136	24	15(26)	lo po	(lo-po)	not here
137	24	15(26)	igul	(ʔigul)	a circle
138	24	15(26)	ipocec	(hitpocec)	explode (3rd person, masculine, singular, past)
139	25	15(27)	bayit	(bayit)	a house
140	25	15(27)	titaf	(?)	the sound of rain
141	25	15(27)	misxa	(mišxa)	ointment
142	25	15(27)	ʔetet	(šaršeret)	a necklace
143	25	15(27)	ʔabaʔaba	(barbaʔaba)	a story character
144	25	15(27)	mudedet	(yom-huledet)	a birthday
145	25	15(27)	ner	(ner)	a candle
146	25	15(27)	kom	(makom)	a place
147	25	15(27)	erer[1]	(sveder)	a sweater
148	25	15(28)	ʔuax[1]	(liftoax)	open (infinitive form)
149	25	15(28)	ʔec	(ʔec)	a tree
150	25	15(28)	ʔabaita	(habaita)	to the house
151	25	15(28)	pes	(lexapes)	look for something (infinitive form)
152	25	15(28)	parpar	(parar)	a butterfly
153	25	15(28)	ʔafal	(ʔafa)	fly (past, 3rd person, feminine, singular)
154	25	15(28	ken	(ken)	yes
155	25	15(28)	irals	(sira)	a boat
156	25	15(28)	pic	(spic)	a point (edge) of something
157	25	15(28)	anak	(arnak)	a purse/wallet
158	25	15(28)	numinumi	(?)	said while putting a baby to sleep
159	25	15(29)	xamiday	(xam-miday)	too hot (masculine, singular)
160	25	15(29)	ala	(nafla)	fall (past, 3rd person, feminine singular)
161	25	16(0)	afa	(džirafa)	a giraffe
162	25	16(0)	gilgul	(gilgul)	a somersault
163	25	16(0)	lyla	(layla)	night
164	25	16(0)	ʔica	(xulca)	a shirt/blouse
165	25	16(1)	kumi	(kumi)	get up (imperative, feminine, singular)
166	25	16(1)	xut	(xut)	a string
167	25	16(1)	ʔenayim	(ʔenayim)	eyes
168	25	16(1)	usi	(kuši)	a dog's name

Table A: continued

Word no.	Week of study	Child's age	Child's word	Conventional form	English translation
169	25	16(1)	uca	(roca)	want (present, all persons, feminine, singular)
170	25	16(2)	os	(ros)	the head
171	25	16(2)	miax	(mafteax)	a key
172	25	16(2)	?uci[1]	(ruci)	run (imperative, feminine, singular)
173	25	16(2)	ol-ol	(gadol)	big (masculine, singular)
174	25	16(2)	atnudnik	(at-nudni)	you're a nag
175	25	16(3)	urara	(sukariya)	a sweet
176	25	16(3)	onez	(?ozen)	ear
177	25	16(3)	me?il	(me?il)	a (rain) coat
178	25	16(3)	pupik	(pupik)	bellybutton
179	25	16(3)	cici	(cici xaze)	breast
180	25	16(3)	va va va	(qua qua qua?)	a frog's croak
181	25	16(3)	ricrac	(ričrač)	a zipper
182	25	16(3)	ixa	(smixa)	a blanket
183	26	16(4)	sus	(sus)	a horse
184	26	16(4)	rina	(margarina)	margarine
185	26	16(4)	aviva	(aviva)	a name
186	26	16(4)	orl	(lisgor)	close, shut (infinitive form)
187	26	16(4)	erer	(sefer)	a book
188	26	16(4)	?id	(lehorid)	get/take (something) off (infinitive form)
189	26	16(4)	is	(?iš)	a man
190	26	16(4)	gufia	(gufiya)	an undershirt
191	26	16(4)	?uci	(lehoci)	take out (infinitive form)
192	26	16(5)	abis	(lehalbiš)	put on/dress (infinitive form)
193	26	16(5)	lalot	(laalot)	get up/get on (infinitive form)
194	26	16(6)	bakbuk	(bakbuk)	a bottle
195	26	16(6)	kar	(kar)	cold (masculine, singular)
196	26	16(6)	nim	(taxtonim)	underpants
197	26	16(6)	sayim	(mixnasayim)	pants, trousers
198	26	16(6)	taic	(taic)	pantyhose
199	26	16(6)	bayim	(garbayim)	socks
200	26	16(7)	pak	(pkak)	a cork
201	26	16(7)	?adur	(kadur)	a ball, a pill
202	26	16(7)	?efi	(sefi)	a name
203	26	16(7)	iri	(ya?iri)	a name
204	26	16(7)	ara	(sara)	a name
205	26	16(7)	?axel	(raxel)	grandmother's name
206	26	16(8)	mici	(?)	a common name of a cat
207	26	16(8)	miba	(mi-ba)	who comes? (present/past, all persons, masculine, singular)

Table A: continued

Word no.	Week of study	Child's age	Child's word	Conventional form	English translation
208	26	16(8)	ba-bau-bo	(ba)	come (present/past, all persons, masculine, singular)
209	26	16(8)	nake	(lenakot)	clean (infinitive form)
210	26	16(9)	ofa	(rof?a)	a doctor (feminine)
211	26	16(9)	anav	(zanav)	a tail
212	26	16(9)	uax	(ruax)	wind
213	26	16(10)	kise	(kise)	a chair
214	26	16(10)	nora-nora	(nora)	very
215	26	16(10)	onana	(šošana)	a name
216	26	16(10)	ubi	(bubi)	a name
217	26	16(10)	ubiya	(kubiya)	a playing block
218	26	16(10)	al	(gamal)	a camel
219	27	16(11)	uboxe	(hu-boxe)	he is crying
220	27	16(12)	alom	(albom)	an album
221	27	16(12)	kesef	(kesef)	money
222	27	16(12)	galgal	(galgal)	a wheel
223	27	16(13)	?emem	(?ecem)	a bone
224	27	16(14)	avizia	(televizia)	a television
225	27	16(14)	pazel	(pazel)	a jigsaw puzzle
226	27	16(15)	halax	(halax)	go (past, 3rd person, masculine, singular)
227	27	16(15)	ma?ayim	(misparayim)	scissors
228	27	16(15)	aniya	(agvaniya)	a tomato
229	27	16(15)	?anuka	(xanuka)	a Jewish holiday
230	27	16(15)	gimel	(gimel)	a Hebrew alphabet letter
231	27	16(15)	?um?um	(kumkum)	a kettle
232	27	16(16)	abar nusnus	(?axbar)	a mouse/ run away
233	27	16(16)	akov	(ya?kov)	grandfather's name
234	27	16(16)	matate	(matate)	a broom
235	27	16(16)	nika	(nikra)	tear (past, 3rd person, masculine, singular, passive)
236	27	16(17)	atan[1]	(katan)	small
237	27	16(17)	ira	(?arye)	a lion
238	27	16(17)	ses ses	(šeš)	the number six
239	27	16(17)	?amana	(matana)	a present
240	27	16(17)	das	(dvaš)	honey
241	27	16(17)	tuk tuk	(?)	the sound of knocking
242	27	16(17)	gai	(gai)	a name
243	27	16(17)	ali	(naftali)	a story character
244	27	16(17)	mocec	(mocec)	a pacifier
245	27	16(17)	?ika	(sika)	a hairpin
246	27	16(17)	?atiax	(šatiax)	a rug
247	27	16(17)	po	(po)	here
248	27	16(17)	yage	(yafe)	nice/pretty (masculine, singular)

Word no.	Week of study	Child's age	Child's word	Conventional form	English translation
249	28	16(18)	cafcat	(?)	the sound of a car horn
250	28	16(18)	atan	(yonatan)	a name
251	28	16(18)	iax	(yareax)	the moon
252	28	16(18)	maus	(Mickey Mouse)	Mickey Mouse
253	28	16(19)	yadayim	(yadayim)	hands
254	28	16(19)	snayim	(šnayim)	the number two
255	28	16(19)	akin	(sakin)	a knife
256	28	16(19)	ola ola	(gdola)	big (feminine, singular)
257	28	16(19)	ukar	(sukar)	sugar
258	28	16(20)	iti	(?iti)	with me
259	28	16(20)	tov	(tov)	good (masculine, singular)
260	28	16(21)	orez pac pac	(picpucei - orez)	rice krispies
261	28	16(22)	ladlik	(lehadlik)	put on/turn on (infinitive form)
262	28	16(22)	byby	(by-by)	bye-bye
263	28	16(23)	iganu	(higanu)	arrive (past, 1st person, masculine & feminine, plural)
264	28	16(23)	ulam	(sulam)	a ladder
265	28	16(22)	o yo yoi	(?)	oh oh/oh no
266	28	16(23)	aken	(letaken)	fix (infinitive form)
267	28	16(24)	?edim	(?edim)	vapor/ steam
268	28	16(24)	balon	(balon)	a balloon
269	28	16(24)	saga	(safta)	grandmother
270	28	16(24)	bumbum	(?)	the sound of hitting
271	29	16(26)	midod	(limdod)	try something on (infinitive form)
272	29	16(26)	imera	(migmera)	finish (past, 3rd person, feminine, singular, passive)
273	29	16(26)	arim	(leharim)	lift up (infinitive form)
274	29	16(26)	uxan	(muxan)	ready (masculine, singular)
275	29	16(26)	isa	(kvisa)	laundry
276	29	16(26)	atuva	(retuva)	wet (feminine, singular)
277	29	16(26)	?izama	(pidžama)	pyjama
278	29	16(27)	iton	(?iton)	a newspaper
279	29	16(27)	ila	(hila)	a name
280	29	16(27)	nama	(na?ama)	a name
281	29	16(27)	gili	(gili)	a name
282	29	16(27)	eusalaim	(yerušalayim)	Jerusalem

Table A: continued

Word no.	Week of study	Child's age	Child's word	Conventional form	English translation
283	29	16(27)	?umonit	(slomit)	a name
284	29	16(28)	inim	(garʔinim)	seeds
285	29	16(28)	ipox	(lišpox)	spill, pour (infinitive form)
286	29	16(28)	zuzi	(zuzi)	move (imperative, feminine, singular)
287	29	16(30)	alom	(šalom)	hello/ good-bye
288	29	16(30)	as	(naxaš)	a snake
289	29	16(30)	cipor	(cipor)	a bird
290	29	16(30)	rut	(rut)	a name
291	29	17(0)	saba	(saba)	grandfather
292	30	17(1)	afanayim	(?ofanayim)	a bicycle
293	30	17(1)	midal	(migdal)	a tower
294	30	17(2)	uda	(afuda)	a vest
295	30	17(2)	tuki	(tuki)	a parrot
296	30	17(2)	ir	(sir)	a potty/night pot
297	30	17(2)	lirot	(lirot)	see(infinitive form)
298	30	17(2)	mirara	(mitriya)	an umbrella
299	30	17(3)	?ocec	(korenfleiks)	cornflakes
300	30	17(3)	adar	(hadar)	a name
301	30	17(5)	bambi	(bambi)	a fawn
302	30	17(5)	ipaon	(?iparon)	a pencil
303	30	17(5)	gumi	(gumi)	a rubber band
304	30	17(5)	cvi	(cvi)	a deer
305	30	17(5)	?alina	(plastelina)	play-dough
306	30	17(5)	?axer	(?axer)	different
307	30	17(5)	yešena	(yešena)	she is sleeping
308	30	17(5)	al	(su?al)	a fox
309	30	17(5)	arum	(?avram)	a name
310	30	17(7)	dani	(dani)	a name
311	30	17(7)	roni	(roni)	a name
312	30	17(7)	šir	(šir)	a song
313	30	17(7)	?abon	(sabon)	soap
314	30	17(7)	kos	(kos)	a cup
315	30	17(7)	arek	(masrek)	a comb
316	30	17(7)	ivit	(biskvit)	a biscuit
317	30	17(7)	onoa	(?ofnoa)	a motorcycle
318	31	17(8)	mipo	(mipo)	from here
319	31	17(8)	šeli	(šeli)	mine
320	31	17(8)	guliver	(guliver)	a name
321	31	17(8)	baybibig	(beibibig)	a nickname
322	31	17(9)	semsa	(semes)	the sun
323	31	17(9)	anut	(xanut)	a store
324	31	17(9)	levad	(levad)	alone/ by myself
325	31	17(9)	regel	(regel)	a foot
326	31	17(9)	sama	(šama)	there
327	31	17(9)	cili	(cili)	a name
328	31	17(9)	rak	(rak)	only
329	31	17(9)	xaruz	(xaruz)	a bead
330	31	17(9)	?ata	(?ata)	you (masculine, singular)
331	31	17(9)	?udit	(yehudit)	a name

Table A: continued

Word no.	Week of study	Child's age	Child's word	Conventional form	English translation
332	32	17(16)	aba mak	(luna-park)	an amusement park
333	32	17(16)	mama	(?)	a nickname
334	32	17(16)	alef	(alef)	the first letter of the Hebrew alphabet
335	32	17(16)	para	(para)	a cow
336	32	17(16)	kelev	(kelev)	a dog
337	32	17(23)	tiyul	(tiyul)	a walk

[1] Words that were recorded repeatedly in a single context.

Appendix B. Keren's reconstructed lexicon

In the present investigation, nine morning sessions of one to three hours each were audio-recorded and subsequently transcribed phonetically. The transcripts of the audio-recorded sessions were incorporated into the main body of handwritten data and were also used to conduct reliability measures on its accuracy (see Chapter 7). The phonetic transcriptions contained a total of 5,134 child utterances. The reconstructed lexicon was prepared from this pool of words. It is a list of all the different child words (types) that appeared in the transcripts of the audio-recorded sessions. The reconstructed lexicon is organized by sessions and presents only new words that were recorded. It consists of 223 different lexical entries. Words are numbered in Table B below in the order of their occurrence in a given transcript. Numbers are successive across transcripts in order to approximate a real lexicon. Table B gives information on the day of recording and the day of acquisition of each word to allow for comparisons between these two dates. The date of acquisition is taken from the original lexicon and appears as day of study. The first day of study was *July 10, 1980*, and this was the date of the third recording of the first word in the child's lexicon (see appendix A). The last date of study was *February 20, 1981*, day number 226 of study. Child words appear in the table as they were transcribed at the specified time of recording. The English translations are based on the meaning of the word in colloquial Hebrew.

Table B.   Keren's reconstructed lexicon

Word no.	Day of acquisition	Child's word	English translation
Transcript no. 1	Day of Study: 107	Age: 13(26)	
1	61	buba	a doll
2	75	myau	a cat's meow
3	147	dubi	a teddy bear
4	107	tutu	the sound of a train
5	114	?ia	a donkey's bray
6	70	hupa	accompanying the perception of something making sudden contact with the ground
7	75	hine	here
8	63	cifcif	a bird's tweet
9	68	tiktak	the sound of a clock
10	99	?ima	mother
11	58	pil	an elephant
12	53	mu	a cow's moo
13	104	pica	a sore/cut/wound
14	104	toda	thank you
15	66	?oto	a car
16	62	bamba	a type of snack
17	35	?aba	Father
18	37	ham	said while feeding
19	1	haw	a dog's bark
Transcript no. 2	Day of Study: 132	Age: 14(21)	
20	147	kaki	bowel movement
21	132	ze	this
22	150	?ix	said in relation to a disgusting thing
23	73	?ein	all gone

Table B. continued

Word no.	Day of acquisition	Child's word	English translation
24	131	ʔapci	sound made when sneezing
25	81	ʔor	light
26	132	baʔat	a ring (finger ring)
27	78	nadned	accompanying a swinging motion
28	80	mayim	water
29	170	ken	yes
30	116	niyar	paper
31	113	ʔapit	a spoon
32	132	cet	go/get out
33	107	ʔuga	a cake
34	118	dod	an uncle
35	88	etze	this (volition)
36	130	ʔet	a pen
37	103	ʔod	more
38	99	dai	no more
39	88	ʔimaima	----

Transcript no. 3   Day of Study: 147   Age: 15(5)

40	147	tik	a bag/handbag
41	143	boi-boily	come/ come to me (imperative feminine, singular)
42	123	mita	a bed
43	147	nuf	an owl
44	142	mod	stand (infinitive form)
45	114	tei	tea
46	143	xam	hot (masculine, singular)
47	136	ʔinok	a baby
48	182	noranora	very
49	99	kuku	peekaboo
50	125	kax	take (present, 2nd person, masculine singular)

Table B. continued

Word no.	Day of acquisition	Child's word	English translation
Transcript no. 4	Day of study: 162	Age: 15(20)	
51	162	ga ga ga	a duck's quack
52	96	pita	a type of Arab bread
53	75	na?al	a shoe
54	166	piax	a flower
55	128	af	a nose
56	156	?iti	a pillow
57	170	parpar	a butterfly
58	147	tator	a tractor
59	106	avoda	work
60		manak	a needle
61	169	titaf	the sound of rain
62	176	sus	a horse
63	136	?amala	up
64	170	numinumi	said while putting a baby to sleep
65	142	?agala	a stroller
66	175	ixa	a blanket
67	166	mus	the toilet
68	63	pipi	urine
69	162	xalav	milk
70	162	beiga	bagel
71	150	nor	an apron
72	162	dag	a fish
73	178	taic	pantyhose

Table B. continued

Word no.	Day of acquisition	Child's word	English translation
74	167	isa	laundry
75	162	an	a rabbit
76	162	kukiko	a rooster's crow
77	128	pe	mouth
78	144	tik tak	a snap
79	66	hita	said while going out for a walk
80	144	?edet	get down (infinitive form)
81	157	deli	jelly
82	150	yeled	a boy
83	144	ul	a diaper
84	150	tova	said while patting
85	162	teip	a small tape recorder

Transcript no. 5   Day of study: 170   Age: 15(28)

86	170	?ec	a tree
87	170	?afa	fly (past, 3rd person, feminine, singular)
88	175	pupik	bellybutton
89	174	ol ol	big (masculine, singular)
90	137	kova	a hat
91	169	ner	a candle
92	187	ma?ayim	scissors
93	208	cvi	a deer
94	168	igul	a circle
95	169	misxa	ointment
96	169	erer	a sweater
97	159	bayit	a slipper
98	169	bayit	a house

Table B. continued

Word no.	Day of acquisition	Child's word	English translation
99	173	kumi	get up (imperative, feminine, singular)
100	150	lo	no
101	170	ira	a boat
102	170	?uax	open (infinitive form)
103	156	puke	a drumstick
104	150	apuz	an orange
105	159	mina	a tangerine
106	170	pes	look for something (infinitive form)
107	175	cici	breast
108	108	mudedet	a birthday
109	189	ira	a lion
110		?em	cream
111	172	afa	a giraffe
112	166	evet	sit (down) (infinitive form)
113	169	kom	a place
114	175	ricrac	a zipper
115	176	or	close/shut (infinitive form)
116	150	mize	who is this?
117	159	maze	what is this?
118	170	pic	a point (edge) of something
119		ma?at	hear (present, all persons, feminine, singular)

Transcript no. 6   Day of study: 174   Age: 16(2)

120	168	ipocec	explode (3rd person, masculine, singular, past)
121	174	atnudnik	you're a nag

Table B. continued

Word no.	Day of acquisition	Child's word	English translation
122		titim	olives
123	171	xamiday	too hot (masculine, singular)
124	196	safa	grandmother
125		mutok	
126	181	anav	a tail
127	175	urara	a sweet
128	152	abatia	a bath/bathtub/bathroom
129	174	os	the head
130	175	onez	ear
131	173	?enayim	eyes
132	167	even	a stone
133		budi	
134	200	zuzi	move (imperative, feminine, singular
135	159	?alai	on me
136	170	?abaita	to the house
137	194	o yo yoi	oh oh/oh no
138	173	uca	want (present, all persons, feminine singular)

Transcript no. 7	Day of study: 189	Age: 16(17)	
139	187	halax	go (past, 3rd person, masculine, singular)
140	176	?id	get/take (something) off (infinitive form)
141	187	?um?um	kettle
142	113	itot	drink (infinitive form)
143	143	kaxa	like this, this way
144	178	bayim	socks

Table B. continued

Word no.	Day of acquisition	Child's word	English translation
145	172	gilgul	a somersault
146	189	?amana	a present
147	179	pkak	a cork
148	178	kar	cold (masculine, singular)
149	114	dli	a pail
150	138	mic	juice
151	189	das	honey
152	189	tuk tuk	the sound of knocking
153	133	tnili	give me (imperative, feminine, singular)
154	168	lo po	not here
155	166	acic	a flower pot
156	189	ses ses	the number six
157	173	xut	a string
158	189	?ika	a hairpin
159		manam	
160		?abeti	
161	166	kis	a pocket
162		gavoba	high (up)
163	189	atan	small
164	189	?atiax	a rug
165	160	fafa	a glove/mitten
166	178	bakbuk	a bottle
167	202	as	a snake
168	87	xor	a hole
169	181	uax	wind
170	150	pax	a trash-can
171	191	snayim	two
172	189	mocec	a pacifier
173	196	bum bum	the sound of hitting

Table B. continued

Word no.	Day of acquisition	Child's word	English translation
Transcript no. 8		Day of study: 212	Age: 17(9)
174	199	eusalaim	Jerusalem
175	177	lalot	get up/get on (infinitive form)
176	182	kise	a chair
177	210	?abon	soap
178	114	puax	an apple
179	210	onoa	a motorcycle
180	144	urim	buttons
181		?usa	a box
182	212	xaruz	a bead
183	208	axer	different
184	210	šir	a song
185		kafe	coffee
186	212	levad	alone/ by myself
187	208	?alina	play-dough
188	179	adur	a ball, a pill
189	176	?uci	take out (infinitive form)
190		kelev	a dog
191	196	balon	a balloon
192	176	erer	a book
193	208	ipaon	a pencil
194	192	tov	good (masculine, singular)
195	156	maraki	soup
196	212	sama	there
197	210	kos	a cup
198		lul	a play-pen
199	210	ivit	a biscuit
200	89	po	here
201	210	arek	a comb

Table B. continued

Word no.	Day of acquisition	Child's word	English translation

Transcript no. 9   Day of Study: 219   Age: 17(16)

202	208	gumi	a rubber band
203	202	alom	hello/ good-bye
204	150	on	an airplane
205	205	lirot	see (infinitive form)
206		xaluk	a robe
207	172	?ica	a shirt/blouse
208	198	?izama	pyjamas
209	212	regel	a foot
210		xamor	a donkey
211		ukim	raisins
212	188	matate	a broom
213	202	cipor	a bird
214	219	para	a cow
215	211	mi .o	from here
216	206	ocec	cornflakes
217	205	tuki	a parrot
218	205	ir	a potty/night pot
219	186	pazel	a jigsaw puzzle
220		al	basket
221		cekar	
222	189	yafe	nice/pretty (masculine, singular)
223	180	ba-bau-bo	came (present/past, all persons, masculine, singular)

Note: The day of acquisition is given only for words which also appear in Table A.

Appendix C. Instructions for the phonetic transcription of the audio-recordings

The nine audio-recorded sessions, yielding a total of 13 hours, were transcribed phonetically. Only the mother's contextual notes, which were superimposed on the situation and were audio-recorded on a separate tape, were written in Hebrew orthography. The symbols used in transcribing the tapes were largely those of the International Phonetic Alphabet with minor modifications for non-conventional sounds. Ochs's (1979) general guidelines for displaying verbal and non-verbal contexts on a transcript were followed. Each transcription page was divided into two columns, one for each participant. Superscripts were used to indicate discourse variables such as initiation of conversation, overlap between two speakers, and turn-taking. The notation of intonation and other prosodic information was also adapted from Ochs (1979). The English translation of the guidelines developed for transcribing the Hebrew data is given below.

Instructions for phonetic transcriptions

1. The following information must be written on the cover sheet of every new transcript: subject's name and age, date of recording, number and side of tape and the names of all participants.
2. All the speech productions of the child and the other participants are to be phonetically transcribed. Be careful to transcribe every utterance exactly as it is produced, not as it is supposed to be pronounced in Modern Hebrew.
3. The symbols to be used in transcribing are those of the International Phonetic Alphabet (IPA).
3.1. The Hebrew vowel system consists of the five cardinal vowels: a, e, i, o, u.
3.2. The following are characters used for unique Hebrew sounds:
    ɣ = voiced velar fricative
    X = voiceless velar fricative
    C = voiceless alveolar affricate
    ? = glottal stop
3.3. Consonants and vowels that are slightly deviant from conventional adult articulations are to be transcribed using the closest IPA symbol, and then circled (e.g., Ⓡ).
3.4. When it is difficult to specify the quality of a vowel, it is to be transcribed as a schwa ə.
4. All the suprasegmental features (e.g., intonation, pauses, utterance bound-

aries, repetitions and interruptions) are to be transcribed according to the convention proposed by Ochs (1979).

5. Each transcription page is to be divided into two columns, one for each participant. The non-verbal context and the verbal data of each participant are to be displayed in separate columns.

6. Only short contextual notes or descriptions of non-verbal actions are to be written in Hebrew orthography.

6.1. Descriptions of context, comments and utterances which occur simultaneously are to be written on the same line.

6.2. When the action follows the utterance it is to be written one line below the utterance.

6.3. When the action precedes the utterance it is to be written one line above the utterance.

7. The utterances, descriptions of actions and comments are to be sequentially numbered according to turn-taking structure, as they occur.

7.1. Every initiation of a turn is to be numbered '1'.

7.2. Every change of topic is to be regarded as a new initiation.

7.3. Descriptions of actions and/or utterances which occur simultaneously are to be given the same number.

Table C.   An illustrative example of one transcribed situation

Adult		Child	
Non-verbal	Verbal	Non-verbal	Verbal
¹taking off her pants		¹sees mother taking off her pants	¹pipi/ 'urine'
	² ?he he he (LF)/		
			³ pipi/ 'urine'
	⁴ naxon/ 'right'		
			⁵cici/ 'breast'
	⁶ ?eifo cici?/ 'where (is the) breast ?'		
			⁷ ?əcici/ 'breast'
		pinching mother	
	⁸ ?oi!/ze koev li/ 'it hurts'		

Appendix D. Description and scoring of two video-taped situations

The precision with which the mother-investigator described the non-linguistic and linguistic content of the utterances produced by the subject was measured by the following procedure. From the set of four video-taped sessions (see Table 3) a sample of six situations were randomly selected as examples of the child's productions during the one-word stage. These situations were selected by an independent observer who was also asked to view them in the laboratory as many times as needed in order to write up a full script of each situation. A set of non-linguistic components and a transcript of the verbal interaction was constructed from a written script. The breakdown of components and the transcript were used as base lines against which mother's and other observers' descriptions of the same situations were tested (see Chapter 7, pp. 85–7). A component-by-component comparison between mother's descriptions and the descriptions of other observers was conducted. Cumulative scores reflecting the precision of the descriptions were calculated. Scores ranging from 0 to 2 were given to each component. Thus, 0 reflected missing information, 1 reflected incomplete information, and 2 represented complete or identical information in two descriptions. Two scripts which were written under laboratory conditions are illustrated below with their breakdown into non-verbal components and verbal interactions.

Situation A

K is sitting on her chair. In front of her, on the table, there is a piece of play-dough. F is sitting on the rug, beside K. F pushes his finger into the play-dough and makes a hole. He says: *veaxšav ?af/* 'and now, a nose'. Then, he makes the shape of a mouth and says: *pe/* 'mouth'. K touches the play-dough and helps F to create the shape. F touches the nose again, fixes it up and says: *?af/* 'nose'. F asks:*?eix korim la?iš haze?/* 'what's the name of this man?' K looks at the play-dough face, touches it and says: *is/* 'a man'. F repeats after her: *iš/* 'a man'.

Table D1.   The breakdown into components of Situation A

Non-verbal context		Mother's score	Verbal interaction	Mother's score
Back-ground	K's little chair and table	2	F: <u>veaxšav ?af</u>/ 'and now, a nose'	2
	Some play-dough	2	F: <u>pe</u>/ 'mouth'	2
	F is sitting on the rug	0	F: <u>?af</u>/ 'nose'	0
Event	F speaks while playing with the play-dough	2	F: <u>?eix korim la?iš haze?</u>/ 'What's the name of this man?'	2
	K answers while playing with the play-dough	2	K: <u>is</u>/ 'a man'	2
			F: <u>iš</u>/ 'a man'	2
Total		8		10

K = Keren   M = Mother   F = Father

Situation B

M and K are sitting on the rug. There are some plastic animals between them. M picks up the turkey, shows it to K and says: *?oi tiri mi po?/ mi po?/* 'oh, look who's here? who's here?' K answers: *kukuriku ?odu/* 'cock-a-doodle-doo turkey'. M repeats after her in exaggerated intonation: *kukuriku ?odu/* 'cock-a-doodle-doo turkey'. K imitates: *kukuriku ?odu/* 'cock-a-doodle-doo turkey'. M says: *?u?u kukuriku ?odu/* 'ooh-ooh cock-a-doodle-doo turkey'. K waves her hand and says: *šalom/* 'hello'. M says *šalom kukuriku hodu/* 'hello cock-a-doodle-doo turkey', and waves the hand holding the plastic turkey.

Table D2. The breakdown into components of Situation B

Non-verbal context		Mother's score	Verbal interaction	Mother's score
Back-ground	M and K are sitting on the rug	2	M: ?oi tiri mi po?/ mi po?/ 'oh, look who's here? who's here?!'	2
	Some plastic animals are placed on the rug	2	K: kukuriku ?odu/ 'cock-a-doodle-doo turkey'	2
Event	M picks up a plastic turkey and shows it to K	1	M in exaggerated intonation: kukuriku ?odu/ 'cock-a-doodle-doo turkey'	1
			K imitating M: kukuriku ?odu/ 'cock-a-doodle-doo turkey'	2
			M: ?u?u kukuriku ?odu/ 'ooh-ooh cock-a-doodle-doo turkey'	1
	K waves her hand	2	K: salom/ 'hello'	2
			M: šalom kukuriku hodu/ 'hello cock-a-doodle-doo turkey'	2
Total		7		12

K = Keren   M = Mother   F = Father

References

Anglin, J. M. (1977). *Word, object and conceptual development*. New York: Norton

Anisfeld, M. (1984). *Language development from birth to three*. Hillsdale, New Jersey: Lawrence Erlbaum.

Austin, J. L. (1962). *How to do things with words*. Cambridge, Mass.: Harvard University Press.

Barrett, M. D. (1978). Lexical development and overextension in child language. *Journal of Child Language*, 5, 205–19.

(1982). Distinguishing between prototypes: The early acquisition of the meaning of object names. In S. A. Kuczaj (ed.), *Language development*. Vol. I. *Syntax and semantics*. Hillsdale, New Jersey: Lawrence Erlbaum.

(1986). Early semantic representations and early word usage. In S. A. Kuczaj and M. D. Barrett (eds.), *The development of word meaning*. New York: Springer.

Bates, E. (1976). Pragmatics and sociolinguistics in child language. In D. Morehead and A. Morehead (eds.), *Normal and deficient child language*. Baltimore: University Park Press.

(1979). *The emergence of symbols: Cognition and communication in infancy*. New York: Academic Press.

Bates, E., Camaioni, L. and Volterra, V. (1979). The acquisition of performatives prior to speech. In E. Ochs and B. B. Schieffelin (eds.), *Developmental pragmatics*. New York: Academic Press.

Bates, E., Bretherton, I., Shore, C. and McNew, S. (1983). Names, gestures and objects: The role of context in the emergence of symbols. In K. E. Nelson (ed.), *Children's language*. Vol. IV. Hillsdale, New Jersey: Lawrence Erlbaum.

Benedict, H. (1979). Early lexical development: Comprehension and production. *Journal of Child Language*, 6, 183–201.

Berman, R. A. (1985). Acquisition of Hebrew. In D. I. Slobin (ed.), *The cross-linguistic study of language acquisition*. Hillsdale, New Jersey: Lawrence Erlbaum.

Berman, R. A. and Dromi, E. (1984). On marking time without aspect in child language. *Papers and Reports on Child Language Development*, 23, 23–32.

Bierwisch, M. (1970). Semantics. In J. Lyons (ed.), *New horizons in linguistics*. Harmondsworth: Penguin Books.

Bloom, L. (1973). *One word at a time*. The Hague: Mouton.

Bloom, L. and Lahey, M. (1978). *Language development and language disorders*. New York: John Wiley and Sons.

Bowerman, M. (1973). *Early syntactic development: A cross-linguistic study with special reference to Finnish*. Cambridge, England: Cambridge University Press.

(1976). Semantic factors in the acquisition of rules for word use and sentence construction. In D. Morehead and A. Morehead (eds.), *Normal and deficient child language*. Baltimore: University Park Press.

(1978). The acquisition of word meaning: An investigation into some current conflicts. In N. Waterson and C. Snow (eds.), *Development of communication*. New York: John Wiley and Sons.

(1980). The structure and origin of semantic categories in the language-learning child. In M. Foster and S. Brandes (eds.), *Symbol as sense*. New York: Academic Press.

(1982). Starting to talk worse: Clues to language acquisition from children's late speech errors. In S. Strauss (ed.), *U-shaped behavioral growth*. New York: Academic Press.

Braine, M. D. S. (1963). The ontogeny of English phrase-structure: The first phase. *Language*, 39, 1–13.

Brainerd, C. J. (1976). "Stage", "structure" and developmental theory. In G. Steiner (ed.), *The psychology of the twentieth century*. Munich: Kindler.

(1978). The stage question in cognitive developmental theory. *Behavioral and Brain Science*, 1, 173–213.

Braunwald, S. R. (1978). Context, word and meaning: toward a communicational analysis of lexical acquisition. In A. Lock (ed.), *Action, gesture and symbol: The emergence of language*. London: Academic Press.

Braunwald, S. R. and Brislin, R. W. (1979). The diary method updated. In E. Ochs and B. B. Schieffelin (eds.), *Developmental pragmatics*. New York: Academic Press.

Brown, R. (1957). Linguistic determinism and part of speech. *Journal of Abnormal Social Psychology*, 55, 1–5.

(1973). *A first language: The early stages*. Cambridge, Mass.: Harvard University Press.

(1977). Word from the language acquisition front. Invited address for the Eastern Psychological Association meeting.

(1979). Cognitive categories. Paper presented at the *Houston II Symposium*.

Bruner, J., Roy, C. and Ratner, N. (1982). The beginnings of request. In K. E. Nelson (ed.), *Children's language*. Vol. III. Hillsdale, New Jersey: Lawrence Erlbaum.

Carey, S. (1978). The child as word learner. In M. Halle, J. Bresnan and G. Miller (eds.), *Linguistic theory and psychological reality*. Cambridge, Mass.: M.I.T. Press.

(1982). Semantics and development: State of the art. In G. Wanner and L. Gleitman (eds.), *Language acquisition: The state of the art*. Cambridge, England: Cambridge University Press.

Carey, S. and Bartlett, E. (1978). Acquiring a single new word. *Papers and Reports on Child Language Development*, 15, 17–29.

Carter, A. L. (1978a). The development of systematic vocalizations prior to words: A case study. In N. Waterson and C. Snow (eds.), *The development of communication*. New York: John Wiley and Sons.

(1978b). From sensori-motor vocalization to words: A case study of the evolution of attention-directing communication in the second year. In A. Lock (ed.), *Action, gesture and symbol: The emergence of language*. New York: Academic Press.

(1979). Prespeech meaning relations: An outline of one infant's sensorimotor morpheme development. In P. Fletcher and M. Garman (eds.), *Language acquisition: Studies in first language development*. Cambridge, England: Cambridge University Press.

Chafe, W. L. (1970). *Meaning and the structure of language*. Chicago: University of Chicago Press.

Clark, E. V. (1973). What's in a word? On the child's acquisition of semantics in his first language. In T. E. Moore (ed.), *Cognitive development and the acquisition of language*. New York: Academic Press.

(1975). Knowledge, context and strategy in the acquisition of meaning. In D. Dato (ed.), *Twenty-sixth Annual Georgetown University Round Table on Languages and Linguistics*. Washington D.C. Georgetown University Press.

(1977). Strategies and the mapping problem in first language acquisition. In J. Macnamara (ed.), *Language learning and thought*. New York: Academic Press.

(1983a). Meanings and concepts. In P. H. Mussen (ed.), *Handbook of child psychology*. Vol. III. *Cognitive development*. New York: John Wiley and Sons.

(1983b). Convention and contrast in acquiring the lexicon. In B. Seiler and W. Wannenmacher (eds.), *Concept development and the development of word meaning*. Berlin and New York: Springerverlag.

(1985). The principle of contrast: A constraint on language acquisition. In M. D. S. Braine and B. MacWhinney (eds.), *Proceedings of the 20th Annual Carnegie Symposium on Cognition, Mechanisms of Language Acquisition*.

Clark, H. H. and Clark, E. V. (1977). *Psychology and language: An introduction to psycholinguistics*. New York: Harcourt Brace Jovanovitch.

Clark, R. (1976). A report on methods of longitudinal data collection. *Journal of Child Language*, 3, 457–9.

(1978). Some even simpler ways to learn to talk. In N. Waterson and C. Snow (eds.), *The development of communication*. New York: John Wiley and Sons.

(1982). Theory and method in child-language research: Are we assuming too much? In S. A. Kuczaj (ed.), *Language development*. Vol. I. *Syntax and semantics*. Hillsdale, New Jersey: Lawrence Erlbaum.

Corrigan, R. L. (1976). Patterns of individual communication and cognitive development. Ph.D. dissertation, University of Denver.

(1978). Language development as related to stage 6 object permanence development. *Journal of Child Language*, 5, 173–89.

(1979). Cognitive correlates of language: Differential criteria yield differential results. *Child Development*, 50, 617–31.

Denny, T. (1978). Storytelling and educational understanding. Address delivered at *National Meeting of International Reading Association*, Houston, Texas.

Dore, J. (1973). The development of speech acts. Unpublished doctoral dissertation. City University of New York.

(1974). A pragmatic description of early language development. *Journal of Psycholinguistic Research*, 3, 343–50.

(1975). Holophrases, speech acts and language universals. *Journal of Child Language*, 2, 21–40.

(1978). Conditions for the acquisition of speech acts. In I. Markova (ed.), *The social context of language*. New Jersey: John Wiley and Sons.

Dore, J., Franklin, M., Miller, R. and Ramer, A. (1976). Transitional phenomena in early language acquisition. *Journal of Child Language*, 3, 13–28.

Dromi, E. (1979). More on the acquisition of locative prepositions: An analysis of Hebrew data. *Journal of Child Language*, 6, 547–62.

——— (1982). In pursuit of meaningful words: A case study analysis of early lexical development. Unpublished doctoral dissertation. The University of Kansas.

——— (1983). On identification of the extensional behaviors of new words. *Rassegna Italiana di Linguistica Applicata*, 15, 235–46.

——— (1984). The word context production strategy in the early acquisition of meaning. In C. L. Thew and C. L. Johnson (eds.), *Proceedings of the Second International Congress for the Study of Child Language*. Vol. II. Lanham: University Press of America.

——— (1986). The one-word period as a stage in language development: Quantitative and qualitative accounts. In I. Levin (ed.), *Stage and structure: Reopening the debate*. Norwood, New Jersey: Ablex Publishing Corporation.

Dromi, E. and Berman, R. (1982). A morphemic measure of early language development: Data from Modern Hebrew. *Journal of Child Language*, 9, 403–24.

Dromi, E. and Fishelzon, G. (1986). Similarity, specificity and contrast: A study of early semantic categories. *Papers and Reports on Child Language Development*, 25, 25–32.

Farwell, C. B. (1976). The early expression of motion and location. Paper presented at the *First Annual Boston Conference on Language Development*.

——— (1977). The primacy of goal in the child's description of motion and location. *Papers and Reports on Child Language Development*, 13, 126–33.

Ferrier, L. J. (1978). Some observations of error in context. In N. Waterson and C. Snow (eds.), *The development of communication*. New York: John Wiley and Sons.

Fillmore, C. J. (1968). The case for case. In E. Bach and R. T. Harms (eds.), *Universals in linguistic theory*. New York: Holt, Rinehart and Winston.

——— (1975). Frame semantics and the nature of language. Presented at the *Conference on the Origins and Evolution of Language and Speech*, New York.

——— (1978). On the organization of semantic information in the lexicon. In D. Fakas, W. M. Jacobsen and K. W. Todrys (eds.), *Papers from the parasession on the lexicon*, Chicago Linguistic Society, Chicago: University of Chicago Press.

Fischer, K. W. (1980). A theory of cognitive development: The control and construction of hierarchies of skills. *Psychological Review*, 87, 477–531.

Fischer, K. W. and Corrigan, R. (1981). A skill approach to language development. In R. Stark (ed.), *Language behavior in infancy and early childhood*. Amsterdam: Elsevier.

Fischer, K. W. and Canfield, R. L. (1986). The ambiguity of stage and structure in behavior: Person and environment in the development of psychological structures. In I. Levin (ed.), *Stage and structure: Reopening the debate*. Norwood, New Jersey: Ablex Publishing Corporation.

Flavell, J. H. (1963). *The developmental psychology of Jean Piaget*. New York: D. Van Nostrand Company.

——— (1971). Stage related properties of cognitive development. *Cognitive Psychology*, 2, 421–53.

——— (1982). On cognitive development. *Child Development*, 53, 1–10.

Flavell, J. H. and Wohlwill, J. F. (1969). Formal and functional aspects of cognitive development. In D. Elkind and J. H. Flavell (eds.), *Studies in cognitive development: Essays in honor of Jean Piaget*. Oxford: Oxford University Press.

Fodor, J. A. (1975). *The language of thought*. Cambridge, Mass.: Harvard University Press.

(1980). On the impossibility of acquiring "more powerful" structures. In M. Piatelli-Palmarini (ed.), *Language and learning*. Cambridge, Mass.: Harvard University Press.

Fremgen, A. and Fay, D. (1980). Overextensions in production and comprehension: A methodological clarification. *Journal of Child Language*, 7, 205–11.

Gelman, S. A. and Markman, E. M. (1986). Understanding natural kind terms: A developmental comparison. *Papers and Reports on Child Language Develpment*, 25, 41–8.

(in press). Categories and induction in young children, *Cognition*.

Gentner, D. (1975). Evidence for the psychological reality of semantic components: The verbs of possession. In D. A. Norman, D. E. Rumelhart and L. N. R. Research Group (eds.), *Explorations in cognition*. San Francisco: W. H. Freeman Co.

(1978). On relational meaning: The acquisition of verb meaning. *Child Development*, 49, 988–98.

(1982). Why nouns are learned before verbs: Linguistic relativity versus natural partitioning. In S. Kuczaj (ed.), *Language development: Language, culture, and cognition*. Hillsdale, New Jersey: Lawrence Erlbaum.

Gillis, S. and DeSchutter, G. (1984). Transitional phenomena revisited: Insights into the nominal insight. In *Proceedings of the Interdisciplinary Symposium on Precursors of Speech*. Stockholm.

Globerson, T. (1986). When do structural changes underlie behavioral changes? In I. Levin (ed.), *Stage and structure: Reopening the debate*. Norwood, New Jersey: Ablex Publishing Corporation.

Goldin-Meadow, S., Seligman, M. and Gelman, R. (1976). Language in the two-year old. *Cognition*, 4, 189–202.

Golinkoff, R. M., Hirsh-Pasek, K., Badvini, C. and Lavallee, A. (1985). What's in a word?: The young child's predisposition to use lexical contrast. Paper presented at *The Tenth Boston University Conference on Language Development*.

Greenberg, J. H. (1966). *Language universals*. The Hague: Mouton.

Greenfield, P. M. and Smith, J. H. (1976). *The structure of communication in early language development*. New York: Academic Press.

Griffiths, P. and Atkinson, M. (1978). A "door" to verbs. In N. Waterson and C. Snow (eds.), *The development of communication*. New York: John Wiley and Sons.

Gruendel, J. M. (1977). Referential extension in early language development. *Child Development*, 48, 1567–76.

Guba, E. G. and Lincoln, Y. S. (1981). *Effective evaluation*. San Francisco: Jossy Bass.

Halliday, M. A. K. (1975). *Learning how to mean: Explorations in the development of language*, London: Edward Arnold.

Hamilton, D. (1981). Doing justice in evaluation research. In W. W. Welch (ed.), *Case study methodology in educational evaluation*. Proceedings of the Minnesota Evaluation Conference.

Huttenlocher, J. (1974). The origin of language comprehension. In R. L. Solo (ed.), *Theories in cognitive psychology – The Loyola Symposium*. Potomac, Maryland: Lawrence Erlbaum.

Huttenlocher, J., Smiley, P. and Charney, R. (1983). Emergence of action categories in the child: Evidence from verb meanings. *Psychological Review*, 90, 72–93.

Ingram, D. (1971). Transitivity in child language. *Language*, 47, 888–909.

(1978). Sensorimotor intelligence and language development. In A. Lock (ed.), *Action, gesture, and symbol: The emergence of language.* New York: Academic Press.

Karmiloff-Smith, A. (1979). *A functional approach to child language.* Cambridge, England: Cambridge University Press.

(1984). Children's problem solving. In M. Lamb, A. L. Brown and B. Rogoff (eds.), *Advances in developmental psychology.* Vol. III. Hillsdale, New Jersey: Lawrence Erlbaum.

(1986a). Stage/structure versus phase/process in modeling linguistic and cognitive development. In I. Levin (ed.), *Stage and structure: Reopening the debate.* Norwood, New Jersey: Ablex Publishing Corporation.

(1986b). From meta-processes to conscious access: Evidence from children's meta-linguistic and repair data. *Cognition,* 23, 95–147.

Katz, N., Baker, E., and Macnamara, J. (1974). What's in a name? A study of how children learn common and proper names. *Child Development,* 65, 469–73.

Kay, D. and Anglin, J. (1982). Overextension and underextension in the child's expressive and receptive speech. *Journal of Child Language,* 9, 83–98.

Keil, F. C. (1986). On the structure-dependent nature of stages of cognitive development. In I. Levin (ed.), *Stage and structure: Reopening the debate.* Norwood, New Jersey: Ablex Publishing Corporation.

Kemler-Nelson, D. G. (1984). The effect of intention on what concepts are acquired. *Journal of Verbal Learning and Verbal Behavior,* 23, 734–59.

Kempson, R. M. (1977). *Semantic theory.* Cambridge, England: Cambridge University Press.

Kratochwill, T. R. (ed.) (1978). *Single subject research: Strategies for evaluating change.* New York: Academic Press.

Kuczaj, S. A. (1982). Young children's overextensions of object words in comprehension and/or production: Support for a prototype theory of early object word meaning. *First Language,* 3, 93–105.

Labov, W. and Labov, T. (1978). The phonetics of cat and mama. *Language,* 54, 815–52.

Leean, G. (1981). Illustrative examples of case studies. In W. W. Welch (eds.), *Case-study methodology in educational evaluation.* Proceedings of the Minnesota Evaluation Conference.

Leopold, W. F. (1939). *Speech development of a bilingual child: A linguist's record.* Vol. I. *Vocabulary growth in the first two years.* Evanston, Illinois: Northwestern.

Levin, I. and Simons, H. (1986). The nature of children's and adults' concepts of time, speed, and distance and their sequence in development: Analysis via circular motion. In I. Levin (ed.), *Stage and structure: Reopening the debate.* Norwood, New Jersey: Ablex Publishing Corporation.

Lewis, M. M. (1959). *How children learn to speak.* New York: Basic Books.

Lock, A. (1980). *The guided reinvention of language.* London: Academic Press.

Lyons, J. (1977). *Semantics.* Vol. I. Cambridge, England: Cambridge University Press.

MacWhinney, B. (1978). Processing a first language: The acquisition of morphology. *Monographs of the Society for Research in Child Development,* 43 (1–2, Serial No. 174).

Mandler, J. M. (1979). Categorical and schematic organization in memory. In C. R. Puff (ed.), *Memory organization and structure.* New York: Academic Press.

(1983). Representation. In J. H. Flavell and E. M. Markman (eds.), *Cognitive develop-*

ment. Vol. II of P. Mussen (ed.), *Manual of child psychology*. New York: John Wiley and Sons.

McCarthy, D. (1954). Language development in children. In L. Carmichael (ed.), *Manual of child psychology*. New York: John Wiley and Sons.

McCune-Nicolich, L. (1981). The cognitive bases of relational words in the single-word period. *Journal of Child Language*, 8, 15–34.

McNeill, D. (1970). *The acquisition of language: The study of developmental psycholinguistics*. New York: Harper.

McShane, J. (1980). *Learning to talk*. Cambridge, England: Cambridge University Press.

Merriman, W. E. (in press). How children learn the reference of concrete nouns: A critique of current hypotheses. In Kuczaj, S. (ed.), *Children's acquisition of word meaning*. Baltimore: University Park Press.

Mounoud, P. (1982). Revolutionary periods in early development. In G. T. Bever (ed.), *Regressions in mental development: Basic phenomena and theories*. London: LEA Publishers.

(1986). Similarities between developmental sequences at different age periods. In I. Levin (ed.), *Stage and structure: Reopening the debate*. Norwood, New Jersey: Ablex Publishing Corporation.

Nelson, K. (1973a). Some evidence for the cognitive primacy of categorization and its functional basis. *Merrill-Palmer-Quarterly*, 19, 21–38.

(1973b). Structure and strategy in learning to talk. *Monographs of the Society for Research in Child Development*, 38 (1–2, serial no. 149).

(1974). Concept, word, and sentence: Interrelations in acquisition and development. *Psychological Review*, 81, 267–85.

(1978). Explorations in the development of a functional semantic system. In W. Collins (ed.), *Children's language and communication*. The 1977 Minnesota Symposium on Child Psychology. Hillsdale, New Jersey: Lawrence Erlbaum.

(1982). The syntagmatics and paradigmatics of conceptual development. In S. Kuczaj (ed.), *Language*. Vol. II. *Language, thought and culture*. Hillsdale, New Jersey: Lawrence Erlbaum.

Nelson, K., Rescorla, L., Gruendel, J. M. and Benedict, H. (1978). Early lexicons: What do they mean? *Child Development*, 49, 960–8.

Nelson, K. and Gruendel, J. M. (1979). At morning it's lunch time: A scriptural view of children's dialogues. *Discourse Processes*, 2, 73–94.

(1981). Generalized event representations: Basic building blocks of cognitive development. In A. L. Brown and M. E. Lamb (eds.), *Advances in developmental psychology*. Vol. I. Hillsdale, New Jersey: Lawrence Erlbaum.

Nelson, K. and Lucariello, J. (1985). The development of meaning in first words. In M. D. Barrett (ed.), *Children's single-word speech*. New York: John Wiley and Sons.

Ninio, A. (1980). Ostensive definition in vocabulary teaching. *Journal of Child Language*, 7, 565–73.

Ninio, A. and Bruner, J. (1978). The achievement and antecedents of labelling. *Journal of Child Language*, 5, 1–15.

Ninio, A. and Snow, C. (in press). Language acquisition through language use. The functional forces of children's early utterances. In Y. Levy, M. D. S. Braine and I. M. Schlesinger (eds.), *Categories and processes in language acquisition*. Hillsdale, New Jersey: Lawrence Erlbaum.

Ochs, E. (1979). Transcription as theory. In E. Ochs and B. B. Schieffelin (eds.), *Developmental pragmatics*. New York: Academic Press.

Peters, A. M. (1983). *The units of language acquisition*. Cambridge, England: Cambridge University Press.

Piaget, J. (1926). *The language and thought of the child*. New York: Harcourt Brace.

(1950). *The psychology of intelligence*. New York: Harcourt Brace.

Postal, P. M. (1966). Review article: André Martinet, "Elements of general linguistics". *Foundations of Language*, 2, 151–86.

Reich, P. A. (1976). The early acquisition of word meaning. *Journal of Child Language*, 3, 117–23.

Rescorla, L. A. (1980). Overextension in early language development. *Journal of Child Language*, 7, 321–35.

(1981). Category development in early language. *Journal of Child Language*, 8, 225–38.

Rice, M. (1980). *Cognition to language: Categories, word meanings, and training*. Baltimore: University Park Press.

Richards, M. M. (1979). Sorting out what's in a word from what's not: Evaluating Clark's semantic feature acquisition theory. *Journal of Experimental Child Psychology*, 27, 1–47.

Rist, C. A. (1977). On the relation among educational research paradigms: From disdain to detente. *Anthropology and Education Quarterly*, 8, 42–9.

Rodgon, M. (1976). *Single word usage, cognitive development, and the beginnings of combinatorial speech: A study of ten English-speaking children*. Cambridge, England: Cambridge University Press.

Rosch, E. (1975). Universals and cultural specifics in human categorization. In R. Brislin, S. Bochner and W. Lonner (eds.), *Cross-cultural perspectives on learning*. New York: Halsted Press.

(1977). Human categorization. In N. Warren (ed.), *Studies in cross-cultural psychology*. Vol. I. New York: Academic Press.

Rosch, E. and Mervis, C. O. (1975). Family resemblances: Studies in the internal structure of categories. *Cognitive Psychology*, 7, 573–605.

Sanders, J. R. (1981). Case study methodology: A critique. In W. W. Welch (ed.), *Case study methodology in educational evaluation*. Proceedings of the Minnesota Evaluation Conference.

Schank, R. C. and Abelson, R. P. (1977). *Scripts, plans, goals, and understanding: An inquiry into human knowledge structures*. Hillsdale, New Jersey: Lawrence Erlbaum.

Schlesinger, I. M. (1977). The role of cognitive development and linguistic input in language acquisition. *Journal of Child Language*, 4, 153–69.

(1982). *Steps to language*. Hillsdale, New Jersey: Lawrence Erlbaum.

Scollon, R. (1976). *Conversations with a one year old*. Honolulu: University of Hawaii Press.

(1979). A real early stage: An unzippered condensation of dissertation on child language. In E. Ochs and B. B. Schieffelin (eds.), *Developmental pragmatics*. New York: Academic Press.

Searle, J. R. (1969). *Speech acts*. Cambridge, England: Cambridge University Press.

Shallice, J. (1979). Case study approach in neuropsychological research. *Journal of Clinical Neuropsychology*, 1, 183–211.

Slobin, D. I. (1973). Cognitive prerequisites for the development of grammar. In C. A.

Ferguson and D. I. Slobin (eds.), *Studies of child language development.* New York: Holt Rinehart and Winston.

Soja, N., Carey, S. and Spelke, E. (1985). Constraints on the meanings of words. Paper presented at the meeting of the *Society for Research in Child Development.* Toronto.

Stake, R. E. (1978). The case study method in social inquiry. *Educational Researcher, 7,* 5–8.

(1981). Case-study methodology: An epistemological advocacy. In W. W. Welch (ed.), *Case-study methodology in educational evaluation.* Proceedings of the Minnesota Evaluation Conference.

Sugarman, S. (1978). Some organizational aspects of pre-verbal communication. In I. Markova (ed.), *The social context of language.* London: John Wiley and Sons.

(1983a). *Children's early thought: Developments in classification.* New York: Cambridge University Press.

(1983b). Empirical versus logical issues in the transition from prelinguistic to linguistic communication. In R. M. Golinkoff (ed.), *The transition from prelinguistic to linguistic communication.* Hillsdale, New Jersey: Lawrence Erlbaum.

Tanouye, E. K. (1979). The acquisition of verbs in Japanese children. *Papers and Reports on Child Language Development, 17,* 49–56.

Thomson, J. R. and Chapman, R. S. (1977). Who is "Daddy" revisited: The status of two-year-olds' over-extended words in use and comprehension. *Journal of Child Language, 4,* 359–75.

Turiel, E. and Davidson, P. (1986). Heterogeneity, inconsistency, and asynchrony in the development of cognitive structure. In I. Levin (ed.), *Stage and structure: Reopening the debate.* New Jersey: Ablex Publishing Corporation.

Uzgiris, I. and Hunt, J. (1975). *Assessment in infancy: Ordinal scales of psychological development.* Illinois: University of Illinois Press.

Valsiner, J. and Lasn, M. (n.d.). Contextual differentiation: The development of first word meanings in children.

Veneziano, E. (1981). Early language and nonverbal representation: A reassessment. *Journal of Child Language, 8,* 541–63.

Vygotsky, L. S. (1962). *Thought and language.* Cambridge, Mass.: M.I.T. Press.

Winner, E. (1979). New names for old things: The emergency of metaphoric language. *Journal of Child Language, 6,* 469–91.

Wohlwill, J. F. (1973). *The study of behavioral development.* New York: Academic Press.

Author index

Subject index